# VEDAS
## FOR BEGINNERS

## other recent books from Cosmo Publications . . .

**THE HINDUS.** *Bestseller*
**Encyclopaedia of Hinduism** in 5 Volumes
Edited by Subodh Kapoor

**ENCYCLOPAEDIA OF INDIAN HERITAGE.** in 90 Volumes
**A Descriptive Work of Indological Research in Philosophy, Religion, Sacred Literature, Society, Thought, Traditions, and Ancient Sciences.**
Edited by Subodh Kapoor

**ANCIENT INDIAN SCIENCES** *Bestseller*
in 3 Volumes
Edited by Subodh Kapoor

**ENCYCLOPAEDIA OF VEDIC PHILOSOPHY.** *Bestseller*
**The Age, Literature, Religion, Pantheon, Philosophy, Traditions and Teachers of the Vedas**
*in 9 Volumes*
Edited by Subodh Kapoor

**ENCYCLOPAEDIA OF INDIAN PHILOSOPHERS.** *Bestseller*
**Philosophers, Saints, Sages, Thinkers, Acharyas, Rishis, and great Religious Leaders**
*in 9 Volumes*
Edited by Subodh Kapoor

**ENCYCLOPAEDIA OF VEDANTA PHILOSOPHY.**
*in 5 Volumes*
Ed. S. kapoor

***Also Available . . .***

**INDIAN HISTORICAL RESEARCHES** *Bestseller*
**By Several Authors of International Repute**
*in 78 Volumes*

**REDISCOVERING INDIA** *Bestseller*
**INIDAN PHILOSOPHY LIBRARY**
**By Several Authors of International Repute**
*in 71 Volumes*

# VEDAS

## FOR BEGINNERS

Edited by

Subodh Kapoor

Editor of THE HINDUS. Encyclopaedia of Hinduism, in 5 volumes
THE BUDDHISTS. Encyclopaedia of Buddhism, in 5 volumes
Encyclopaedia of Indian Heritage, in 90 volumes
Encyclopaedia of Vedic Philosophy, in 9 volumes

COSMO PUBLICATIONS

2008 New Delhi

**VEDAS FOR BEGINNERS**


First published by COSMO 2008

ISBN 978-81-307-0910-9

***Published by***
COSMO PUBLICATIONS
*for*
GENESIS PUBLISHING PVT. LTD.
24-B, Ansari Road, Darya Ganj,
New Delhi-110 002,
INDIA

***Printed in India by***
Cosmo Publications

# Contents

# ABBREVIATIONS

AB. = Aitareya Brāhmaṇa.
Āp. = Āpastamba.
AV. = Atharva-Veda.
B = Bombay edition of Mahābhārata.
Bṛh. Up. = Bṛhadāraṇyaka-Upaniṣad.
C = Calcutta edition of Mahābhārata.
GDS. = Calcutta Dharmaśāstra.
H = Harivaṃśa.
Hit. Hitopadeśa.
IS. = Indische Studien.
JAOS. = Journal of the American Oriental Society.
JRAS. = Journal of the Royal Asiatic Society.
M = Manu.
Muṇḍ. = Muṇḍaka-Upaniṣad.
OST. = Original Sanskrit Texts.
PW. = Petersburger Wörterbuch.
R = Rāmāyaṇa, Text of Krishnacharya.
RB = Rāmāyaṇa, Bombay edition.
RG = Rāmāyaṇa, Text of Gorresio.
RV. = Rig-Veda.
S = South Indian (Kumbakonam) edition of the Mahābhārata.
ŚB. = Śatapatha-Brāhmaṇa.
SBE. = Sacred Books of the East.
ŚGS. = Śāṅkhāyana Gṛhyasūtra.
TS. = Taittirīya-Saṃhitā.
VP. = Viṣṇu-Purāṇa.
VS. = Vājasaneya-Saṃhitā.
RV. = Rig-Veda.
Praś. = Praśna-Upaniṣad.

# one

## THE VEDAS: GENERAL ASPECTS

The oldest scriptures of India, and the most important, are the Vedas. Orthodox Hindus, who include all schools of Indian thought past and present except Buddhists and Jains, recognize in them the origin of their faith and its highest written authority. Buddhists and Jains reject them, though in varying degree: the Buddhists renouncing them altogether, the Jains acknowledging their spiritual validity but denying that they are in any peculiar sense sacred. Of Jains there are in India today about a million and a quarter; of Buddhists, in India, proper, there are virtually none. For the vast majority of modern Hindus, therefore, amongst all their sacred writings, the Vedas supreme.

This does not, however, suggest the whole story. For the term *Vedas*, as used by the orthodox, not only names a large body of texts composed in times indefinitely remote, and handed down by generation after generation to our own day, but in another sense stands for nothing less than Divine Truth itself, the inexpressible truth of which the Vedic texts are of necessity but a pale reflection. Regarded in this second aspect, the Vedas are infinite and eternal. They are that perfect knowledge which is God.

Even more than the other scriptures of the world, the Vedas make a special claim to be divine in their Bible, the Koran, and other revelations of the word of God owe their authority to delivery of the sacred message through an angel, or prophet, or other special messenger from God to certain chosen persons. And these revelations must be accepted on faith. No question is raised as to whether any human being today can verify these revelations in his own experience. The Vedas, on the other hand, are said to be *apauruseya*, which means divine in origin. In fact, in the words of Sayanācārya, the learned commentator on the Vedas, *Yo vedebhvah adhilam jagat nirmame*—God created the whole universe out of the knowledge of the Vedas. That is to say, Vedic knowledge existed even before the creation of mankind. The authority of the Vedas does not depend upon anything external. They themselves *are* authority, being the knowledge of God. And, as we shall see later, their truth is verifiable by any spiritual aspirant in transcendental consciousness.

But it is the Vedas in the concrete sense of scriptures with which alone we are henceforth concerned. As such, they are divided into four major parts, and each of these, in turn, is further divided and subdivided—as may be conveniently seen in the following table 1.

Many questions suggested by this classification we shall pass by for the moment, while we inquire how, in the view of orthodox Hindus, this body of sacred texts came into being. The answer involves certain Hindu beliefs with which, if only in preliminary fashion, we should now become acquainted. To the Hindu, creation is beginningless and endless. That it is beginningless he proves by a simple process of logic. If creation had a beginning, then must the creator also have had a beginning, since until there is a creation there can be no creator; but to admit that the creator had a beginning would be to admit that God had a beginning, since God is not God until he creates—and to think of God as having had a beginning would, to the Hindu, be a manifest absurdity. God, who contains within himself the seed, the material cause, of the universe, first brings forth the universe–his own being, and then in due time takes it back again to himself. This process of creation and dissolution goes on for ever and ever for it is as endless as it is beginningless. Eternity is witness, not of one universe only that, for example, of which we are now a part—but of an infinite succession of universes. The birth, life, and destruction of a universe constitutes a cycle. To say that there was never a first cycle, and will never be a last, is only a way of affirming that the creative function of God is, like himself, eternal.

Further beliefs concern the stuff of which the successive universes are composed. This stuff is simply an immense multitude of beinge, some animate, some inanimate. Plants, animals, and men are animate; rocks and stones are inanimate. But all are alike beings. These by their nature,

- Ṛk*
  - Work
    - Saṁhitās
    - Brāhmaṇas
    - Āraṇyakas
  - Knowledge (Upaniṣads)
- SĀMA
  - Work
    - Saṁhitās
    - Brāhmaṇas
    - Āraṇyakas
  - Knowledge (Upaniṣads)
- Yajur
  - Work
    - Saṁhitās
    - Brāhmaṇas
    - Āraṇyakas
  - Knowledge (Upaniṣads)
- Atharva
  - Work
    - Saṁhitās
    - Brāhmaṇas
    - Āraṇyakas
  - Knowledge (Upaniṣads)

**Table 1**

* Ṛ.k, when joined with Veda, become Ṛg, by a regular change of consonant.

are involved in a process the final goal of which is their complete absorption into God—in his quiescent, or noncreative aspect. When an individual being is thus absorbed he is free forever, from the cycles of finite existence; but the process leading to this blessed state may be a long one. Not only may a being be born, live, and die, and then be born again, live, and die, indefinitely, within the bounds of a single universe, but he may also be born again and again into an indefinite series of universes. The history of a particular individual, the number of times he experiences rebirth, or reincarnation as it is called, depends entirely upon the quality of his will upon the moral effort he puts forth. As he rises in moral and spiritual stature he is born into an ever higher plane of existence until at last he returns to the world as man. Birth as a human being is extolled as a sacred birth, not because to be born as man necessarily leads to immediate liberation—far from it—but because the achievement of liberation is possible to man alone.

Against the background of these conceptions the orthodox view of the origin of the Vedas may be quickly sketched. At the very beginning of each cycle, holy seers are born into the world, men who in previous universes have ascended far towards the supreme goal and are therefore especially capable of perceiving divine truth. These blessed saints—ṛṣis, the Hindus call them—meditate on God, and while so meditating discern the everlasting laws of the spirit; and it is the concrete record of these laws, so discerned, that constitutes, in each cycle, the most authoritative or sacred writings. The record of the meditations of the ṛṣis born at the beginning of our own cycle is, then, what we know as the Vedas.

Thus far the account is, to orthodox eyes, literal truth. However, around the origin and early development of the Vedas are clustered many myths and symbols. Some of these we may now glance at—though in so doing we should realize that the gods of the Hindu, or devas as he calls them, must always be sharply distinguished from God. God is the one supreme being, the uncreated; while the gods, though supernatural, belong (together with many other orders of supernatural beings) among the creatures. Like the Christian angels, they are much nearer to man than to God.

'As smoke and sparks arise from a lighted fire kindled with damp fuel'—runs one account—even so, Maitreyi, have breathed forth from the Eternal all knowledge and all wisdom—what we know as the Rg-Veda,[2] the Yajur Veda, and the rest. They are the breath of the eternal.[3] And another, more circumstantial: 'The gods performed a sacrificial rite, meditating on the transcendental being as the sacrifice itself. From out of that sacrifice came Ṛk, Sāma, and Yajur.[4] (The Atharva—see the Table, above—which was probably later than the others, and of minor importance, is not here mentioned.) And another relates, with still more circumstance, how the god Brāhman was once meditating on his creator when there was manifested within the shrine of his heart the eternal word Om—the seed of all knowledge and of all thought. One by one were also manifested the sounds of all the letters, and through these letters there became known unto Brahman the wisdom of the Vedas. Then in order to spread this knowledge through the world he taught it to his disciples—to Marici, Atri, Angiras, and others—and these in turn to the world around them. In this fashion did the Vedas become known to all mankind.

By way of accounting for certain subdivisions of the Yajur a story is told[5] which has about it, like so many of the ancient scriptural narratives, a quaint, childlike humour. On a certain occasion the ṛṣis, it seems, planned a conference. 'Whoever fails to attend', they announced, 'will commit a great sin—equal to that of killing a brahmān.'[6] Now Vaisampayana failed to attend, and, as a consequence, the curse of all the other ṛṣis fell upon him. In order to expiate his offence he requested his disciples to practise austerities. One disciple, however, Yājñavalkya by name, remonstrated thus: 'Master, how can you expiate your sin by the austerities of these thy worthless disciples? I am the one amongst them who alone can bring good unto thee by my practices.' At this Vaisampayana grew angry, and said: 'How dare you speak thus? I want no such hot-headed, egotistical disciple as you! Give back what you have learned from me, and be off!'

So the egotist Yājñvalkya spewed from his mouth all that he had learned, and departed. His fellow disciples, unable to endure this insult to their knowledge, assumed the form of tittiri birds and gathered up the lore that had been ejected and taught it to their pupils. Thus it was that the branch of the Yājur called the Black Yajur, or, with reference to the birds, the Taittiriya, came into being.

Now Yājnavalkya, having cast away his knowledge of the Vedas, felt how empty he was, and realized what a very beast a man becomes who is destitute of this wisdom. But where might he find a teacher? Then it occurred to him that the sun-god never separates himself from the Vedas; for in the morning he is adorned with the Ṛg-Veda, at noon with the Yajur Veda, and in the evening with the Sāma Veda. And so, accepting the sun-god as his master, Yājñavalkya prayed to him for knowledge. The sun-god, pleased with the ardour of his new votary, did according to his desire, and the portion of the Vedas which he taught him was henceforth known as the White Yājur. Yājñavalkya then, in his turn, taught this to his disciples.

For the study of the Vedas, according to long tradition, and even according to the Vedas themselves, one must have—as Yājñavalkya had—a master, or guru: 'Approach a teacher', we read in the Ṛk, with, humility and with a desire to serve'; and in the Upanisads: 'To many it is not given to hear of the Self. Many, though they hear of it, do not understand it. Wonderful is he who speaks of it; intelligent is he who learns of it. Blessed is he who, taught by a good teacher is, able to understand it.[7]

The function of the 'good teacher', as Hinduism conceives it, is twofold. He of course explains the scriptures, the spirit as well as the letter; but, what is more important still, he teaches by his little daily acts, by his most casual words, sometimes even by his silence. Only to be near him, only to serve and obey him in humility and reverence, is to become quickened in spirit; and the purpose of the study of the Vedas is not merely or primarily to inform the intellect, but, to purify and enrich the soul:

> Pleasant indeed are the study and teaching of the Vedas!
> He who engages in these things attains to concentration of mind,
> And is no longer a slave to his passions;
> Devout, self-controlled, cultivated in spirit,
> He rises to fame and is a blessing to mankind.[8]

We have said that the orthodox Hindu regards the Vedas as his highest written authority. Any subsequent scripture, if he is to regard it as valid, must be in agreement with them: it may expand them, it may develop them and still be recognized, but it must not contradict them. They are to him, as nearly as any human document can be, the expression of divine truth. At the same time it would be a mistake to suppose that his allegiance to their authority is, in the final analysis, blind and automatic. If he considers them the word of God, it is because he believes their truth to be verifiable, immediately, at any moment, in his own personal experience. If he found on due examination that it was not so verifiable, he would reject it. If he found that any part of it was not so verifiable, he would reject that. In short, he conceives that his faith in the Vedas is as well founded, and on grounds exactly as critical, as is the natural scientist's belief in any physical law. And in this position these very scriptures themselves, he will tell you, uphold him. The real study, they say, is—not study of themselves—but study of that 'by which we realize the unchangeable'. In other words, the real study, in religion, is first-hand experience of God.

The Vedas teach the knowledge of God, and lay down work as a means to that knowledge—the word work here signifying both sacrificial rites and unselfish performance of secular duty. When through work our hearts are purified, we are ripe for divine knowledge. Work and knowledge—these two are the subjects of the Vedas, and name the parts into which Ṛk, Sāma, Yajur, and Atharva are each divided.

**Foot Notes:**

1. Ṛk. When joined with Veda, becomes Ṛg, by a regular change of consonant.
2. ṚK, when joined with Veda, becomes Ṛg, by a regular change of consonant.
3. Brhadaranyaka Upanishad, II. iv.10.
4. Ṛg-Veda, x. 90: Purusa Sūkta, 9.
5. From the Sanskrit quoted in the Introduction to Durgacharan Samkhyavedanta Tirtha's Bengali translation of the Iśa Upanishad with Samkara's commentary (Calcutta: Kshirode Chandra Majumdar).
6. A member, that is, of the brāhmin or priestly, caste.
7. Katha, I.ii. 7.
8. Śatapatha Brahmana, Mādhyandini sākhā, xi. v. 7, Swadhyāya prasansa, 1.

# two

## WHAT IS THE VEDA?

As the oldest Indian and also the oldest Indo-Germanic literary monument the Veda deserves an outstanding place in the history of world literature. It deserves it also, if we bear in mind that at least for 3000 years millions of Hindus considered the world of the Veda as the word of God and that the *Veda* controlled their thinking and feeling. Just as the Veda is, on account of its age, foremost in Indian literature, so also no one can understand the spiritual life and the culture of the Indians without acquiring an insight into the Vedic literature. Besides, Buddhism, whose place of birth is India, remains for ever un-understandable to one who does not know the Veda. For, the teaching of the Buddha are related to the Veda as the New Testament to the Old. No one can understand the new faith without getting acquainted with the old faith of which the Veda gives us information.

### 1. Now, what is actually the Veda?

The word 'Veda' means 'knowledge' and then the 'knowledge *par excellence*' *i.e.* the sacred, the religious knowledge, and it does not denote any one single literary work like perhaps the word 'Koran', or any compact collection of a definite number of books, completed at any particular time, like the word 'Bible' (the 'book par excellence') or like the word 'Tipiṭaka' the 'Bible' of the Buddhists, but a large extent of literature that came into being in the course of many millennia and was transmitted centuries long from generation to generation by word of mouth, until at last by a later generation—of course in the hoary past—it was declared as 'sacred knowledge' as 'divine revelation' on account of its age as well as its content. Here it is not a question of a 'canon' that was established at the time of any church-council. But the faith in the 'sacredness' of this literature followed in a way from itself and was only seldom seriously disputed.

But what is called 'Veda' or 'Vedic literature' consist of three different classes of literary works; and to each of these three classes belongs also a large or small number of individual work, of which some have been preserved but many have been also lost today. These three classes are:

I. SAṂHITĀS *i.e.* 'Collections' namely collections of hymns, prayers, magic songs, benedictory words, sacrificial formulas and litanies.

II. BRĀHMAṆAS, extensive prose texts which contain theological discussions, especially observations on the sacrifice and the practical or mystical significance of the individual sacrificial rites and ceremonies.

III. ĀRAṆYAKAS (Forest Texts) and Upaniṣads (secret teachings) which are partly included in or appended to the Brāhmaṇas themselves and partly are supposed to be independent works. They contain the meditations of hermits in forests and ascetics on God, world and man. And in them a good amount of Indian philosophy is contained.

There must have been once upon a time a fairly large number of Saṃhitās which originated in several schools of priests and singers and have been handed down further by them. Many of these 'collections' were however nothing but slightly different recensions—Śākhās, 'branches', as the Indians say—of one and the same Saṃhitā. But there are four Saṃhitās which differ sharply from one another and which are preserved to us in one or more recensions. They are:

1. The Ṛgveda-Saṃhitā, the collection of the Ṛgveda. The Ṛgveda is 'the veda or the knowledge of the praise—songs (ṛc, plural ṛcas).
2. The Atharvaveda-Saṃhitā, the collection of the Atharvaveda, i.e. of the knowledge of the magic formulas (*atharvan*).
3. The Sāmaveda-Saṃhitā, the collection of the Sāma veda. *i.e.* 'of the knowledge of the melodies' (Sāman).
4. The Yajurveda-Saṃhitā, the collection of the Yajurveda, *i.e.* 'of the knowledge of the sacrifical formulas (Yajus, plural Yajüṃṣi) of which there are two recensions which differ from each other rather sharply, namely:

   (a) The Saṃhitā of the Kṛṣṇa (Black) Yajurveda which is preserved in various recensions of which the Taittirīya-Saṃhitā and the Maitrāyaṇī-Saṃhitā are most important; and

   (b) The Saṃhitā of the Śukla (White) Yajurveda, which is preserved in the Vājasaneyi-Saṃhitā.

Based on these four different Śaṃhitās, the Indians distinguish four different Vedas—and therefore one also speaks often of the 'Vedas' in plural, namely: Ṛgveda, Atharvaveda, Sāmaveda and (Black and White) Yajurveda. And each one of the works of the class of the Brāhmaṇas, the Āraṇyakas or the Upaniṣads is attached to one or the other of the Saṃhitās enumerated above and 'belongs' as one usually says to one of the four Vedas. We have therefore not only Saṃhitās, but also Brāhmaṇas, Āraṇyakas and Upaniṣads of the Ṛgveda as well as of the Atharvaveda, of the Sāmaveda and of the Yajurveda. Thus the Aitareya Brāhmaṇa for e.g. belongs to the Ṛgveda, the Śatapatha Brāhamaṇa to the White Yajurveda, the Chāndogya Upaniṣad to the Sāmaveda etc.

Every work that belongs to one of the three above mentioned classes and to one of the four Vedas, must be described as 'Vedic'; and thus the whole vedic literature presents itself to us therefore as a large number of works of religious content—collections of songs, prayer-books, theological and theosophical treatises—which belong to several successive epoques, which however form one unit in this that altogether they constitute the basis for the Brahminical religious system and have for Brahminism the same significance as the Old Testament for Judaism and the New Testament for Christianity. And as the Jews and the Christians their 'Holy Scripture', so the Brahminical Indians, hold their Veda in its full extent to be divine revelation. It is however characteristic that corresponding to the expression 'Holy Scripurte' the Indians have the word 'Śruti', 'hearing' because the revealed texts were not written and read but only spoken and heard. However, that not only the ancient hymns of the Ṛgveda were supposed to have been 'breathed out' by Brahman and 'seen' by the ancient seers, but also that every word in the Upaniṣads, the latest products of the vedic literature were considered as indisputable truth coming from God Brahman, is testified by the whole history of Indian philosophy. Although the various systems of Indian philosophy differ widely from one another, they all agree on this that they hold the Veda as revealed and that they all quote the Veda, especially the Upaniṣads, as authority. There is certainly a high degree of freedom and arbitrariness as regards explaining these texts, and every philosopher reads out of them whatever he wants to find. It is highly characteristic that even the Buddhists who reject the authority of the Veda admit that it was originally proclaimed (or 'created') by God Brahmā; only, they add, that it was falsified by the Brahmins and therefore it contains so many mistakes.

The expression 'Veda' is justified only for this literature considered as revealed. There is however one more class of works which most closely follow the vedic literature but cannot be described as belonging to the Veda. They are the so called Kalpasūtras (sometimes also called shortly 'sūtras') or text books of rituals, which are written in a peculiar, aphoristic prose style. Among them we find.

1. The Śrautasūtras, which contain the rules for the execution of the great sacrifices often lasting for many days, during which several sacrificial fires burn and a large number of priests must be employed.
2. The Gṛhyasūtras, which contain rules for the simple ceremonies and sacrificial acts of every day life (at birth, wedding, death etc.) and
3. The Dharmasūtras, the text books of spiritual and wordly law—the oldest law books of the Indians.

Just like the Brāhmaṇas, Āraṇyakas and Upaniṣads these works are appended to one of the four Vedas; and there are Śrauta, Gṛhya and Dharmasūtras which belong to the Ṛgveda, others which belong to the Sāmaveda, to the Yajurveda or to the Atharvaveda. They have originated evidently from particular vedic schools which have set to themselves the task of the study of any one particular Veda. But these text books are considered as man's work and not as divine revelation any more. They do not belong to the Veda but to the 'Vedāṅgas', the 'Vedāṅgas', the 'parts' *i.e.*, 'the auxiliary sciences of the Veda.'

To these 'Vedāṅgas' belong, in addition to the works on rituals also a number of works on phonetics, grammar, etymology, prosody and astronomy. We shall treat these at the end of this chapter.

After this general survey of the Vedic literature and its connected literature, we shall apply ourselves to discussing the most important works belonging to the Veda, above all the Saṁhitās.

# three

## THE VEDIC SCHOOLS AND TEACHERS OF THE BRĀHMANAS

THOUGH the Puranas say very little about secular history after the Bhārata battle, yet the Pruanic brahmans incorporated notices of the Vedic schools and later teachers. The development of those schools among Vyāsa's disciples is described best in the Vāyu and Brahmaṇḍa less fully in the Viṣṇu, and the Bhāgavata has copied less clearly and intelligently.[1] Many of the teachers named[2] are alluded to in Vedic literature, but their assignment in those several schools does not, I believe always tally with their assignment in that literature; yet there may be truth in both, since teachers were no doubt masters of more than one Veda. The account in the first two Puranas mentioned was obviously drawn up and added by the Puranic brahmans themselves, and deserves attention, because they had knowledge of those schools, and because the account was endorsed by the brahmanic Viṣṇu and again by the still more brahmanic Bhāgavata. As I have not studied Vedic literature closely, I cannot venture to discuss intricacies, and so merely set out the account briefly here with a few comments. Care must be taken not to confuse different persons of the same name, for the account shows there were many such; thus, as will appear, there were two Sumantus and several Yājnavalkyas, and the Jaimini who taught Pauspiṇḍya was great grandson of Vyāsa's disciple Jaimini.[4]

***Rigveda.***[5] Paila made two versions and gave them to his disciples, one to Indrapramati[6] and the other to Vaṣkala. Vāṣkala made four samhitas of his version and gave them severally to his four disciples, Bodhya, Agnimāṭara, Parāsaṛa[7] and Yājnavalkya. Indrapramati taught his version to Madnūkeyā; he taught it to his son Satyaśravas; he to Satyahita; and he to his son Satyaśri. Satyasri had three great disciples, Devamitra Sākalya. Rathitarra Sakapurna'[8] and Vāskali Bharadvāja; and they established sakhas. Sakalya made five saṁhitās and taught them to his five disciples, Mudgala, Golaka, Khālīya, Vatsa and Śaiśireya. He was very conceited,[9] and King' 'Janaka' of Videha performed a horse-sacrifice and a great concourse of rishis attended it. He offered great wealth (including slaves[10]) to whoever should be the greatest among them, so they challenged one another to discussion. Yājñavalkya, son of Brahmavāha vanquished them all with his questions, and then challenged Śākalya with the penalty that whichever failed should forfeit his life. He answered all Sakalya's questions, but Sakalya could not answer his single question and so perished.[11] Yājnāvalkya then carried off the prize.[12] Śākapurna Rāthītara made three samhitas and also a nirukta. He had four disciples, Ketava, Dalaki,[13] Śatabalāka and Naigama.[14] Vāskali Bharadvāja made three samhitas, and had three disciples, Nandāyaniya, Pannagāri and Aryava.

***Yajurveda.***[15] Vaiśampāyana made 86 saṁhitās and all his disciples received them except Yājñavalkya, who was discarded because of his presumption. Those 86 disciples fashioned samhitas, and comprised three groups distinguished geographically, the northern, the madhyadeśya and the eastern, the chiefs of which were respectively Śyamāyani, Asuri and Ālambi. They were all called Carakas and Carakadhvaryus, and (says the Viṣṇu) Taittirīyas. Yājñavalkya, called Brahmarāti[16] fashioned independently separate yajrs,[17] and had 15 disciples, Kaṇva, Madhyamdina, &c. (names given) they were called Vājins. So there were 101 recensions altogether.

All these occurrences and names are explained in a story,[18] which consists largely of fable and grew out of a misunderstanding of names. It says (among other things) that Yājñavalkya Brahmarāti when discarded had to disgorge the yajuses he had learnt from Vaiśampayana, and the other disciples picked them up; that he then worshipped the sun and obtained his own special yajuses from the sun; and that the name Vajin arose because he was *aśva-rūpa*. Now *vājin* can be synonymous with *vāja-sani*, the name of a Yājñavalkya; this Yājñavalkya was (either Vejasani or) Vājasaneya; hence his disciples, the Vājasaneyas of the White Yājus, were called shortly Vājins: but *vājin* was misunderstood as a horse and so he is styled *asvarupa*.[19] Similarly, Tittiri was apparently the chief of the disciples of the Black Yajus,[20] and his followers were the Taittiriyas.

This Yājñavalkya as Vaiśampāyana's disciple would have been prior to Janmejaya III, and his teaching appears to have been adopted by that king, for, it is said, Janmejaya established the Vajasaneyaka school in disregard of a Vaiśampāyana and in spite of his curse, but ultimately abdicated.[21] In other respects this account of the Yajurveda, and especially of the Black Yajus, appears from its brevity and indefiniteness and the large number of disciples and recensions to have contracted the succession of teachers; and the three leader of the Taittirīyas, Syāmayani, Asuri and Ālambi, should be placed soon after Adhisīmakṛṣṇa's time if this Āsuri is the same a Pāncasikha's teacher (see *infra*).

***Sāmaveda***.[22] Jaimini taught this to his son Sumantu, he to his son Sutvan, and he to his son Sukarman. Sukarman Jaimini made a thousand saṁhitas of it.[23] He had two famous disciples, Pauspiñji or Pauspiyaji[24] and Hiraṇyanabha Kausalya. Pauspiñji made 500 samhitās and taught them to his four disciples who were called the northern sāman chanters. Hiranyanābha made 500 also and taught them to his disciples, who were called the eastern sāman chanters. Pauspiñji's disciples were Laugaksi (or Lokāksi), Kusītin and

Lāngali. Laugaksi had five disciples and their school were those of Rānayanīya, Taṇḍiputra, &c. (names given). Kuthumi had his three sons as his disciples, Aaurasa, Parāśara[25] and Bhāgavitti, and these Kauthumas formed three sections. Śauridyu and Śrṅgiputra were apparently disciples of Aurasa or Bhāgavitti,[26] and Śrṅgiputra declared three saṁhitās, those of Caila, Pracīnayoga and Surāla. Pārāsarya Kauthuma declared six saṁhitās, those of Āsurāyaṇa, a Patañjali, &c. (names given). Lāngali and Silihotra[27] each declared six Saṁhitās. Lāngali's six disciples were Bhāluki, Jaimini, Lomagāyani, &c. (names given); and they promulgated saṁhitās.

Hiranyaṇabha Kausalya's, disciple was prince Kṛta. He made 24 samhitās, and declared them to his disciples, Rāda, Gautama, Parasara, &c. (names given); and they were the Kārta[28] sāman chanters. Pauspiñji and Kṛta were the most famous of all sāman chanters. This statement, about Hiraṇyanābha, Kṛta and his disciples is wrongly introduced here, for they belonged to a much earlier period: it has been inserted in order to bring them into the scheme of Vedic schools derived from Vyāsa.

***Atharvaveda.***[29] Sumantu divided it into two and taught it to Kabandha. Kabandha divided it into two again and gave one part to Pathya and the other to Devadarsa (or Vedasparsa). The latter made four versions and taught them to his four disciples, Moda, Brahmabala, Pippalāda and Šaulkayani. The Pathyas had three divisions, those of Jājali,[30] Kumudādi and a 'Śaunaka.' Śaunaka made two saṁhitās, and gave one to Babhru and the other to Saindhavāyana. Saindhava gave that to Muñjakeśa and it was again made into two. The best *vikalpanas* of the samhitas are the Naksatrakalpa, Vaitāna, Saṁahitāvidhi, Aṇgiras's kalpa and Sāntikalpa.

This account of the Vedic schools has brought them well into the Brāhmaṇa period, and the chronology of that period may be considered. The great Brāhmanas[31] were composed in the country of the Kurus or allied, Kuru-

Pañcalas,[32] hence the fusion of those two peoples is important, which occurred more than a century after the Bhārata battle or about 820 B.C.

The Pañicavimsa and Taittirīya Brāhmanas are the most archaic of the regular Brahmanas.[33] The Pañcavimsa, though its home apparently lay farther east, yet contains a minute description of sacrifices performed on the rivers Sarasvatī and Drasadvati, and has no allusion to the Kuru-Pancālas; hence it was apparently composed before the blending,[34] and while the Kurus still reigned at Hastināpur and over Kuruksetra (say) about, 880 B.C. The Taittirīya refers to the united Kuru-Pañcalas,[35] and was therefore composed after the fusion, (say) soon after 800 B.C. A more recent group is formed by the Jaiminiya, Kauṣitaki and the Aitareya Brahmanas. The first of these is probably the oldest, while the third seems, on linguistic grounds at least, to be the latest of the three. The Satapatba is posterior to these. Latest of all are the Gopatha Brahmana and the short Brahmanas of the Samaveda.[36] All these would be posterior to the fusion of' the Kurus and Pañcalas, and so the Jaiminiya refers repeatedly to' the Kuru-Pancilas, and they ,are mentioned in the Satapatha and Gopatha.[37] The Brahmana period ended apparently before or about 600 B.C.;[38] hence the Satapatha may be placed somewhat before that date, and it will probably not be far wrong to put the Jaiminiya, the Kausitaki and the Aitareya about half-way between the Taittiriya and the Satapatha, in the last quarter of the eighth century and the first quarter of the seventh, the Jaiminiya first and the Aitareya third.

By the end of the seventh century B.C., the original Puranas had been compiled, and the old traditions became known to a certain extent to the recluse brahmans who composed the Brahmanas: hence the Satapatha notices much legend, though seemingly with doubtful success.[39] The fact that the Brahmanas make no reference to the Pandavas or the Bharata battle has been explained;[40] and the reason why the Bharatas are not mentioned in the geographical lists of the Aitareya Brahmana, in Manu, or in the Buddhist texts,[41] term Bharata had become too wide for particular use. The futility of expecting to find secular history in the Brahman as, which are purely priestly literature; is emphasized by the fact that they take very little notice even of contemporary kings.

The foregoing succession of teachers of the Vedic schools during the Brāhmana period may be supplemented by notices of various brahmans who were contemporary. Many are mentioned in Vedic literature and in the Mahābhārata and Puranas, but generally in brahmanie statements without definite historical connexions:[42] yet here may be noticed certain of them on whom light can be thrown so as to suggest their mutual, and approximately real, positions.

A near relative probably of the Pandavas purohita Dhaumya was Āyoda Dhaumya, who lived in the time of their successor Pariksit II and his son Janamejaya III.[43] He had three disciples, Upamanyu, Āruni Uddālaka Pāncālya and Veda. Veda became Janamejaya's purohit.[44] Uddālaka[45] was son of Aruna Aupavesi Gautama. Aruna had learnt of Upaveśa and of Asvapati[46] prince of the Kekayās, who instructed also Prācinasala. Aupatmnyava. Uddālaka learnt also of Patancala Kapya. He was contemporary with Svaidāyana Saunaka and Sauceya Prāclnayogva,[47] and he or his son Auddalaka were, contemporary with that Pracinasala, four other brahmans and Asvapati.[48] Uddālaka had a son begotten of his wife by a disciple at his request, Śvetaketu Auddālaki Aruneya.[49] He had a favourite disciple Kahoda, (Kausitaki[50])and gave him his daughter Sujata in marriage, and their son was Astavakra. Kahoda was vanquished by Vandin in a controversy before king 'Janaka' and was drowned. Svetaketu and Astavakra, uncle and nephew, were of the same age, and were brought up in Uddālaka's hermitage. When Astavakra learnt of his father's faιe, they both went to Janaka Ugrasena Puskaramalin and over-came Vandin.[51] Contemporary with Śvetaketu were the Pancala king Pravahana Jaivala[52] and Jala Jatūkarnya.[53]

It is said Svetaketu, who was reckoned a rishi,[54] established strict monogamy for women; in relation to brahman women.[55] It is amazing that such a story should have been fabricated and preserved, if not true; and if true, it would indicate that laxity among brahmans (which various stories suggest in early times) did not disappear till some time later, than the Bhārata battle. [56]

Uddālaka had as pupils Yājnavalkya Vajasaneya[57] and Proti Kausurubindi. The Vājasaneya school was established in or by Janamejaya Iii's time. Yājnavalkya had Āsuri as pupil.[58] Āsuri's first disciple was Pāncasikha who was of Parāsara's gotra, was a bhiksu,[59] and was called Kāpileya (it is said) after his foster mother Kapila and shortly Kapila by the Sankhyas.[60] He went to Janaka Janadeva, king of Mithila, and the king gave up his hundred teachers and followed Pancasikha, who taught him moksa according to the Sankhya;[61] and Janaka Dharmadvaja also was his disciple.[62] Two stages below Asuri was Asurayana with whom Yaska was contemporary.[63] This Yājnavalkya also taught Madhuka Paingya, he taught Cūda Bhagavitti, he Jānaki Ayasthuna, and he Satyakama Jabala.[64]

In a chronological succession of teachers are names (downwards) Upavesi, Aruna, Uddālaka, Yājnavalkya, Āsuri and Āsurayana:[65] and Vodhu (or Vodha), Kapila, Āsuri and Pancasikha are mentioned as connected teachers,[66] treating Kapila and Pañcasikha as distinct.

These particulars yield something like a chronological scheme, and all the more important of these teachers[67] are shown in the following table, which is in continuation of those mentioned earlier. It starts with teachers contemporary with the Pandavas, Pariksit II and Janamejaya III, and nearly all the persons 'in the first four columns' are connected by Synchronisms. There are few synchronisms touching the teachers, in columns 5-8, yet something may he done to

| | Kuru-Pauravas | Janakas of Videha | Other kings | Various teachers |
|---|---|---|---|---|
| 92 | Victravīrya | Dhati | ... | Kaṣṇa-Dvaipāyana-Vyāsa |
| 93 | Dhatarāṣṭra | Bahulāśva | ... | Śuka |
| 94 | Pāṇḍavas | Katakṣaṇa | ... | Bhariśravas,&c. (p. 214) |
| 95 | Abhimanyu | ... | ... | Upaveśa |
| 96 | Parikṣit II | ... | Aśvapati of Kekaya | Āyoda, Patañcala, Aruṇa, Prācīnaśāla |
| 97 | Janamejaya III | ... | ... | Uddālaka, Veda, 'Upamanyu,' Svaldāyans, Prācīnayogya |
| 98 | Śatānīka | Janaka-Ugrasena | ... | Kahoda, Vandin, Yājñavalkya-Vājasaneya |
| 99 | Aśvamedha-datta Śvetaketu, | ... | ... | Pravāhaṇa of PañcālaAṣṭāvakra |
| 100 | Adhisimakaṣṇa | ... | ... | Yājñavalkya (son of Brahmavāha) |
| a | ... | ... | ... | Āsuri, Madhuka |
| b | ... | Janaka-Janadeva | ... | Pañcaśikha |
| c | ... | Janaka-Dharmadhvaja | Caḍa-Bhāgavitti | |
| d | ... | ... | ... | Asurāyaṇa, Yāska |
| e | ... | Jānaki-Āyasthaṇa | ... | ... |
| f | ... | ... | ... | Satyakāma-Jābāla |

| Of Rigveda | Of Yajurveda | Of Sāmaveda | Of Atharvaveda | |
|---|---|---|---|---|
| ... | ... | ... | ... | 92 |
| ... | ... | ... | ... | 93 |
| Paila | Vaiśampāyana | Jaimini | Sumantu | 94 |
| Indrapramati, Vāṣkala | ... | Sumantu-Jaim- | Kabandha | 95 |
| Bodhya, 'Yājñavalkya,' Pāraśara, Māṇḍakeya | Yājñavalkya-Brahmarāti | Sutvan-Jaimini darśa | Pathya, Deva- | 96 |
| Satyaśravas | Tittiri | Sukarman-Jaimini | Pippalāda, &c. | 97 |
| Satyahita | ... ... | Pauṣpiṇḍya | Jājali, Śaunaka | 98 |
| Satyaśrī | Madhyaṁdina, Kaṇva, & | Laugākṣi, Kuthumi, Kuśitin, Lāṅgali | Saindhavāyana Babhru | 99 |
| Śākalya, Vāṣkali. Śākaparṇa | 'Yajnavalkya' | Rānāyaniya, Tandiputra, Parasara, Bhagavitti, &c. | ... | 100 |
| Pannagāri, Šaiśireya, Vatsa, Śatabalāka | Śyāmāyani, Āsuri, Ālambi ... | ... | Muñjakeśa | a |
| ... | ... | Lomagāyani, Pārāśarya, Prācīnayoga | ... | b |
| ... | ... | ... | ... | c |
| ... | .... | Asuryana, a | ... | d |
| ... | ... | 'Patanjali' | ... | e |
| ... | ... | ... | ... | f |

estimate their positions for the notice of some of them in the Brāhmanas would no doubt warrant the inference that such a person flourished well 'before the Brāhmana which mentions' him, at least a quarter of a century prior. The steps are numbered as far as 100, but beyond that there are, no clear royal synchrnisms to mark definite steps.

Thus the Taittiriya Brāhmana above that Aruna Aupavesi[68] lived well before, 800 B.C., and the synchronisms coupled, with date of the Bharata battle assign him to the early half of the ninth century B.C. Similarly the Jaiminiya shows that Yājnavalkya Vājasaneya lived well before 725, and his position in the, table places him more than a century earlier. The Satapatha notices Uddālaka, Śvetaketu, Śakalya, Āsuri, Madhuka, Prācinayogya and Satyakāma, and shows that Satyakāma, the latest of them, lived well before 600 B.C. The Kausitaki mentions' Uddalaka, Svetaketu and Madhuka, and fixes their time closer in that Madhuka, the latest .of, these, lived well before 700. The most effective indication is that to the Tandins belonged the Tandya or Pañcavimsa Brahmana of the Samaveda,[69] so that Tandiputra and all the prior teachers of that Veda in column 7 were anterior to 830 B.C.

If then we work on these inferences according to the sequence in the table and with the scale proposed, we may estimate the periods when the teachers *flour ished* excepts as regards those of the Atharvaveda for whom there are no synchronisms. In the ninth century B.C. flourished Uddalaka in the first quarter, Śvetaketu about the middle, and Śakalya and Tandiputra in the third quarter. In the eighth century Āsuri and Madhuka at the beginning, Pancasikha in the middle, and Asuriyana and Yāska in the fourth quarter. In the seventh century Satyākama in the second quarter. This estimate for Pāncasikha agrees with Buddhist legends, which speak of him as long prior to Buddha.[70]

The account of the Vedic schools shows that Vyāsa's successors exercised individual liberty in dealing with the text of the Vedas as arranged by him, and so there grew up a multitude of modifications which constituted different 'uses'. Five Puranas' explain briefly how that happened.[71] The differences arose from the idiosyncrasies (*drsti-vibhrama*) of the various teachers, and consisted in their arrangement of the mantras and Brāhmanas and in their transposition of tones and syllables (*svara-varna*), but the essential text itself remained fixed apparently.[72] The multiplicity and variance of the different uses must have worked their own remedy in the gradual salection of the best versions and the elimination of the rest, until at length one use became generally accepted as the established Saṁhitā text.[73] The table shows that the growth of diversities continued during at least eight succession of teachers, that is, nearly two centuries according to the above estimated dates. The reverse process could hardly have taken much less time. The two processes therefore probably occupied .nearly four centuries, and this may be suggest as one reason why the Saṁhitā text did not come into existence till after the complation of the Brāhmanas or about 600 B.C.[74]

Moreover, when we compare the teachers in column 4 with those in columns 5-8, we notice that there is no agreement between the two classes (except perhaps as regards No. 100, Yājnavalkya) until we reach Asuri and Āsurāyana. This want of agreement is entirely what should he expected, because the Vedic schools could not have dominated all the religious teachers forthwith, and had gradually to make good their special province and authority, each as regards its own Veda. That process would have been slow not only because of religious conservatism and jealousy,[76] but also because the multiplicity of competing version's would have weakened their prerogative. It would have required a long time; and the table shows that from Vyāsa's disciples to Āsuri (when the influence began to appear) was more than a century and a half. During that period religious teachers of the old order would have continued to flourish independently alongside the growing Vedic schools, and that is what column 4 shows.[77] The two streams of teaching would have persisted, with gradually diminishing difference, even longer than that, and may not have blended till the close of the Brahmana period. Hence that condition may be suggested as another cause why 'the Saṃhitā, text did not come' into existence till after the completion of the Brāhmanas.

Here notice historical tradition on the religious side closes, for the Puranas and epic contain nothing noteworthy about later' teachers. Their account stops with Āsurayana, who has been assigned' to about the, end of the eighth century B.C. It was drawn up by the Puranic brahmans as mentioned above and the fact that, they continued the lines of religious teachers, beyond the stage where their secular tradition closed, down to about 700 B.C. with precise statements, and allude to nothing later personal, except to Buddha curtly or vaguely, indicates that these additions were made then as a second stage while personal knowledge was fresh. Not long afterwards Jainism and Buddhism challenged the supremacy of the brahmans, and no traditions about later teachers, were added., Secular chronicles preserved knowledge of the dynasties and kings who reigned in the chief countries, and were incorporated in the Bhavisya Purana, and copied later into the Matsya,[78] and, other Puranas in the third, century A.D. and afterwards. Religious tradition about the same period would seem to have become too scanty, uncertain or confused amid the religious conflicts to gain admittance into the Puranas.

Ancient tradition was compiled into the original Purana about the ninth century B.C., later religious historical tradition was added till the end of the eighth century B.C., and the chronicles of the kings of the Kali age were incorporated in the Puranas in prophetic guise down to the early part of the fourth century' A.D. Such were the three main stages of the compilation of historical tradition in the Puranas.

**Foot Notes:**

1.Cf. kūr i, 52, 17-18; Va 1, 180; 61, 73-7; Bd ii, 35, 83-6.

2.Also in Bd ii, 33, 3.17 (not in Vā): Kur I, 53, 5-25: lg I, 7, 14-52; 24, 11-132: but the lists are jumbled. There is much variation in many of the lesser names, and Va is generally followed when they are uncertain.

3.Weber, *Hist. of Ind. Lit.*, p.142, note, refers to the Viṣ and Vā accounts, but doubts their trustworthiness—gratuitously.

4.They are treated as one, Weber, op. Cit., p.240, note.

5.Vā 60, 24-32, 63-6; 61, 1-4. Bd ii, 34, 24-33; 35, 1-7. Viṣ iii, 4, 16-26. Ag 150, 25-6; 258 (a disquisition); 270, 2-3. Bhag xii, 6, 53-60.

6.To be distinguished from the earlier Indrapramati, p.214.

7.To be distinguished from earlier Parāśaras, p.213.

8.Śākapūni, Weber, *op. Cit.*, p.85.

9.*Jnanahañkāra-garvita*; hence called *Vidagdha*, Weber, pp.33, 129: *Vedic Index* ii, 296, Cf. MBh xiii, 74, 589-92.

10.Videha slaves, *Vedic Index*, ii, 212.

11.Vā 60, 32-62, Bd ii, 34, 33-68. Referred to, Mbh xiii, 14, 689 Vā adds—Śakalya's disciples on his death incurred the guilt of brahmancide, but went to Bādaditya tīrtha at Pavanapura and were purified (60, 67-75 and 59, 108-30).

12.This might explain the name Vājasani of a Yājnavalkya (Weber, p.104), except that the name Vājasāneya appears to have arisen earlier; *see infra* under Yājurveda.

13.Here Vā (60,65-6; 61, 1) has apparently confused the text and inserted six names wrongly.

14.Viṣ says, the fourth disciple made a nirukta.

15.Vā 61, 5-10, 23-6. Bd ii, 35, 8-13, 26-30. Viṣ iii, 5, 1-2, 12-13. Ag 150, 27-8; 259 (a disquition) ; 270, 3-5. Bhāg xii, 6, 61-74.

16.Viṣ says son of Brahmarāta: Bhāg son of Devarata.

17.Called *ayatayama*, which Vaisampayana did not know; so Viṣ. Bhāg copied this.

18.Vā 61, 11-23. Bd ii, 35, 14-26. Viṣ iii, 5, 3-28, embellishing.

19.Viṣ, misunderstanding, makes the sun appear *asvarupa*. Bhag copied.

20.Weber, pp.41, 87, 90-1. Vis misunderstanding, turned him and the other disciples into partridges; and so also Bhāg. Tittiri was a name, see p. 105.

21.Mat 50, 57-65. Vā 99, 250-6. This Vaiśampayana can hardly have been Vyāsa's disciple, chronologically. He may have been confused with Vyāsa's disciple, and so Vyāsa and the earlier Vaiśampayana have been wrongly introduced.

22.Vā 61, 27-47. Bd. ii, 35, 31-55. Partially, Viṣ iii, 6, 1-8: Bhāg xii, 6, 75-80: Ag 150, 28-9; 260 (a disquisition); 270, 6-8.

23.Here Vā and Bd tell a fable about him and Indra.

24.*Pausyaṇji* (va, Bd) is a misreading of Pauspinji (Vis), *i.e. Pauspindya; Vedic Index*, ii.27.

25.To be distinguished from other Parāśaras, p.213.

26.The text is defective.

27.Śālihotra may = Kuśtin, but Bd makes him = Lāngali.

28.Vā and Bd misread this as Kranta (p.173).

29.Vā 61, 49-55. Bd ii, 35, 55-62. Vis iii, 6,9, 9-15. Ag 150, 30; 261 (a disquisition); 270, 8-9. Bhāg xii, 7,1-4.

30.Jājali in Hv 142, 7999 (if genuine) was much earlier

31.Their formation, ten functions (*Vidhi*),&c.; Bd ii, 33, 47-58: Vā (incompletely) 59, 130, 132-41. Their declarers are styled *rsi-purakas*. Bd ii, 33, 1.

32.*Vedic Index*, i. 165.

33.*Macdonell, Sansk*, Lit., p.203.

34.Id., p.210. Weber, *Hist of Ind.* Lit., pp.67-8.

35.*Vedic Index*, i.165.

36.*Macdonell, Sansk*, Lit., p.203.

37.The Kuru-Pancala dynasty ended about 400 B.C. (P.180).

38.*Macdonell, Sansk. Lit.*, pp.50,215. Winternitz, in his *Geschichte der Indischen Litteratur* (i. p.25) makes the landmark the rise of Buddhism. Which practically agrees.

39.e.g. its story of Gotama Rahugana, pp.224, 311.

40.P. 283. See also Macdonell, *Sansk. Lit.*, p.216.

41.*Vedic Index*, ii, p.98.

42.MBh I, 53, 2044-50 is a brahmanical jumble.

43.Dhaumya was a Kāśyapa (p.233). So Aitar Brahm (vii, 5, 27) says the Kaśyapas were Janamejaya's hereditary priests.

44.Mbh I, 3, 673-97, 740-6; 53, 2047. Weber, *Hist of Ind. Lit.*, p.71.An Arunj, Var 37, 7.

45.He was an Āngirasa, Mat 196, 4,6,8. He must be distinguished from Uddala or Uddālaki, an Atreya (mat 197, 2.) whose son was Nadketas, called also Nāciketa. They appear in brahmanical fables; Mbh xiii 17, 1291-2; 71, 3486-7: var 193, 12 f. *Vedic Index* i. pp.88-9, 432. Katha Upanisad I, 1.1. and 11; ii, 4.5. apparently identifies them.

46.There were more than one Asvapati, see p.164, and Mat 28, 5.

47.Satapatha Brāhm xi, 4, 1-9; 5,3.

48.Chāndogya Up. V, 11-17.

49.Mbh I, 122, 4724, 4735: iii, 132, 10599: xii, 34, 1229: xiii, 165, 7671. Weber, pp.71, 137. Called by abridgement, ' son of Gautama,' SBE I, pp.76-7; *Vedic Index* ii, p.409. Mentioned, Mbh ix, 39, 2207-9.

50.*Vedic Index*, i, p.145.

51.MBh iii, 132, 10599 to 134, 10690. Rām vi, 121, 16. Fables about Astāvakra, Mbh xiii, 19, 1390 f.; Br 212, 72 f.

52.Chandogya Up. V, 3.1. Bṛhadaraṇyaka Up, vi, 2 ,1.

53.*Vedic Index* ii, p.409.

54.Apastamba I, 2,4,5, 4-6.

55.MBh I, 122, 4724-35. Yet the same is attributed far earlier to Dīrghatamas, 104, 4204-3. Both possibly true.

56.Cf. the story of Jabālā and her son Satyakama, who were later (*infra*); Chandogya Up. Iv, 4, 1-2. Cf. Vedic Index I, 273, 479-80; ii, 84, 259. As regards polyandry, Mbh I, 195, 7244 to 196, 7271. Was the description of

a brahman by adding putra to his mother's name see Bracta practice that prevailed about this period) due to such laxity? Weber, *Hist. of Ind. Lit.*, pp.71, 131: where Kṛṣṇa Devakiputra the scholar, is plainly different from Kṛsṇna the king; so *vedic Index*, I, p.184. Kṛṣṇa was a very common name, Devaka (and therefore the feminine Devaki) an ordinary name.

57.Bhāg ix, 22, 38, if correct would refer to an earlier Yājnavalkya. There were many yājuavalkyas (p.237).

58.Weber, op. Cit., pp.128. 131, 235-6. *Vedic Index* I, 72.

59.MBH xii, 322, 11875.

60.Cf. Mat 3, 29. He is confused with the mythical Kapila, MBH vi, 34, 1230: xii, 342, 13078-9; 341, 12932; 344, 13254; 51, 13703: iii, 220, 14197: Mat 171, 1-4: story of Ṡagara's sons (p.271): Pad ii, 75,2—and so called cira-jivin, MBH xii, 218, 7890.

61.Mbh xii, 218, 7883-7900; 219, 7930-4. Fable, 269, 9600-4.

62.MBh xii, 322, 11855, 11875 with 321, 11839-40.

63.Weber, pp.128, 235-6. *Vedic Index* i. 72.

64.Weber, pp.130, 134. Brhadāraṇyaka Up. Vi, 3, 7-11.

65.Brhadāranyaka up. Vi, 5, 2-3.

66.Vā 101, 338, Bd iv, 2, 273-4. Mat 102, 18 and Kūr I, 53, 15 (both placing Vodhu third). Cf. Va 23, 141: Lg I, 7, 41: 24 41: MBh xii, 320, 11783-4 (which all omit Voḍhu).

67.Cf. Bd ii, 33, 1-17; which is wanting in Vā. For the references for the following statements see Vedic Index generally. The dates of the Brāhmaṇas are those suggested above.

68.*Vedic Index* I, 35.

69.Macdonell, *Sanek*, Lit., pp. 209-10. Weber, op. Cit., p.68.

70.Weber, *op. cit.*, p.236.

71.Vā 58, 12-18. Bḍ ii, 31, 12-18. Mat 144, 11-17. Lg i 39, 58-60. Kur i, 29, 44-6.

72.So Macdonell, *Sansk. Lit.*, p.49.

73.Weber, *op. cit.*, pp. 13-14.
74.Macdonell, *op. cit.*, p. 50.
75.Not certain, because there were several yajnavalkyas.
76.Weber, *op. cit.*, p. 13. This would have restricted the citation by one school of teachers of another school.
77.Such must have been the position that naturally resulted from the establishment of the Vedic schools, however they were established.
78.It existed before (p. 51).

# four

## INTRODUCTION TO THE RIG-VEDA

### 1. Introductory

The *Ṛigveda* is the Vedic book *par excellence.* Chronologically, it is the oldest book in Hindu literature. Theoretically, it is the most sacred, as it heads[1], the list of books which come under *sruti* or 'revelation'. The word *Veda* means knowledge or wisdom[2], and Ṛig (*Rik*) is the name for laudatory verse or stanza. Hence the compound word Rig-Veda may be translated as 'Verse-Wisdom'[3]. It is the earliest and most sacred wisdom of the Indian Aryans set forth in the form of stanzas which are grouped in hymns. The unit of revelation, as in the Quran, seems to be the verse.

The *Ṛigveda* is a great collection (*saṁhita*) of a thousand or more hymns. It is, however, only one out of four collection. For besides the Ṛv., there is the Sāman or chant-Veda, the *Yajus* or Veda of sacrifical formulae, and the *Atharvan* or Veda of 'popular religion'. The four Vedas are not unconnected with one another. Thus all the stanzas of the Sāmaveda except seventy-five are found in the Ṛv. The Yajurveda and the Atharvaveda also have a considerable amount of material in common with the Ṛv. What we really have, then, in the four Vedas is the distribution of the original Vedic material into four *saṁhitas* or 'collection'[4]. The four Vedas are a fourfold presentation of the primitive Veda, in some such way as the four Gospels are a fourfold presentation of the primitive Gospel. By 'primitive Veda' of course is meant the poetic material of the Vedic age before it was collected. Such material existing in the various Vedic clans and priestly families consisted, as the four historic collection show, of 'a heterogenous combination of old hymns, charms, philosophical poems, and popular songs, most but not all of which are of religious content'[5]. This primitive Vedic material was in part 'hieratic' or priestly, having to do with the worship of the great gods, such as Agni, Indra, Soma; and in part, popular, consisting of house ceremonies, charms and magic spells'[6]. The Ṛigveda, while containing some popular material, especially in the tenth, first and seventh books", is pre-eminently a text-book of popular religion.

The process of the formation of the Ṛigveda as a collection of hymns must have been complete by about 800 B.C., and the true date may be still earlier. The complete Ṛik is presupposed in the existing Brāhmanas, which, according to the most moderate possible estimate, cannot be dated later than 800 to 600 B.C. The other three Vedas were collected rather later than the Rik, but we need not discuss the dates of their formation here. It is, besides, quite probable that long before the fourfold collection was formally made, the Vedic material began to break up into four groups on the basis f religious use. Thus the reference in the *Puruṣa-Sūkta*[8] may be only to an incipient classification of the Vedic material into laudatory verses (ricaḥ) used by the *Hotṛi* or invoking priest,chants (sāmāni) used by the *Udhatri* or singing priest, and sacrificial formulas (yajus) used by the *Adhvaryu* or officiating priest. The final redaction of the four collections may very well have been only *a de-jure* recognition of what had for some time been a *de facto* state of things.

The motive which determined the fourfold collection of Vedic material was, then, primarily *practical*—to serve the interests of the ritual[9]. Of course, there was in operation at the same time a more theoretical motive namely, the preservation from change and destruction of the ancient heṛitage of sacred song.

But though the Ṛigveda as a collection is not to be dated later than 800 B.C., the final settlement of the exact spelling of the text as we have it to-day, did not take place until after the completion of the older Brāhmaṇas, about 600 B.C., when the Saṁhita text[10], *i.e.* the text settled in accordance with the rules of *samdhi*, which control Classical Sanskrit, was formed. Since that date the text of the Ṛigveda has been preserved with almost faultless accuracy.

The Ṛigveda deserves to be called 'the most important'[11] of the Vedas, because, it is the oldest and largest collection of Vedic hymns and the source of much of the material found in the *Saman*, *Yajus* and *Atharvan*. Of the 20, 000 metrical stanzas in Vedic literature (omitting variants) bout 10,000, or fully one-half occur in the Ṛik[12]. Of the 1549 stanzas of the Sāmaveda 1474 are derived from the Ṛik, and also one-fourth of the matter of the Yajurveda. Besides a considerable portion in prose, the Atharvaveda contains about 6000 poetic stanzas, one-fifth of which, namely 1200 stanzas, occur also in the Ṛv.[13] The Ṛigveda, then is a great documentary source for the other three Vedas, very much as the Gospel of Mark is an important source for the Gospels of Matthew and Luke.

Vedic literature covers three classes of literary productions in the Vedic age, viz. (1) *Mantras* or Vedic stanzas produced largely in the creative period and afterwards collected in the form of the four Vedas; (2) *Brahmaṇas*, exposition and also of the philosophical element[14], and (3) *Sūtras*, mnemonic compendia dealing with Vedic ritual and customary law. Thus by Veda we mean, in a narrow sense, the Ṛigveda; in a wider sense, any or all of the Four Vedas; and, in the widest sense of all, the whole cycle of Vedic literature according to the threefold division of *Mantra*, *Brahmaṇa*, and *Sutra*. The extent of the existing Vedic literature may be estimated from the fact that about one hundred and twenty texts have contributed to the *Vedic Concordance* of Prof. Bloomfield[15]. The Ṛigveda is about equal in bulk to the Iliad and Odyssey combined. Being 'the most ancient literary monument of India', it is the foundation not only of Vedic literature, but of Indian literature in general. Thus for Indian history, religion, philosophy and civilization the Ṛigveda is a book of origins. As prophetic of the lines of future development it may also be called a collection of 'first fruits'.

## 2. The text of the Ṛigveda

The Ṛigveda contains 1017 hymns, or 1028, if we add the supplementary *Valakhilya* hymns. But the number can be easily increased by breaking up some of the large wholes into separate hymns, as we seem forced to do on critical grounds [16]. Thus out of the total collection of 1028 hymns E.V. Arnold finds about 200 which are composite and consist of 780 parts, usually short hymns of three verses each[17]. The hymns are arranged in ten books or mandalas (lit. 'cycles').

Books II-VII are the so-called 'family books', because each is assigned by tradition to the eponym ancestor of a particular priestly family[18]. That these groups of hymns were produced within the families to which they are ascribed is sufficiently probed by internal evidence. The hymns of the family books are arranged on a uniform plan, which seems to reveal the editorial work of a single school. Each major group of mandala is a collection of smaller groups of hymns arranged according to the deities addressed, the first sub-group consisting of hymns to Agni, the second to Indra, and so forth. Within these smaller groups the position of any hymn is determined by the number of stanzas being placed first, and so on. Hymns which break this rule are to be regarded either as complexes of smaller hymns, or as containing later additions. Again books II-VII seems to have been arranged according to the number of hymns, they severally contain (not counting later additions); for the second book contains the smallest number of hymns (43) found in any of the family books, and the seventh book the largest number (104). Thus the'family books' clearly form one great group.

The first, eighth and tenth books agree together in the fact that the groups of which they consist are based on identity of authorship, actual or assumed. The eighth book and Part A (hymns 1-50) of the first book have a certain affinity with each other due to the strophical arrangement which exists more or less in both and also to the fact that the family of the Kāṇvas figures in the authorship of each. The ninth book is unique, in that all of its hymns are addressed to Soma. Its groups depend upon identity of metre[19]. We see, then, that there are three principles which lie at the basis of the groups within the several books, viz. identity of the deity addressed, as in the first, eighth and tenth books, and identity of metre, as in the ninth books. The first and tenth books have each the same number of hymns (191), and together they contain the great mass of all the Atharvanic or 'popular' stanzas in the Ṛigveda.

On the basis of these uniformities of arrangement by which various sections of the Ṛv. are linked together it, is plausible to assume more or less independent redaction for seveal of the larger wholes of which the Ṛv. consists Professor Hopkins[20] thinks that a threefold process of grouping lies at the basis of the present arrangement; books II-VII, the 'family books', furnishing the nucleus, books I and VIII adding a framework, and books IX and X completing the collection. This, or something like it, must have taken place. If Hopkins view is correct, then we have a kind of threefold canon in the Ṛv.

The canonical form of the Ṛv., as we have seen, is

known as the Samhita text, that is, the text in which the words are united according to the rules of combination current in Sanskrit, and is not earlier than 600 B.C. Several schools existed, each with its own text, distinguished by unimportant differences; but the text has come down to us only in the recension of the of the Śākala school[21].

As soon as the Ṛv. 'collection' was made, an extraordinary set of devices was invented, in order to guard the purity of the text. Soon after the formation of the Saṁhitā or synthetic text, the *Pada* or analytic text was constructed. In the *pada* or 'word'—text each word of the *Saṁhita* was reproduced in its separate, unmodified and (generally) older form. It is easier to read metrically from the *pada* than from the *saṁhita* text. Further devices for safeguarding the text were the *Krama-patha* 'step-tect', the *jaṭa-paṭha* 'woven text', and the *ghana-paṭha*, still more complicated text. Representing the words of a Vedic stanza by the letters of the alphabet, we may illustrate the three safeguarding texts by the three following formulas: (1) abs-bc-cd-de, etc., (2) ab-ba-ab; bc-cb-bc, etc. (3) ab-ba-abc-cba-abc; bc-cb-bcd, etc. By these complicated processes of dislocation and repetition forwards and backwards, the aim was to make impossible the slightest change in the sacred text. Besides the five forms of the text mentioned above, there were two more safeguards in the shape of the Pratisakhyas, which explain all the changes necessary for converting the pada into the samhita text, and the Anukramanis or 'Indices', which define the contents of each hymn from various points of view, and also furnish a statistical account of the Ṛv. as a 'whole'. The result was that from the time that these safeguarding devices began to be applied, the Sakala recension of the Quran, was preserved in a unique state of purity. Before that time, however, some textual corruption had taken place.[23]

It should be mentioned also that for a long time the Vedic texts were in all probability orally transmitted. If writing was introduced into India in the 8th century B.C., as

Bühler thinks, its use for ling centuries was confined largely or entirely to commercial transaction and the like. Doubtless the Brahmanical community had an interest in keeping the sacred texts as kind of priestly monopoly. Such a monopoly could be maintained only if the texts were taught orally and not reduced to writing.

The extraordinary machinery for safeguarding the text of the Ṛv., the like of which is not found elsewhere in the world, indicates the existence of a well-ground fear that the textual history of the Vedic hymns in the past would repeat itself in the future, in other words, that "the text would continue to be corrupted, modified, modernized, as without such precaution it had been changed in the pst"[25]. The tectual history of the hymns of the Ṛv. before the 'collection' was stereotyped in the form of the canonical text, was undoubtedly a history of linguistic levelling. On this point the testimony of experts may be cited. Macdonell admits that "there are undeniable corruption is detail belonging to older period". Hopkins[26] holes that the hymns of the Ṛv. collection hymns of very different periods originally had been already reduced pretty much to one linguistic level, at the time the canonical text was formed. Grierson and Barnett[27] also remark that the songs of Lallā, or Lāl Ded, the Kashmiri female ascetic, furnish a valuable example of the manner in which the language of the Vedic hymns must have changed from generation to generation, before their text was finally established. The effect of such linguistic levelling was to obscure more or less the data for the existence of different dialects in the Ṛv. and the evidence for different periods of composition. The samhita text stereotyped the form of the Ṛv. very much as the grammar of Panini fixed the form of Sanskriṭ.

What has the extant text of the Ṛv. to say regarding the material out of which it is composed? As an answer to this question Bloomfield[29], the editor of the great Vedic Concordance, remarks: "Of the 40,000 lines of the Ṛigveda about 5000 are repeated[30] lines...Not for from 2000 verse-lines occur two three, or more times...This collection as a whole is the last precipitate, with a long and tangled past behind it, of a literary activity of great and indefinite length...Every part seems to be conscious of and assimilated to every other part." And in another place the same scholar[31] writes that "the earliest books of the Ṛv. are not exempt from the same processes of secondary grouping and adaptation of their mantras, though they are less frequent and less obvious than is the case in the Atharvaveda". In harmony with this Hopkins[32] declares that "the Ṛigveda Collection itself is a composite consisting largely of the same material disposed in various ways". And he draws the conclusion that "the hymns are founded on older material, the wreck of which has been utilized in constructing new poetic buildings, just as many of the temples of India are to a great extent built of the material of older demolished temples". This is certainly true to some extent. But may not many of the phenomena of repetition in the Ṛv. even as in the O.T. Psalms and in the Quran, be due to a stereotyped religious vocabulary, in which the same phrases would naturally tend to recur?

### 3. The language of the Ṛigveda

The centre of gravity of the Indo-Aryan world at the time that the Ṛv. collection was made (circa 600 B.C.) was most probably in *Brahmarsidesa*[33] (the country of the Holy Sages) in the region between the upper Jumna and Ganges. It is clear that the earlier hymns were composed further East and probably largely in the vicinity of the sacred river Sarasvati[34]. Now an outstanding fact in the linguistic history of Aryans India is the distinction emphasized in Sanskrit literature between the 'Midland' (Madhyadesa) and the 'Outland'[35]. The midland extending approximately from the Himalayas to the Vindhya Hills and from Sirhind to Allahabad was regarded as the true home of the Aryan people, language, religion and culture. The Outland, namely, Punjab, Sind, Gujarat, Rajputana, Oudh and Bihar, was also peopled by

Aryan tribes, each with its own dialect. Now in the opinion of Grierson, the Superintendent of the Linguistic Survey of India, "a comparison of the modern venraculars[36] shows that these outer dialects were more closely related to each other than any of them was to the language of the Midland". The account for this linguistic condition of things, he assumes that the latest invaders "entered the Punjab like a wedge into the heart of the country already occupied by the first immigrants, forcing the latter outwards in three directions, to the East, to the South and to the West"[37]. The result of course would be the creation of a kind of linguistic cleavage between the language of the Midland, on the one hand, and the various dialects of the Outland, on the other, such a cleavage as is suggested by the linguistic facts imbedded in the modern Indo-Aryan vernaculars. If this is correct interpretation of the facts, then the Aryans of the Midland as distinguished from the Aryans of the Outland, were the last to arrive, but the first to achieve great things.

This interpretation of the linguistic facts lies at the foundation of the assumption of two widely separated gates by which the Aryans entered India, the Khyber Pass and the route through Chitral and Gilgit. This view is not supported by the general consensus of opinion. If certain scholars, such as Hoernle, Grierson and Risely[38] favour it, other equally great scholars like Macdonell,[39] Keith,[40] and Rapson,[41] who occupy the Sanskrit chairs at Oxford, Edinburgh, and Cambridge, oppose it. Rapson suggests an alternative theory to account for the linguistic facts.

The language of the Ṛigveda was naturally the dialect of the region where the hymns were composed, namely, the northern and eastern part of the Punjab, with its centre probably at the sacred river Sarasvati. It was, without doubt, the literary form[42] of a living vernacular, and Grierson[43] sees in it "the earliest Prakrit, of which we have any cognizance". The language of the Ṛv. doubtless represents a more archaic dialect than was commonly spoken. The later hymns, we have reason to believe, were largely imitative and presuppose a fixed tradition of the kind of speech proper for a sacred song. If, as Hopkins holds, the earlier Ṛigveda hymns have suffered from 'linguistic levelling', it is probably equally true that the later hymns have suffered from the opposite process of linguistic heightening, so to speak, through the conscious archaizing of their authors[44].

The speech of the Ṛv. may be called Vedic to distinguish it from the elaborate and artificial form given to the language by the grammatical cannons of Pāṇini (circa B.C.). The main difference, then, between Vedic and Sanskrit it the difference between an earlier and relatively unpruned popular speech and a later pruned and polished speech. In fact, Vedic as the vernacular of a limited religion in and near the upper Gangetic Doāb is referred to by Grierson as the only known specimen of "the Primary Prākrits of Inida"[45]. The language of the Ṛv., then was in its time as truly a vernacular speech as the Hebrew of the Old Testament or the so-called 'Biblical' Greek of the New testament; at the same time, as the hieratic speech, it was "the first literary dialect of India"[46]. There are of course other differences between Vedic and Sanskrit. Vedic is much richer in conjugational forms, having numerous subjunctive, infinitive, and aorist forms, which do not occur in Sanskrit. Phonetically, there is little difference between the two. Of course, many Vedic words were obsolete by the time of Pāṇini and the beginnings of classical Sanskrit. On the whole, Vedic and Sanskrit differ from Classical Greek or as the language of Chaucer differ from that of Milton.

The processes of levelling down and levelling up, to which reference has already been made[47]—the old being assimilated to the new and the new to the old—have naturally more or less obscured any traces of dialectical differences which might otherwise have existed in the Vedic text. The distinction between 'hieracitc' and 'popular' language in the Ṛv. is a real distinction, if priestly and popular hymns belong to the same age; if not, it may mark simply chronological sequence. Such a distinction, however, between two varieties of Vedic speech, one more learned and technical, and the other more popular, would be very natural according to all analogy. We would except that the priests as the learned class of the Vedic age would have a 'class' speech, technical and professional. There are also some linguistic phenomena in the Ṛv., which suggest as their causes the existence of different Indo-Aryan dialects, notably the multitudinous present, aorist and infinitive forms.[48]

The language of the Ṛv. is closely akin to that of the Avesta, the Bible of the Zorastrian religion. In fact, as already shown[49], Vedic and Avestan are simply dialects of the same Indo-Iranian speech. Entire passages of Avestan can be rendered into Vedic and *vice versa* merely by making the necessary phonetic changes[50]. And a knowledge of Vedic is the best preparation for the study of Avestan.

But Vedic, as we have seen[51] is related not only to Avestan, but also to Greek, Latin, Celtic, Teutonic and Slavonic. It is, in other words, a member of the great Indo-European family of languages, the only rival of which in historic importance is the Semitic family. If Assyro-Babylonian, Hebrew and Arabic were important vehicles of ancient culture, none the less were Vedic, Avestan, Greek and Latin. But in modern times the languages of the Indo-European family have far outstripped in importance the languages of the Semitic family (except pehaps Arabic). As modern representatives of the Indo-European family there may be mentioned nearly all the languages of Europe, including such tongues as English, French, German, Russian and Italian, and in Asia Persian[52], Hindī, Bengāli, Punhābi, Marāthi, etc. Thus Vedic belongs to that potent and widely conquering family of languages which more than any other (except possibly the Semitic) has furnished literary vehicles for the best thought of the ages past, and is apparently bound up, to a large extent, with the future linguistic destiny of mankind.

Vedic, as the Indian branch of the Indo-European family, has shared with the other branches in the common tendency to spread and conquer. What was first simply the dialect of a district became the language of a caste and a religion and afterwards (in the form of Sanskrit) the language of religion, politics and culture throughout India[53]

## 4. The chronology of the Ṛigveda

Brief reference have already been made to the migration and settlements[54] of the Western Indo-Europeans, as bearing upon the problem of the date of the Ṛigveda. It seems desirable to consider this question from the point of view also of Indian history and archaeology. There is as yet no unanimity among scholars concerning the age of the Ṛigveda. Brahmanical orthodoxy hods that the Vedas are eternal[55]. Modern critical scholars have hitherto been divided into three camps, according as they have favoured an early, a late, or an intermediate date. Professor Hopkins[56] of Yale, a great authority on the Epic literature of india, and Professor Jackson of Columbia, well known as a Zorastrian scholar, both agree in urging a late date, 1000-600 B.C. Briefly stated their grounds are as follows: (1) The date of Zoroaster is now generally fixed at B.C. 660-583[57] by *e.g.* Geldner's[58], West[59] and Jackson[60], and since there is only a dialectic difference between the language of the Ṛv. and that of the Avesta, there can be no great interval in time between the two works, the date of Zoroaster, of course, determining the date of the oldest part of the Avesta. (2) the change in language between the Ṛigveda and the Upaniṣads is not greater than that between Chaucer and Milton, and hence it is fair to suppose that about 200 years would suffice in the one case as well as in the other. The two hundred years within which Hopkins and Jackson place the bulk of the Ṛigveda hymns are B.C. 800-600. (3) The Rishis who composed the hymns may very well have been in large measure contemporary with one another, and certain differences in vocabulary and style may be accounted for simply by variety of authorship. According to this view, then the Ṛigveda is roughly contemporaneous with the bulk of early Hebrew literature.

At the opposite pole from Hopkins and Jackson stand Tilak[61] and Jacobi[62], who on the basis of astronomical calculations would carry the period of the composition of the Ṛigveda back beyond 2500 B.C., as far at least as 3500, and according to Tilak farther still. Jacobi places the Vedic age within the period 4500-2500 B.C., but refers the composition of the Ṛigveda to the second half of this period. Tilak dates the oldest period of Aryan civilization between 6000 and 4000 B.C., when he thinks certain 'sacrificial formulae' were 'probably in use'. He places the composition of the Ṛigveda hymns as we have them, within the period 4000-2500 B.C.[63] The Tilak- Jacobi thesis has met with severe criticism from Wever, Whitney, Oldenberg[64], Thibaut[65], Hopkins, Macdonell, and Keith[66]. Apart from the assumed astronomical data, however, Jacobi urges that the norm of European progress cannot be applied to India on account of its isolated position and the consequently independent character of its development. And he emphasises the fact that the dates assumed by himself for the Vedic period are not greater than are accepted by scholars for the civilization of the Euphrates and Nile[67]. The late Professor Bühler[68] was of the opinion that the conquest and brahmanizaion of India requires a much earlier date than 1200-100 B.C. Following him, Winternitz[69] declares that from the standpoint of Indian history there is nothing against the view that Vedic literature goes back to the third millennium and the beginnings of Indian culture to the fourth millennium B.C. Prof. Bloomfield[70], too, declares himself "now much more inclined to listen to an early date, say 2000 B.C., for the beginnings of Vedic literary production, and to a much earlier date for the beginnings of the institution and religious concepts" thereof.

The third group of scholars stands between these extremes. Their conviction are based largely upon considerations of the time necessary for the linguistic, literary and historical development in India. It was Max Müller who suggested the chronological system we refer to, in his brilliant pioneer volume, *A History of Ancient Sanskrit Literature*, published in 1859. Here are the essential features:—

1200-1000 B.C. the *Chhandas* period, when the earlier hymns of the *Ṛigveda* were composed.

1000-800 B.C. the *Mantra* period, when the later hymns were composed and the *Samaveda* and the *Yajurveda* were compiled.

Most British scholars and many belonging to other lands have followed him; and it now seems as if his ideas were likely to have a far wider range. The first volume of *The Cambridge History of India*, published in April 1922, is a magnificent piece of collaborative scholarship. The book consists of chapters written by fourteen great scholars – eleven British, two American, one Swedish, Sir Halford Mackinder, Prof. Rapson, Peter Giles, Master of Emmanuel Collage Cambridge, Prof. A. Berriedale Keith, Prof. Jarl Charpentier of Upsala, Prof. T.W. Rhys Davids, Mrs. Rhys Davids, Prof. Hopkins of Yale, Prof. Jackson of Columbia, Dr. George Mackonald, Mr. E. R. Bevan, Dr. F. W. Thomas, Dr. Barnett and Sir John Marshall—and the whole group accept for the early Vedic period the chronological scheme proposed sixty-three years ago by Max Müller. It is noticeable that the two brilliant men, who are mentioned above as favouring later dates, are included in this group. Their views have doubtless been modified during the intervening years.

But, although this scheme seems to be steadily gathering the suffrages of a larger number of scholars, the grave differences which separate them from those thinkers who favour far earlier dates make it quite clear that positive dates are as yet lacking for determining the chronology of the Vedic period. Scholars who bring forward considerations based upon the length of time assumed to be necessary for a particular development, linguistic, literary or historical, as the case may be, sometimes forget that in literature and history as well as in religion one day may be as a thousand years and a thousand years as one day[71]; that is to say, the literary and political development may at one time drag very slowly and at another time proceed with leaps and bound. If the development of the invading Aryan tribes was rapid—and the development of an invading population is more likely to be rapid than that of a stationary population then a period of four hundred years might well suffice for the composition of the Ṛigveda hymns, as is shown by the development of the new world after its discovery in 1492. If, on the contrary, the development was slow, then the period suggested by Jacobi and Winternitz may be none too large.

What is needed in order to set all this uncertainty at rest is discovery of positive data. Such data must clearly be *archoaeological.* The appearance of Iranian proper names[72] in one of the Tel-el-Amarna letters (1400 B.C.), the occurrence of the name *Assara-Mazas* (Ahura Mazda) in an Assyrain list of gods[73], and Winckler's discovery at Boghaz-Köi[74] are suggestive of the kind of evidence needed. And there is good reason to hope that the needed evidence will be forthcoming in the future. If it is true, as Bloomfield[75] says that "from the entire Vedic period we have not one single piece of antiquarian or archaeological material, not one bit of real property; not a building, not a monument, not a coin, jewel or utensil", it is equally true that "the archaeology of India is, at present almost an unworked field[76]", at least so far as pre-Buddhistic sites are concerned. One needs but to visit the Punjab and see the numerous ancient mounds scattered over its surface, in order to be convinced that material bearing upon the Vedic period will almost certainly be forthcoming, when these mounds have been adequately explored.

A glance at the map of Asia is also instructive. Leaving

out China, there are three river basins which are among the earliest culture-centres of manking, viz. the Nile, the Euphrates-Tigris, and the Indus-Granges. The Euphrates-Tigris basin lies between the Indus on the east and the Nile on the west. It is well known that there were close relation, political, diplomatic and commercial, between Babylonia and Egypt at a remote period. While there were probably no political relations equally ancient between the Euphrates and the Indus, it is certain that there was an early trade[77]. Bühler's[78] conclusions concerning the origin of the earliest Indian script presuppose such trade relations at least as early as the 8th century B.C. kennedy also on the basis of all the evidence available concludes that "in the ninth century B.C. some trade existed between the Punjab and Assyria", and that "maritime commerce between India and Babylonia flourished in the seventh and sixth century B.C.[79]. The sea-route between Babylonia and the mouth of the Indus was relatively not a long one, the distance from the base of the Persian Gulf to the Indus being less than from the same point on the Persian Gulf to Babylon. Hitherto archaeological research in the Punjab, as already stated, has done practically nothing toward the discovery and excavation of the earliest sites of Vedic culture. We may well cherish the hole that there may yet be found some dateable objects such as inscribed seals or tablets or other articles from Babylinia or Egypt, which by establishing a lucky synchronism, may solve the chronology of the Vedic age. But as yet Winternitz's formula, x to 500 B.C., expresses the facts of our knowledge or lack of knowledge concerning the chronology of the Vedic period. Theoretically x may mean any date between 1000 and 6000 B.C. as determined by future investigation. This is but giving to the Indus valley a chance to prove for its culture a like antiquity with that of the Euphrates and Nile. In the light of the extraordinary discoveries of recent years (*e.g.* the discovery of the relics of Buddha at Pashawar) Max Müller seems to be too pessimistic when he says that "the date assigned to the poetry of the Veda is and well always remain hypothetical". As yet it is hypothetical. That it will always be so, remains to be seen.

While, then the lack of evidence precludes the fixing of the Vedic age with anything like certainty, yet a tentative and provisional chronology may be adopted, subject to modification or even rejection in the light of future discovery. The present writer would accordingly present the following system of chronology found in the *Cambridge History of India* as the best availlable to-day:

| B.C. | |
|---|---|
| 2500 | Probable date of the beginning of the Indo-European migrations. |
| 1800 | Period during which, in Northern Asia Minor ownward. and eastward through Northern Mesopotamian to Media, Indo-European peoples can be traced. |
| 1500 | Probable date of first Aryan invasion of In dia. |
| 1400 | The Böghaz-Koi tablets, containing Indo-Aryan deities in Vedic form. These clearly come from Aryan who have not made "the Iranian snift". Possibly we should think of them as Aryan tribes, who had stopped on the way, while their brethren had already passed on and settled in Iran and in India. At a later date we find Aryan gods at Babylon, whose names are still of the old forms. |

| B.C. | |
|---|---|
| 1200-1000 | Early hymns of the *Ṛigveda* composed probably for the most part in the western Punjab, notably the hymns to Uṣas and to Varuṇa. |
| 1000-800 | Lather hymns of the Ṛigveda composed in Brahmāvarta. The *Samaveda* and the *Yajurveda*. |

Beginnings of the Brāhmaṇa literature.

800-600 The existing Brāhmanas.

600 Formation of the *Saṁhitā* text of the Rik.[81]

This scheme has the merit of not being extremist either upwards of downwards. It fits into the latest and most trustworthy ethnological opinion as to the chronology of the dispersion of the Indo-European peoples, and harmonizes well with the conclusions of students of prehistoric IE. archaeology, such as Schrader, Hirt, Feist and Giles[82], and students of ancient history such as Eduard Meyer. It makes possible a reasonable interpretation of all the evidence recently found in Asia Minor, Mesopotamia and elsewhere. The Indian dates were originally based on the literary and cultural evidence of Indian literature; and the majority of our greatest scholars still agree that from this point of view, these are most natural. Finally it makes possible a common chronology for Indian and Persia. If we place Zoroaster circa 1000 B.C., as Oldenberg, Moulton and others suggest then the linguistic phenomena of the early Avesta and of the early Vedic hymns become clearly comprehensible; while we are able to understand at once the Zoroastrian reformation in Persia, and in India the rise of Varuṇa and the composition of the great Varuṇa hymns. This becomes all the more natural and intercourse in those days between the early Zoroastrians in Bactria and a special group of their brethren in the Punjab. It is altogether within the limits of possibility that the personal influence of Zoroaster reached the Punjab, whether by the actual sending of preachers or in the ordinary intercourse of trade. It is certainly not too much to believe that some reverberation from that mighty voice for as a personality he is surely comparable with the Buddha himself would be heard in Punjab.

## 5. The Interpretation of the Rigveda

The Ṛigveda is not only 'the most ancient literary monument

of India', but also 'the most ancient literary document of the Indo-European peoples'[84]. Covering, as it does, several centuries at least, it may be characterized as nothing less than 'a library and a literature[85]. As already pointed out, it forms a connecting link between India and the West. For while, on the one hand, it fulfils itself in the later history and literature of India, on the other, its roots run deep into the Indo-Iranian and even Indo-European period. Its discovery laid the foundation of the sciences of Comparative Philology and Comparative Mythology. In view of its intrinsic importance in so many field of thought, linguistic[86], mythological, religious, literary, and historical, it is not at all strange that an unusually large proportion of Sanskrit scholars have been attracted to its study.

The Ṛigveda is not an easy book. Its dialect is archaic, and there are a very large number of words which occur only once. The vocabulary is priestly, full of mystic allusion to the technique of the sacrifice. Hence, while a considerable part of the Ṛv. is fairly clear, there are many single stanzas and even whole hymns which still remain obscure. Moreover, there is hardly a single hymn in the Ṛv., in which there is not some obscure word or difficult phrase. A comparison together of the various translations is the best proof of the difficult of the Ṛiveda text.

The traditional text of the Ṛigveda and its traditional interpretation constitute, as it were, the *given element*, the data to be critically examined. The traditional text was fixed (circa 600 B.C.) in the form of the *Saṁhitā* text. This is open to a limited amount of conjectural emendation[87], in correction of errors which preceded the final editing of the Ṛv. When Yaska wrote his Nirukta (Etymology) about 500 B.C., the meaning of many Vedic words had already become unintelligible; for he quotes one of his predecessors as saying that the Vedic hymns are 'obscure, unmeaning and mutually contradictory. This was only one of seventeen predecessors of Yaska, whose opinions often disagreed. Accordingly Yaska has a way of assuming altenative roots and meaning for the same word, from which we conclude that there was no unbroken tradition. Yaska's weakness is his too great dependence on etymology.

About eighteen centuries after Yāska, Sāyana (14th Cent. A.D.) wrote his great commentary on the Ṛv. It is extremely valuable[88] as setting forth the Indian tradition,in Sāyana's time, of the meaning of the Ṛigveda. Sāyane leaned heavily upon Yaska, and like him put too much dependence upon etymology. He fails to deduce the meanings of words by a comparison of parallel passages. We may note in passing that the Vedic interpretation of *Swāmi Dayānad*a Sarasvati (1824-1883), the founder of the Arya Samāj, outstrips Yāska and Sāyaṇa in its over-emphasis on etymology, neglect of the consideration of parallel passages, and appeal to later and non-Vedic usage.[89].

The history of the modern interpretation of the Ṛigveda is the story of various attempts to pentrate its secret, different schools of investigators emphasizing different points of view. The traditional interpretation as represented by Sāyaṇa was regarded by H.H. Wilson[90] as adequate and trustworthy; and so he reproduced it in his English translation of the Ṛv. Roth, the founder of the 'critical' school, was impressed with the primitive and natural poetry in the Ṛv. For him it was 'the oldest religious lyric[91]. His principle was that we must gather the meaning from the texts themselves with the help of çomparative philology. He overlooked, however, the importance of the Indian commentators and of a knowledge of the ritual literature. His merits and defects are both reflected in his lexicographical work[92]. Bergaigne[93] employed an allegorical method and emphasized the single meanings of words, but interpreted the Ṛv. from too narrow a standpoint. Dayānad Sarasvati[94] built upon the theistic element in the Ṛv., especially on such passages as I. 164, 46 ad X. 114, 5, which seemed to him to indicate that the multitudinous divine names in the Ṛv. refer to a single exalted divine being; and on the basis of this interpretation helped out by his gift for etymologizing, he laid the foundation of an indigenous theistic society in North India. Pischel and Geldner[95] represent a reaction against the school of Roth in favour of a more indigenous method of interpretation. Their principle is that the Ṛigveda is a purely Indian book, and that accordingly. It was a vigorous attempt, in the words of Oldenberg[96], to rehabilitate the indigenous Vedic exegesis which had fallen into disrepute. In the opinion of Pischel and Geldner the Ṛv. hymns do not reflect a primitive state of society, but rather an culture with all its evils, such as greed for gods and a highly developed *demimonde*. The weakness of Yāska and Sayana are reproduced along with their method, namely endless etymologizing and the assumption of multitudinous meanings for words. The one solid contribution of Pischel ad Geldner is their emphasis upon the necessity of making the fullest use of the resources of indigenous scholarship in the elucidation of the Vedic text. Brunnhofer[97], the Ishmael among Sanskritist, lays hold of the fact that the roots of the Ṛv. run deep into the Indo-Iranian period. It is for him almost as much an Indo-Iranian as an Indian book. Hillebrandt and Oldenberg stress the importance of the later Vedic ritual for the understanding of the Ṛv. Macdonell and Keith cherish well-balanced views on Vedic topics and avoid eccentric opinions.

Such are some of the different points of view from which the Ṛigveda has been studied,—the adequacy of the traditional interpretation, the allegorical method, the Indian or the pre-Indian character of the Ṛv., and the presence in it of a primitive lyrical, a theistic, and a ritualistic element. Devotion to a particular point of view has inevitably meant exaggeration, but has at the same time accomplished the end of bringing out whatever truth is contained therein. The exaggerations of opposing scholls of Vedic research tend to correct one another, very much as in the case of Old Testament research. The truth lies in the middle[98].

The tendency of the best Vedic scholarship at the present time is to emphasize the largeness of the context in which the Ṛigveda is to be set and studied. In the first place, the Ṛv., as Roth held, is its own best commentary. Moving out from this in ever enlarging circles we should use as aids to Vedic interpretation the indigenous exegesis as found in Yāska and Sāyans, the Avesta, the younger Vedic texts containing the 'ritual' literature, the later literature of India, present day religious custom and folklore as found, *e.g.* in the writings of Crooke[99] and Mrs. Stevenson[100] the great Western IE. literary works, Iliad, Odyssey, AEnied, Eddas and Niebelungenlied, and the mythology and anthropology of all the nations. To illustrate the new emphasis on the importance of studies in the modern religion and folklore of India in their bearing on the elucidation of the Ṛigveda, attention may be drawn to the bibliography at the end of Hopkins chapter on *The Vedic Religion of India*[101] in which Crooke's *Popular Religion* and *Folklore of Northern India* occupies the first place, standing even ahead of Macdonell's *Vedic Mythology*. In like manner as illustrating the contribution, which general mythology and folklore may make to Vedic study, Caland[102] points out the striking similarity which exists between the sacred formulas of the Cherokees[102] and those of the Kausika *Sūtra*.

**Foot Notes**

1. In the *Purusa Sūkta* (Ṛv. X. 90.9) the stanzas (richa) of the *Rik* are mentioned before the verses (*samani*) of the Saman, and the *Yajus*.
2. Cognates of *Veda* are Fr. οιδα, Lat. vid-εο, Eng. *wit*.
3. Hopkins, ION. 23.
4. Hopkins, ION, 24.
5. Hopkins, ION. 23.
6. Bloomfield, AV. 2, and *On the Relative Chronotogy of the Vedic Hymns*, JAOS. 21 (1901 p. 46).
7. "Considerably more than one half of the ṚV. stanzas which correspond to the AV. belong to the tenth book of the ṚV., largely to the last *anuvaka* of that book; about one-sixth to the first-book; about one-tenth to the seventh book; about one-eighth to all the other books put together." Bloomfield AV. 46.
8. ṚV. X. 90.
9. Bloomfield refers to his own "rapidly growing conviction that the Ṛv., as we have it, in common with the other Vedas, is a liturgic collection". *Relative Chronology*. JAOS., 1901, p. 45.
10. Macdonell, SL. 46-50; Hopkins ION. 27.
11. Macdonell. SL. In IGI. II. 209.
12. Bloomfield, *op. cit.* 42-43.
13. Macdonell *op. cit* 227-229.
14. The elaboration of the philosophical element in the Vedas if, of course, the work of he *Upanisads*, philosophical to the Brāhmaṇa.
15. Bloomfield, ṚV. 18.
16. Hillebrandt, *Alt-Indien*, 83.
17. The *Ṛigveda and Atharvaveḍa*, JAOS. 1901. P.312.
18. The names of these *Rishis* are: Gritsmada, Visvamitra, Vamadeva, Arti Bharadvāja, Vasiṣtha.
19. See for this whole section Macdonell, *Sanskrit Literature*, Chap. III.
20. ION. 26-27.
21. This single recension of the Ṛv. reminds us of the similar textual history of the Quran, the single recension of Othman being reponsible for all later copies of the Bible of Islam.

22. 1028 hymns, 10, 402 verses, 133, 826 words and 432,000 sylables. Max Muller, *Physical Religion*.
23. For evidences of this see Oldenberg, *Hymns to Agni*, SBE., XLVI.
24. Indian Palegraphy in IA. vol. XXXIII. appendix 1516.
25. Hopkins, ION. 26.
26. Sanskrit Literature 47.
27. op. cit. 26.
28. *Lalla-Vakyani*, 1920, p. 128, note 1.
29. *On Certain Work in Contiuan of the Vedic Concordance*, JAOS. 29 (1908) pp. 287-288.
30. Cf. Bloomfield, *Ṛigveda Repetitons* in HOS., Vol.20.
31. SBE. XLII, p. LXXII.
32. ION. 24.
33. Rapson, CHI. I. 46.
34. *Manusmriti* II. 17; Hopkins ION. 34.38, and JAOS 19, p. 20; Grierson JRAS. 1904, p. 476.
35. See chapter on *Languages* by Grierson in IGI. 1. 349 ff.
36. Grieson's classification of the Indo-Aryan Vernaculars of India is as follows:—

    A. Language of the Midland, *Western Hindi*.

    B. Intermediate Languages.

(a) More nearly related to the Midland; *Rajashandi*, *Pahari*, *Gujarati*, *Punjabi*.

(b) More nearly related to the outer band, *Eastern Hindi*.

C. Outer Language.

(a) North Western Group: *Kasmiri*, *Kohisham*, *Lahuda*, *Sindhi*.

(b) Southern Group: *Marathi*.

(c) Eastern group: *Bihari*, *Oriya*, *Bengali*, *Assamese*.

37. Grierson IGI. 1. 358 (following Hoernle).
38. IGI. I. 303 ff.
39. Vedic Index.
40. CHI. I. 119, 123.
41. CHI. I. 50.
42. Deith, CHI., 1, 109, 110.
43. *op. cit.* 360.
44. This may be illustrated from the religious hymns or *bhajans* of North India. Even to-day Hindi, hymns are usually written in the archaic dialect of the *Rāmayana* of

Tulsi. Das.

45. Grierson distinguishes between primary, secondary and tertiary Prakrits. The language of the Ṛv. illustrates the first; the Pali of the Buddhistic writtings, the second; and the modern Indo-Aryan vernaculars, such as Hindi and Punjabi, the third. It is noticable that these various vernaculars, Vedic, Pali, Hindi and Punjabi, have furnished the literary vechicles for such religious books as the *Ṛigveda* the *Tripitka* of Buddhism, the *Ramayana* of Tulsi Das, and the *Granth Sahib* of the Sikhs.
46. Farquhar, ORLL 8.
47. pp. 61, 64.
48. "The wealth of inflectional forms in the Vedic age may be partly explained as the result of a mixture of dialects". Rapson, JRAS. 1904, p. 440.
49. p. 21.
50. Jackson, *Avesta Grammar*, Part 1 (1892), p. XXXI.
51. pp. 2-6.
52. If the superstructure of Persian is Semitic (Arabic), its foundation is Indo-European.
53. Rapson, *op. cit.* 456.
54. p. 19.
55. *Manu* I. 21-23, XII. 94-100. The view embodied in *Manusuriti* (circa 100 A.D.) is that in the beginning Brahma fushioned from the words of the Veda the several names, foundation and conditions of all creatures, and that in order to the performace of sacrifice he drew forth from *Agni*, *Vayu* and *Sūrya* the triple eternal Veda. According to Brahmanism, then the Veda is at once a *creative* and a *sacrifical* program. Kuluka-Bhatta (15th Cent, A.D.) who builds on Govindaraja (12th Cent. A.D.) interprets Manu to mean that at the beginning of the present mundane are (Kalpa) Brahma drew forth the Vedas from, Agni Vayu and Sūrya. The Arya Samāj, which has broken with Brahmanical tradition at so many points, holds fast nevertheless to the Brāhmanical theory of the antiquity of the Vedas and traches that the Four Vedas were revealed to four sages, Agni, Vayu, Sūrya and Angiras at the beginning of the present mundane age over one hundred billion (!) years ago.
56. ION. 30.

57. Oldenberg demons. See *Orientalische Religonen, 78, Die Kuttar de fragnment* (1906), 1. 3, 1.
58. Art on *Zoroasrianism in Encylopedia Biblica*, IV. 5431.
59. SBE. XLVII, p. XLII.
60. *Zoroaster the Prophet of Iran*, 16.
61. *Orion or Resqarches into the Antiquity of the Vedas*, Poona, 1916.
62. ZDMG. XLIX. 218-230: JRAS. (1909) 721 ff. and (1910) 156 ff.
63. Tilak, *Orion*, 206.
64. ZDMG. ZLIX. 470 ff.
65. *Antiquity of Indra Literature and Civilization* (Hindustan Review, January (1904).
66. JRAS. (1909), 1905 ff., and (1910), 464 ff.
67. The Tilak-Jacobi hypothsis is, to some extent, recommended by the fact that each sponsor discovered and formulated is independently of the other.
68. IA, XXIII. 245 ff.
69. GIL. 254.
70. ṚV. 20. and JAOS (1908) p. 287 ff.
71. 2 Peter III.
72. Blommfield calls this "the earliest direct record of Indo-European chronology". AJP. XXV. 10.
73. Hommel, PSBA. 21 (1899) p. 137.
74. Meyer GA. I$^2$ (1909), p. 802.
75. ṚV. 20.
76. Quoted from Prof. Rhys Davids by Vincent Smith, JRAS. 1902, p. 288. During the last twenty years (1900-1920) there have been great developmets in Indian archology, but the sits selected for excavation have been largely Buddhistic. For example, at Taxila, the first and oldest city represented by the Bhir mound, the occupaton of which probably reaches back to the Vedic age, is as yet hardly touched by the spade.
77. Kennedy, *The Early Commerce of Babylon, with India*, JRAS, 1898, p. 241 ff.
78. Indian Pateography in AL. Vol. XXXIII, Appendix, 15-16.
79. *op. cit.* 264, 270.
80. Physical Religion (1891) p. 22.
81. CHI. Vol. I. 1922, pp. 76, 112-113, 697.

82. Schrader, RIA. and Indogermanen; Hirt, Indogermanen II and I; Feist KAHI.; Giles, CHI. I. 65 ff.
83. Oldenberg, *Vedaforschung*; Gray, *Interpretation* (*Vedic*). ERE. CII; Macdonell, VRS. XXIX-XXXI, and Principles (Bhandarkar, CV. 3 ff.).
84. Bloomfield, ṚV. 17.
85. Arnold, *Vedic Metre*. p. 1.
86. Sanskrit lies at the foundation of Indo-European Comparative Grammar.
87. The late Prof. Oldenberg while at Lahore in 1913, expressed in the hearing of the author his regret at having carried the conjectural emendation of the Ṛv. text too far, an example of the humility of the true scholar. Compare Macdonell, *Principles* (Bhandarkar, CV. 18): "Advancing study has proved many emendation made by earlier scholars owing to imperfect knowledge, to be unneccssary. Conjectual correction of the text should, therefore, be resorted to only in extreme cases".
88. At the basis of all modern study of the Ṛv. is Prof. Max Muller's *magnum opus*, his critical edition of the *Ṛigveda-Samhita* together with the Commentary of Sayauacurya, vols. I-VI, 1849-1871, a library in itself.
89. Griswold, *The Dayanandi Interpretation of the word 'Deva' on the Ṛigveda*, Ludhiana, 1807 (out of print).
90. Ṛigveda Samhita, Eng. trans., vols. I-VI, 1850 and following years.
91. PW. I-VII.
92. *La Religion Vedique*, I-111, Paris, 1897-1883.
93. *Ṛigvedaibhasyabhamika*, Ajmer (Sanskrit with explanation in Hindi).
94. *Vedische Studien*, I-III.
95. *Vedaforachung* 21.
96. *Urgeschichte der Arier*, I-III, 1889-1893, and *Arische Urzeit*, 1910.
97. Winterninz, gil., 65.
98. PR.
99. RT. and RJ.
100. Chapter XI of *The History of Religions*, N. Y. 1918.
101. *Allindisches Zauberritual*, 1900, pp. IX-XI.
102. Pablished by James Morney, 1891.

# five

## INTRODUCTION TO SAMA-VEDA

1. (a) The Sāma Veda is one of four Vedas which has been handed to us over a period of thousands of years by oral tradition, without an error of even a syllable, before they were reduced to writing in very recent times. The Vedas are of varying lengths with varying number of mantras or hymns as stated below:

| | | |
|---|---|---|
| (1) Sama Veda | 1,875 | mantras |
| (2) Yajur Veda | 1,976 | ,, |
| (3) Ṛg Veda 1,028 hymns | 10,552 | ,, |
| (4) Atharva Veda | 5,038 | ,, |

The mantras are mostly in the form of couplets of varying metres ranging from 24 to 40 or 50 syllables. The hymns in the Ṛg-Veda comprise groups of mantras ranging from 3 to 40 or 50 even. The Yajur Veda is partly in prose form.

(b) Although the Ṛg Veda is credited with 10,552 mantras, this number is reduced to 8,629, which represents its own contribution, if we deduct 1,442 mantras from the Sāma Veda and 481 mantras from the Yajur Veda which the Ṛṣis of the Ṛg Veda have quoted or adopted. This however is our view although it is generally erroneously believed that Sāma and Yajur Veda have adopted from Ṛg Veda. This cannot be true as both Sāma and Yajur Vedas are very much more ancient as we will show later while discussing the antiquity of the Vedas.

## 2. Origin of the Vedas

It is generally believed, even by some scholars of repute, that the Vedas are eternal and were directly communicated to some inspired ṛṣis or old. This view is held because of the scholars not having been able to determine the period from which the oral tradition had been persisting. This belief is no longer true as we are now in a position to determine with some exactitude the dates of the Vedas. But, apart form this fact, the claim that the Vedas are direct utterances of God revealed to some ṛṣis arises from a confusion between the expression Veda meaning knowledge in general and "The Vedas" referring to the works discussed here. No doubt all knowledge arises only from God, otherwise how could creation have taken place which involves a vast amount of concealed knowledge divulged in the manifestation processes themselves. Knowledge was there which arose as ideas of the creator. Then it is unbelievable that god gave utterances to any knowledge. The process by which God reveals his ideas is to endow man with the faculty of speech and to inspire him with ideas through his brain and to induce him to the utterances. Such ideas as form the content of the Vedas are revealed only to profound thinkers who had gone through life's experiences and gathered wisdom.

## 3. Revelation—What it Means

The expression "Revelation" used to indicate the source of the Vedas has been thoroughly misunderstood. What was meant to be conveyed by the word was that the knowledge which remained locked up in man's brain, before language had developed to such an extent as to enable one's thoughts and ideas to be translated cogently into speech, was revealed to the outside world when speech was perfected. Thus man himself was the author of the revelations and not God direct. This truth is borne out by the Ṛg Veda itself as stated in Maṇḍala X.71.1-2.

See *Call of the Vedas* by A. C. Bose, Bhavan's Publication.

"Of the first and foremost speech that you sent
Giving names to things, O Bûhaspati,
Whatever was nobles and stainless and secretly treasured
With love you revealed.
When sages have created the word straining it through
Their spirits as flour through a sieve
Therein have friends recognised their mutual friendships
Whose blessed signs lay hidden in words."

So here we see what revelation signifies.

(a) This truth receives further confirmation by statements in Sāma and Yajur Vedas which declare repeatedly that the knowledge conveyed by them was derived by tradition. No authorship is mentioned in these two Vedas. The mantras then must have accumulated over a long period little by little. Knowledge is a growing experience and accumulates with the efflux of time. (See Appendix III)

(b) Thus it is seen that the Vedas themselves do not claim divinity for the knowledge revealed by the mantras. Still people attributed divinity of origin to them. It can only be for all knowledge in general.

**4. Special Features and Content of Sāma Veda**

Sāma Veda alone of the four Vedas is set to music and is intended to be sung. The present day music is derived from it. Evidently there was no script at the time and all knowledge had to be committed to memory and transmitted by oral tradition to succeeding generations. In musical form it is easier to commit to memory. The text of the Veda or Saṃhitā is divided into two sections namely: (1) Gaṇa or songs being the first part containing 640 mantras, some of which are based on musical notes. These mantras are again subdivided into two groups namely those which are to be sung in the villages and those which are meant to be using only in the forests and not in the villages. (2) The second part containing the remaining 1,235 mantras is called Ārcika or prayers. The subject-matter of the two sections is the same and there are 222 mantras of the first part repeated in the second part often-times addressed to a different Deva or lending itself to be interpreted differently.

### (a) Subject-matter

As regards the content or subject-matter of the Veda, it is to be noted that a number of translations are available with divergent trends and interpretations. The Veda lends itself to be so dealt with, because of the economy in words and brevity of expression devised for easily committing to memory. Often times the mantras read like the Delphic oracle "the Greeks the Romans conquered", leading to different renderings.

### (b) Transcriptions

Another circumstance which has accentuated the confusion is that the transcription to writing from oral tradition has been made several thousand years later when the Veda had become more or less a faint memory in the lives of the people. Again the transcription has been done from musical chanting in which the syllables are often tacked on to a previous or a succeeding word, which give different meaning altogether. In our translation we have resorted to this artifice to a great extent to arrive at proper ideas consistent with the trend of the subject-matter.

### (c) Our Line of Interpretation

We hold that in whatever other ways the Veda may have been translated and presented, it lends itself to be correctly presented as we have done in our effort. This leads us to a cogent and consistent system of ideas bearing on two subjects principally, namely: (1) Evolution and (2) How the operations of the brain and the sense organs and the body take place and what Devas are responsible for carrying them out. All prayers for one's own welfare and prosperity are addressed to these Devas. The entire Veda is devoted only to these subjects.

### 5. The Home of the Veda

The Sāma Veda as well as the Yajur Veda were the gift of the Deva race to us who along with the kindred Asuras were the inhabitants of the Arctic circle originally and were uprooted from their homes when they were invaded by glaciation. These races were mistakenly thought to be divine beings even in very early times and so represented by the Purāṇic writers. Actually they were human beings who, after they abandoned their original homes in the Arctic belt settled down in Central Asia, in the trans-Himalayan regions west of the Gobi desert up to and including the present day Iran. Of these two sections of a kindred stock of people, the Asuras after a ceaseless struggle with their kindred folk settled down in the present day Iran and imparted their culture to the local people the Parsees who have chronicled the memory of their past, their faiths and beliefs in their sacred books and religious writings similar to out Vedas.

#### (a) The Devas

The Devas on the other hand settled down towards the east of the Asura lands as in Afghanistan and further east known as Ilāvrata Varṣa in ancient times. They were hill lovers and so had their homes and settlements on the slopes of hills, where the plains were occupied by our own forefathers the patriarchs and their own people. That our forefathers were of a different stock from the Devas and Asuras has been made plain in all ancient writings and all our Purāṇas. The Devas and Asuras were in ceaseless warfare among themselves they were on friendly terms with the local population and got on well with them.

**(b) Deva Culture**

The language Sanskrit called Davanāgarī originated from them and is their mother tongue i.e. of Devas and Asuras. Other expressions in current use like "deva gaṇa" "deva bhāṣā" all confirm that the Sanskrit language originated from them and also the Sāma and Yajur Vedas. The Devas had a superior culture which exercised a wholesome influence on our remote forefathers the patriarchs who seem to have absorbed the Deva culture in toto, their language, their customs and manners, their faiths and beliefs and also their Vedas, Sāma and Yajur. The Deva clans were headed by leaders like Indra, Agni, Mitra, Varuṇa, Vāyu, Yama, Brahmā and so forth, everyone of whom had his own distinct hill settlement in the Ilāvrata Varṣa. Brahmā was the supreme head and Indra a subordinate leader under him. Brahmā's residential area was known as Manovatī and on this hill every other leader had a place of residence to live in whenever he had to call on the supreme head. Indra's region was known as Amarāvatī. Here in their new homes the devas lived their lives amicably with the local people imparting their culture, language and art to them.

**(c) Our Forefathers**

The people of present day India whose distant forefathers were the patriarchs marīci, Atri, Pulastya, Pulaha, Kratu, Vasiṣṭha, Aṅgiras, Bhṛgu, Pracetas and Nārada and their followers were living in the plains of Central Asia among whom the Devas also lived but on the hills. There were 11 other Prajāpatis too making up 21 in all. That the Prajāpatis followed the Vedic way of life is evident from the Yajña which Dakṣa I arranged, to which he had not invited his own son-in-law Śiva, at which his daughter Satī felt insulted and immolated herself in fire and the dire consequences which befell Dakṣa himself. During this patriarchal period, peace seems to have prevailed between the Devas and Asuras—at least there is no record of strife between them.

But at a much later period during the reigns of the Solar and Lunar dynasty kings, descendants of the patriarchs, the Devas frequently resorted to help from these kings in their wars against the Asuras. Ṛg Veda was unknown during the sojourn of the patriarchs in Central Asia. It had its origin in the Indian soil after the migration to India of the descendants of the patriarchs, owing to a great flood. The Ṛṣis of the Ṛg Veda spoke of the distant and forgotten forefathers when referring to the patriarchs, the originators of their race.

**(d) The Arctic Home of the Devas and Asuras**

That these people had their original homes in the Arctic belt is established form the mantras which refer to natural phenomena observable only in the Arctic belt. There are 7 such mantras in the Sāma Veda, 8 in Yajur Veda. Unless one has lived in that area and had been an eye-witness it would not have been possible to describe them. But these references have been made only to illustrate that similar phenomena take place in our own system. These two Vedas inculcate that the phenomena in the external world is similar to what takes place within us but on a magnified scale. Their conviction is that the external world is what one conceives as perceiving. So these two Vedas do not deal much with the external world separately.

**(e) Peculiarities of Natural Phenomena in the Arctic Circle**

The peculiar features of the Arctic region are:

1. A six-month long continuous day followed by a six month long continuous night at the pole.
2. A period of 7 to 10 months of daily sunshine and darkness of varying durations as in other places, according to the latitude of the place.
3. A period of continuous darkness varying from 2 to 100 days according to the latitude of the place.
4. A revolving dawn of 2 to 30 days followed by the

reappearance of the Sun above the horizon succeeded by days and nights as in lower latitudes followed by a period of continuous sunshine.

5. The rising of the Sun from the South.

Independent of the mantras from Sāma and Yajur Veda Tilak has established beyond doubt quoting extensively from the Ṛg Veda and other sources that the home of the Vedas was in Arctic circle originally. But we have already mentioned that the Ṛg Veda originated from Ṛṣis on Indian soil who had only vague memories of their remote forefathers in the Central Asian plains. So, whatever references are made to the Arctic phenomena in the Ṛg Veda cannot be from personal experiences but gleaned from the older Vedas and from traditional knowledge. Thus Tilak's finding can be applied only to Sāma and Yajur Vedas and under no circumstances to Ṛg Veda, as the former had their homes in the Arctic belt while the latter in the Indian soil. Further they were so remote in time from each other, as will be shown presently.

## 6. The Age of the Veda

The Sāma Veda gives us no sort of indication to determine its age except by references to the Arctic home. It has to be established only from indications given in the Yajur Veda and the Parsee scriptures. Although scholars try to fix the age of the Vedas with reference to Ṛg Veda considering it to be the oldest Veda, which however it is not, as pointed out above, we have to fall back on the sources stated by us which enable us to fix the date with great exactitude.

### (a) Yajur Veda Mantas

Mantra XXX. 18 reads as follows:

"The imperishable is the origin of all, now Kṛta (yuga) is gone (cheated us), Tretā is being witnessed by us newly to be followed by the closely connected Dvāpara, I determine from my immaculate gift from beyond that assemblies of men and plant life (stationary objects) will perish, hour of death will control men, hunger and destruction of cattle will follow, there will be deformity (internal transformation) begging and evil doings will be resorted to with sinful minds and robbery." This mantra is followed by a few more predicting dire calamities to people, breakdown of morality, society etc. and the resulting evils thereof. There will be endless wanderings in search of a new home. We have however no clues to know whether the prognostications did come out to be true, in our own ancient records. The only information left behind by the Veda is (1) that a dire calamity will overtake the race and (2) that it will be in the beginning of Tretā Yuga.

**(b) Confirmation from Parsee Scriputres**

The Parsee race who were originally in Iran and adopted the culture of the Asuras, of the same stock as Devas but with different beliefs and hostility to their kindred folk, confirms that what was foretold did come to pass. Their holy book *Zend Avesta* mentions that glaciation set in the Arctic area and destroyed the homes of their forefathers who in consequence had wander over many lands, as many as 16, and for several hundreds of years, suffering untold calamities and death and destruction until they finally settled in safe homes in Iran.

**(c) Glaciation early in Tretā Yuga**

Thus, if we fix the date of glaciation, we can be certain that the two ancient Vedas were current in inter-glacial times. The date of commencement of Tretā Yuga can be fixed only by settling the period covered by Mahāyuga. The Purāṇic writers assign a period of 43,20,000 years on the assumption that Devas were gods and that a year of 360 days is but a day for the Devas. But we know now that the Devas were human beings and so the period of time is the same for both and that a Mahāyuga of 12,000 years as fixed by Manu and Vyāsa is the same for both races and has not be multiplied by 360 to arrive at human Mahāyuga period.

A Mahāyuga comprises four sub-periods comprising (1) Kṛta—4,800, (2) Tretā—3,600, (3) Dvāpara—2,400 and (4) Kali—1,200 including Sandhi periods of 10 per cent both before and after, making 12,000 years altogether. Since now 5,078 years have elapsed from the commencement of Kaliyuga, the date of commencement of Tretāyuga is 5,078+6,000 =11,078 years. Glaciation then occurred about this time and the two Vedas had been accumulating their traditions earlier over several hundreds of years possibly.

#### (d) Glaciation—Other Determinations

Other Researchers have estimated the age of glaciation variously from 8,000 to 23,000 years. Tilak fixes the date from astronomical data and statements from Parsi scriptures at 8,000 to 10,000 years from now. A more recent determination appeared in the *Reader's Digest,* March 1974, pages 44-48 under the title "Solving the great confield Mystrey" by Ronald Schiller on the researches of archaeologist Stuart Struver. Explorations were made by him in the Koster Valley near the river Illinois in North America in 1969. The lowest layers of the excavations revealed Red Indian settlements of about 8,000 years old. Struver states that the earliest evidence of the presence of this tribe is variously estimated at from 13,000 to 26,000 years. These Red Indians are said to have migrated from Asia across the Behring Strait about 10,000 years ago as the glaciers receded and the climate turned warmer and drier in America. There is no doubt that these Red Indians were one of the races who fled from the Arctic area on the onset of glaciation. It appears to us that among all these determinations the Yajur Veda statement stands out as the most precise one.

### 7. Evolution According to Sāma Veda

#### (a) General

The conceptions of Sāma Veda on Evolution on earth

are unique but at the same time most rational carrying the stamp of conviction. This Veda shares its views on the subject to a great extent with Yajur Veda. Since this creation had a beginning at some remote time it is natural to enquire what was there before. All this illimitable and vast space was filled completely with his presence. All that exists now and which may appear in the future are his manifestations (619). There can be nothing that is not he. Three parts of this Puruṣa of the nature of pure intelligence, named Savitā or Viṣṇu, and of the nature of activity also, constituting the heaven; beyond our perceptions, is all about us and filling all space. We are at his feet taking on repeated existences (mantra 618). The Puruṣa has thousand heads, a thousand eyes and a thousand flights of imagination. He envelops the entire universe, transcends it and looks upon it as at a finger (617). Since the creator is of the nature of activity, he should have pursued that activity within himself i.e. he was in a state of browsing and planning for the future. From what followed this state of single blessedness, it is natural to infer that he was seized with a desire to know himself and as it is possible only in the presence of a multitude of others, he came out of his reverie, which may be called the state of cosmic sleep, and indulged in creating his objective states. This great and irrepremsible zeal to externalize his activity and create his objective states as ideas is known as Agni in the mental world and he is represented on earth by fire, both possessed of the same qualities i.e. to devour everything to be identified with what is devoured.

**(b) The World of Idea**

This Veda, in common with the Yajur Veda, holds the view, what everyone of us knows and experiences, that no activity or achievement is possible on earth or in heaven without prior thought or planning. Activity in the material world is only a transfer of ideas to matter. This universal truth is equally valid for the manifestation process on earth.

What truly happens in manifestation is to provide a mantle or cloak to envelop the idea received from heaven for their activity from within. Nothing new takes place on earth. Whatever happens here then is what has already happened in the world of ideas in heaven which surrounds us, though unseen. So, the manifested world was evolved first as ideas in heaven by the intelligent creator; the creator woke up from sleep to dream, what we call the cosmic dream.

### (c) Idea are only Objective States of Creator

Since there was only the creator present, he had himself to play the role of object. Intelligence in activity creates only ideas and these formed his objective states. But when he is an object there is no subject and when he next resumes his role of subject there is no object at that instant. During this activity several gods or Devas appeared on the scene. In the first place appeared the Aśvins with their twin arms, along one arm of which he passed on to be an object which he deposited in himself, as he was present all over, and returned by the other arm of the Aśvins to resume him subjective role. This activity spelt out two new ideas namely, (1) the sense of differentiation and (2) the sense of touch by which the objective states were constantly recharged. These two functions form part of the seven-pronged or-armed activity of Vaiśvānara called also simply Activity or the seven celestial rivers, the other arms being the other four sense perceptions and speech. And now an activity once initiated is repeated again and again to confirm the object unshakeably. This role of repeating activities was taken over by Ṛta. And now, from what we said above the object of the creator to know himself is not realised as this entails the simultaneous presence of both subject and object which however is not possible as it stands. So the creator was committed to unending activity which persisted even in the manifestation process.

### (d) Evolution in the World of Ideas

The creator was compelled, therefore, by his own resolve, to produce ideas continually until the whole of the vast space was completely filled with ideas which were to take part in the subsequent manifestation. These ideas formed the foundation of knowledge. Knowledge furnished the basis for the evolution of creatures in the subtle world at first. Hundreds of the likenesses of all creatures were released from the depths of knowledge (321). This established the dharma for the subsequent manifestation. The Self or Jivas were born foremost in ancient times prior to Ṛta (594). Man was the first being to be created by Vaiśvānara possessing the sense of differentiation, the five sense perceptions and speech but without the scope to exercise these faculties till late (1,116). As manifestation was the ultimate goal and as that was not possible until the ideas reached the stage of matter, other creatures with less and less sense faculties were evolved. All the creatures which subsequently appeared on earth during manifestation were evolved now in prototype forms by suppressing at first speech, then hearing, then sight, smell and taste when the lowest forms of creatures were reached. Where only the sense of touch remained the stage of trees and plants was reached. The suppression of this sense too paved the way for the inanimate world. It must be borne in mind that the suppressed sense faculties remained latent in the creatures making the other faculties more acute. Agnideva sensed us in the story of creation and bestowed many creatures beginning with men (1,782). The Puruṣa bestows births of creatures first, unites with them, then he created the worlds (621).

### (e) (i) Evolution of the Inanimate World of Ideas

Manifestation depends on matter or inertia equally with ideas, for life process is an association of both. But this matter of no external activity cannot be derived from ideas of unimaginable activity in one jump. Ideas have to slow down their activity in stages and it is during this process we come across the world of radiation and energies. Cosmic radiation, gamma, beta, alpha, x-Ray ultra-violet, light, infra-red, heat and sound are all varying forms of ideas more and more densely packed and in varied configurations accounting for their various properties. Then we come down to air, water and earth in which ideas are wholly deprived of external activity and in which the activity is internal with electrons spinning round a central nucleus. The Veda says that followers of Agni i.e. ideas were roped together to form impenetrable ignorance (matter) giving diverse guileless objects (1,748). The elements of the periodic table were formed in this manner, more and more ideas entering into the composition of the elements. Automatic radiation in elements like uranium indicates that excess of ideas had been packed in, leading to their escape from imprisonment. The world of energies and matter were evolved out of ideas thus. The external world of Stars, Sun, Moon and the planets with their contents were evolved thus. This external world is constituted only of the percepts of the creatures and hence it came into existence after the creatures. Anyhow all energies and all matter exist only as ideas at times. All the properties which they are endowed with are percepts of the creatures induced by the creator. (e) (i) The descent from ideas to matter *through energy* is our own inference and is not expressly stated in the Veda. But we consider it a reasonable inference. The stage was now set for manifestation.

(ii) Since man was the first creature to be created and since the manifestation terminated with man, the Veda considers man as having undergone the travails of experiences through the various stages of evolution.

**(f) Time Involved in Evolution**

We have some means of ascertaining with reasonable guesses the period that has expired since manifestation began. We assign it a period of 4,000 to 5,000 million years. But we have no means of even guessing at the period taken for evolution in the subtle plane. But ideas function with unimaginable rapidity, far superior to the speed of light and other radiations. So, the period involved must have been very very little, perhaps a 100 years or less in our reckoning. The ideas had not to contend with inertia.

**(g) Manifestation**

In manifestation the various types of Jīvas or creatures with varying number of sense activities already evolved are provided with a shelter enclosing them, for them to engage in activity with the outside world. This shelter is the body with the sense organs. Agni bestowed sense object on the Jīvas in heaven who were browsing in ancient times and he bestowed on them ideas. He bestowed many youthful creatures freeing them from their slumber in the fight for life and honoured them with gifts from sense activities (1, 782). What was hindering manifestation was Vṛtra or inertia of matter. Indra overpowered him in water and laid the foundation for life-activity.

**(h) Cell Life**

Cell organisms were the foremost to be organised in water. They are the building blocks of organised life. Agni invoked water and announced his desire to them for supporting the bodies of creatures with its latent heat (18). Water was chosen for organising cell life as it was easier to split it up and as the latent heat furnished the energy requirements. The first step in producing creatures taken by the creator was in the ocean waters (529). Life-activity in the form of these cells came into being when Vṛtra (inertia) in water was overcome, which was a hindrance (1,429). In ancient times the intelligence of Prajāpati perceived homes (cells) in water and he bestowed Activity to control them (1,495). Consciousness bestowed protection on the cells like lightning and also existence (1,496). In very ancient births Agni adorned the lives of the species (1,711). The protector of creatures nourishes all cells like milch cow (1,720). Indra assaulted the water for the sake of the cells desiring existence to the Jīvas (1,858). Indra cut off the head of Namuci with the foam from the water of the oceans and won him for the bodies of creatures (211). See the explanations give under the mantra. The cells sprouted from water, Indra bestowed them, enveloped and roused them up (1,327). These cells grew combined and finally developed to become the brain. Devas (ideas) from heaven bestow wealth from the waters by overflowing and riding them which the brain cells sip (55). The earliest creatures of ancient times were very odd which the sense activities brought to light, on whom the brain depended (1,494).

**(i) Plant Life**

The cells gave rise to plant life in the waters at first and by the combined action of the wind and waves they were wafted ashore and in due course established plant life on land as well. Birth is the dharma of the yonder world which unites with life and grows with existence (90). In ancient times when the cells were without a mind as in plants Indra used to move to release impulses (1,677). The plants in which only the sense of differentiation and sense of touch were active initiated the process of building up a physical body. Indra ruled over them, over the sense activity and consciousness (1,678). They furnished the food for survival of the forms of life which followed them. The stationary trees and plants are sunk in fearful dependence and they rejoice to grow collectively (1,698). The ruddy rays of the sun are helpful to the plant kingdom (1,783). Prāṇa was not the cause of delighting manifestation in ancient times i.e. in plants, the sense of touch was the comrade of the sap (1,010). Plants do not have a mind as this comes into existence only through sense organs which the trees and plants do not have.

**(j) Mobile Creatures**

(I) Since trees and plants with a stationary existence

were so utterly dependent on help from the other world for their existence, the creator conceived introducing mobile creatures who to some extent can held themselves by their own activity. This thought brought out the mobile creatures on earth which exist already in heaven as idea groups. In these mobile creatures the sense activities and Uṣas together with the external world (Varuṇa) and sense organs play mighty roles.

**(ii) *Vṛtra***

In these mobile creatures matter formed part of the existence of the creatures. Known as Vṛtra in the Veda, it formed the outer shell or body providing a shelter and armour for the ideas within to have scope for their activity. At the same time this inertia had to be overcome within in the brain, before sense activities or ideas can function. Consciousness honours sense activities and strikes down Vṛtra through Indra (89). Consciousness honours the head after striking down and pushing away Vṛtra (126). Indra bestows understanding and supports it by opposing Vṛtra whom he struck down to give newer and newer forms of creatures (179). Indra after striking down Vṛtra makes him form the other half of creatures (181). Indra cut off the head of Namuci i.e. inertia and won him for the bodies of creatures (211). Indra strikes down Vṛtra for newer and newer creatures to be created (913). Life-activity came into being when Vṛtra was overcome, who was hindering it (1,429). Life-activity was born out of it and consciousness also took a hand at it (1,430). After Vṛtra is shattered and devoured the Aśvins turn round to Activity for establishing the brain (1,719). But it was Agni who first put down Vṛtra when he established cell life and plants and offered sense objects (4).

**(iii) *Agni-activity***

After inertia is overcome, Activity or Vaiśvānara controlled by Agni established the mobile creatures on earth after the plant kingdom. Agni from heaven visualised a variety of creatures in the waters through ideas (629). Agni in ancient times ran to create many forms of creatures and bestowed his favours on mind through the nerves (69). Vaiśvānara has his source in Agni and man is his guest (67). The sense activities from the source preside over the brain and bestow it mightily from heaven to bring out creatures (77). Various colourful creatures are born of sense activities and then man enters (352). The sense activities are bestowed by the Aṅgiras' (Agni-activity and Aśvins) (1,641). Sindhu (sense activities) envelops us, subdivides itself into the five activities and bestows on the head impartially (1,652). All paths of sense activities were released in the early morning of creation in the waking state; consciousness arose in midday in man (1,754). In the early morning of creation Agni let in the motley sense activities (85). When the brain cells were young Agni established mammoth creatures (359). In ancient times when the brain cells were young, Agni established odd creatures from the source (1,250). Agni churns the external world through sense activities. Aditi rains ideas from Varuṇa's dominion through Indra (1,857). Alone Indra ran to the conflict of life and bestowed many youthful creatures (325).

**(iv)** ***Sense-organs***

The sense activities function through the sense organs. These organs are developed progressively with higher and higher forms of life with greater complexities of life. The Veda does not expressly mention the sense organs of the very low forms of life. But as food is the basis of their lives and activity we can infer that they are all provided with a mouth for consuming food and some sort of breathing apparatus for taking in air for oxidising the food. The sense of taste and smell for selecting the food must have been developed in course of time. As we ascend the scale of evolution the sense of sight was imparted to the creatures first both for searching prey and to look out for enemies. The great Activity chose the sense of sight as desired by the creatures (303). Later on the creatures were equipped with ears as a further protection bestowed by heaven disclosing concealed enemies (1691). The sense of smell also falls in this category. The brain drinks the intoxicating honey, sense perception and there Indra supports the sense of hearing (356). The sense organs constitute though of matter (or ignorance) themselves are gateways to knowledge. They open the doors to the external world. Lastly when man came on the world scene he was endowed with the faculty of speech. Indra supports us by uniting with us; he mixes with all for yoking them to speech. The function of speech is to reveal the ideas stored or received by the brain. The Vedas were said to be revelations and what was meant by this was that the knowledge stored in the brains of men was revealed to the outside world through speech. Speech is said to be agni's minister and it is speech that tells us that we are born from the source and appeared first in water (1,382).

**(v) (a) *Sense-perceptions—Ideas***

Sense activities only establish a physical connection between the creator and the objects he created in the external world or the creatures. They do not reveal anything more. The sense activities are however accompanied by ideas from heaven and they make their imprint on the objects they meet with and give a content to them, when they become sense impressions or perceptions contributing to knowledge stored by the brain. Agni! You cultivate (educate) the devotee with ideas (11). Indra arouses sense activities to bestow sense perceptions creating forms of objects. What is available in the external world a moment before the first sense perception of an object is formed is a group of unformed ideas pell-mell fashion. The idea from heaven gives them a form and consolidates them to a specific object. Such contacts are repeated by Ṛta and the shape and content stabilised. Further contacts give rise to sense impressions in the creatures of a pure nature. It is well-known that ideas attach themselves to the brain, unite with it and strive to help the brain cells (170). Ideas nourish the sense organs praise worthily (324). Every organ of the body is a home of ideas i.e. it is constituted of ideas and responds to other ideas (636). Ancient creatures sought ideas and these hastened to mind. Such Ideas either induced them to activities, or constitute their sense perceptions or added to the store of knowledge. Indra rains ideas boldly with Aditi (sense activities) in Varuṇa's dominion vigorously (1,857). Troops of ideas move to Indra from beyond emulating sense activities (1,860). In ancient times troops of ideas supported the body watching it like a swan steadily and unperturbed (770).

**(v) (b) *Sense-perceptions Tinged and Untinged***

Although the objects of the external world remain constant they arouse differing reactions in the observing creatures or men, primarily tinged and untinged. The tinged sense reactions arise out of desires for which ideas are furnished by heaven through Soma. Soma is universal mind who fulfils the desires of the individual mind. The individual mind cultivates desires from sense perceptions with which it is fed and its longing are fulfilled by Soma allied to ideas from heaving furnished by Agni. The latent heat in the brain fluids shines and pleases the sense activities releasing them untiringly (1,385).

**(vi) *Nervous System***

A miniature nervous system is already in evidence in the cell organisms. As these developed to a complicated brain as evolution progressed with higher and higher scale of beings with increasing number of sense organs a complicated system of nerves grow apace organised by Indra first to receive the sense activities from heaven and then distribute them among the brain cells and from there to spread them out selectively to the mind and sense organs, then to receive the sense perceptions and reactions from the external world and redistribute them among the brain cells and finally to pass them on to mind also. Rudra is said to be in charge of this nervous system. He is considered the younger brother of Indra who is in overall charge and who receives the sense activities from heaven for distribution. Among these nerves, the spinal cord with two long nerves commencing in the region of the rectum and running parallel, crossing at the base of the spine to opposite lobes of the brain, are the most important. These two nerves at the sides are said to be controlled, one by Indra and the left one by Viṣṇu. Normally Indra functions in conjunction with the left lobe of the brain and only when this lobe is damaged and rendered useless the right lobe of the brain and Viṣṇu come into operation. The function of these two nerves is to energise the brain cells and prepare them to receive sense activities from heaven and sense perceptions and reactions coming from the sense organs. The central spinal cord conveys messages from the brain to all parts of the body and conveys the reactions of all bodily cells to the brain. The Veda says that above the spinal cord unites with the brain like a river, the source i.e. heaven unites with it (143). The footless brain cells release us from ignorance (145). All paths of sense activities i.e. the nerves were released in the early morning of creation in the waking state (1,754).

**(vii) *Consciousness—Uṣas***

We are not aware of all that goes on in the brain, the centre of all activities. These are all however transferred to mind by Indra through the nerves and then Uṣas or Consciousness, her father, reveals them to the mind of the creatures. This is the second birth for idea, the first birth being in heaven. Consciousness with his full blaze of light is associated only with man. The feeble light of Uṣas is associated with all other creatures. The Veda says that in the early morning of creation in ancient times the effulgent consciousness looked within the head which gave us the waking state (20). Consciousness as a relative of Activity draws out the image of Savitā for existence, as men (1,547).

Uṣas terminated herself in favour of consciousness when man appeared (1,725). In ancient times Uṣas sought to cut off her own activities (1,728). The highest Deva is consciousness bestowing the variegated rays on the sense activities, Savitā likewise created night and day (sleeping and waking states) (1,749). Consciousness arose in midday in man. The ruddy light of Uṣas protects the paths of sense perceptions of the new creatures (1756). The motley sense activities eagerly bestowed powerful atmospheric creatures in the earlier half of creation. Soma tells us that we men have descended along the line of animals (boar) (524).

### (viii) *Evolving New Creatures from Existing Ones*

How the successive species of creatures in bewildering variety came on the world scene remains a mystery. Modern Evolutionists attribute it to random mutation and goal directed activity. It does not explain how the phenomena took place. The Sāma Veda gives a rational explanation. Since most of the creatures are womb-born, transformation must take place in the brains of an existing creature to influence the genes to be transmitted to the new creature.

Ideas relating to the new species awaiting manifestation in heaven enter the brain of a selected existing species and effect transformations in the brain cells without the knowledge of the creatures themselves. This happens when prāṇa is not in contact with the brain cells i.e. when prāṇa is on its downward journey to the body. So, the Veda says that the paths of the ideas are below consciousness (172). Agni helps to produce transformation (1,348). Viṣṇu nourished the new creatures with oblations; Indra and the Aśvins approached the creatures with ideas. Indra fosters the growth of only such creatures which have to continue existence and lets others become extinct (1,639). Man is anxious not to suffer transformations himself and says "let not the form of my body be changed to another form by Activity" (1,625). Prāṇa carves out new forms in the home with Tvaṣṭā (440).

Besides the transformations in the brain cells the bone structure is also changed through idea. For, it is said, according to the sacred ordinances of old times the bones of creatures were split and jointed for new creatures (244). Indra fosters life-activity in whatever creature which subsists and which he envelops (121).

**(ix)** ***Mind***

Mind appeared in evolution with the advent of mobile life on earth. The individuality of a creature is known only from its own private experiences which together make up its mind. Mind is not strictly necessary for existence, as we do exist during sleep when mind is dissociated from the brain. Men are known to continue in existence during the state of Samādhi stretching over several days or when men go into a state of come extending over several years even. Mind's presence is however necessary on other counts. Mind is like a nagging wife. It forms desires and goes on complaining about its wants, inadequacies and so forth and in this way it was instrumental in the creation of higher and higher species of creatures, with increasing number of sense organs and better equipped to face the battle of life. Continued evolution depended on it. And then it plays an even more important role in continuing existence after death. The brain with all its experiences is buried or burnt and it is only the mind, which knows all the current experiences and which are conveyed for an after-life. It fulfils the creator's purpose of continued existence. The Veda says that the brain and sense organs bestow on mind (622). Ancient creatures sought ideas and they hastened to mind (1,264). Indra! You bestow a new gift on women for which you arouse the girl and bestowing it guide it. (1,460).

(x) The Jīvas from heaven were born in ignorance (467). They gather knowledge only on this earth through the sense organs from the external world and from heaven, all as ideas. In the state of ignorance the brain is restive like a horse, Agni bestows a variety of gifts on it (1,871). The source itself is glad that its activity depends on ignorance being devoured to establish existence on earth (1,872).

### 8. Man and his Internal Activities

Man as well as all other creatures are sustained by universal Devas whose functions we speak of in physiological terms alone forgetting the divinities behind them. We realise however that the activities go on in spite of ourselves and that we cannot control except at grave risk to ourselves. There are a large number of mantras spread out on this aspect, too numerous to be presented in brief, but they are the aspect, too numerous to be presented in brief, but they are the activities of the following Devas:—

#### (a) Savitā

Savitā is the arbiter of the destinies of the universe and the creature and the stimulator of their activities. He is also known as Viṣṇu or worker and the equivalent of the later Brahman. He is immanent in all both subtle and gross. Unlike Brahman who is conceived to be in eternal repose, Savitā is eternally and incessantly active, sustaining the activity of every creature, sustaining all energies and the inertia of matter. In fact he is all these at all times. His various attributes or activities are personified as various divinities mentioned below.

#### (b) The Aśvins

The Aśvins have twin arms and are said to be the vehicle of Savitā by whom the creator is enabled to play the part of both subject and object moving along one arm to the momentary object and returning among the other arm to resume being the subject. The Aśvins also bridge two levels of activities transforming each other and assist the other Devas. They carry on the cooking of the various component part of the body translating ideas into matter. By virtue of their twin arms they are often referred to by cloven footed animals like sheep, goat etc. in the Veda.

**(c) Consciousness**

The creator next brought consciousness into being to bestow all his beneficences on the creatures by revealing them and so consciousness is termed his hands. Consciousness brings out the identity of the universal with the particular and the differences among the particular themselves. It is an instantaneous activity.

**(d) Agni**

Agni is the flaming zeal for activity and knowledge. This furnishes the basis for every activity of man and the creator included. This aspect of Savitā is the leader of the Devas and organiser of the creatures and the worlds.

**(e) Activity**

Activity also known as Vaiśvānara or seven Ṛṣis or celestial rivers, is the basic activity establishing the creatures and the worlds contributing to their knowledge. This Activity is constituted of seven limbs or illuminating principles namely: (1) sense of differentiation as subject and object; (2) the five sense perceptions also known as Aditi, Sarasvatī etc.; and (3) speech which releases ideas of the brain to the external world.

**(f) Indra**

Indra is the architect of the bodies of creatures. Agni inspires activity through the seven ṛṣis but it is Indra who is directly involved in breaking up mạtter, overcoming inertia and building up bodies with the help of Aśvins and ideas. Ideas are the building blocks of the body. He builds up the nervous system too and Indra's younger brother Rudra is said to be the leader of the nervous system. The spinal cord and the afferent and efferent nervers are together known as the three Ṛbhus who are said to be the first to reach heaven (head or brain) from the terrestrial world (body). Indra is also known as the Bull, Destroyer of a hundred forts etc. and is the universal prāṇa. Indra comprises the five prāṇas (1) Udāna, (2) Prāṇa, (3) Apāna, (4) Samāna, and (5) Vyāna.

**(g) Soma**

Soma is the universal mind sustaining Activity through his reacting with desires instructed by Agni. Activity and Soma sustain each other and neither can function without the other. Soma representing desires has sway over all creatures. So desires discarded by soma take hold of other as their victims. Desires unfulfilled in the current life are carried over by Soma to the next.

**(h) Prāṇa**

Prāṇa is the controller of individual bodies representing Indra. Prāṇa controls the body by inciting the brain cells and functioning through the nervous system. We have explained under mantra 1,685 the five-fold activity of Indra of which prāṇa is one. This prāṇa actuates the brain cells towards receiving sense impressions from outside or calls from inside the body. Prāṇa does this by ascending along one of the two long nerves running parallel to the spinal cord on either side of it and cross each other at above neck level and ascend to both sections of the brain. The nerve on the right side of the spinal cord is traversed by Indra-Prāṇa and the one on the left, which comes into operation when the left section of the brain becomes inoperative due to damage to it, is under the control of Viṣṇu. Regarding the other prāṇas please see the explanations under mantra 1,685. The prāṇa is called the horse (aśva) which draws the chariot (body) and Indra is the charioteer.

**(i) Mind**

Mind is the individual man or creature sustained by the universal Devas who import all their gifts to the brain and carry on their activities; impart knowledge and understanding to it. The brain in turn imparts all these to the Mind. Ordinarily we attribute all subtle activities to Mind whereas they all emanate from Soma who acquaints Mind with them through the brain. Mind comprises sense perceptions, sense reactions and desires.

**(j) Mitra**

Mitra is the brain comprising the brain cells variously referred to as grains, drops, caves and the nerve fibres referred to as grass, hair, threads etc. The brain too is referred to as fat, porridge etc. The brain may be said to be the computer of the creator who feeds the brain and sustains it to carry on life-activity through his assistants. The brain mediates between the universal Devas and the external world and acts as a central exchange between them. All the universal Devas enter the brain through the skull which is not impervious to them.

**(k) Varuṇa**

The whole of the external world, of land, seas and air is referred to as Varuṇa. Ideas of the external world conveyed by the perceptions are imparted to Mitra so that Varuṇa resides in Mitra as ideas and so these two Devas are always spoken together. Varuṇa is said to be a stern upholder of truth in the sense that he presents for cognition ideas invested with from and substance so that there can be no mistake about them.

**(l) Viśvedevas**

The brain-cells like the stars in the sky are referred to as Viśvedevas.

**(m) Devas Maruts**

Ideas are referred to by these names. Ideas form the building blocks of the non-material and the material worlds. Devas are said to have been slaughtered, by depriving them of their natural activity, in building up the bodies of creatures which need inertia to retain their forms.

**(n) Vṛtra, Vala, Namuci etc.**

These Asuras or non-Devas represent matter which is another class of ideas deprived of their natural voluntary activity by which they acquire inertia or inactivity which is so essential for life-activity to be carried on successfully. In the course of evolution in the subtle plane in heaven the Jīvas shed one perceptive faculty after another, which successively became latent, until all seven became latent reaching the state of matter but still remaining an idea floating about in space like the rest of the ideas. A legend in the Purāṇas says that Indra smote down these floating inert ideas to settle down as land, mountains and rivers. It is evidently a picturesque way of describing what took place subsequently to the inert ideas by getting very densely packed by cohesive forces among them variously as land, sea and air of various groups of ideas. Perhaps the radioactivity of soma of the higher elements of matter is an effort at breaking fee from this repressed state presaging life-activity to follow with the cooperation of matter.

The characteristic of matter is that it preseves carefully what is entrusted to it. This essential feature contributes to memory in the brain cells without which life-activity would be impossible. This matter forms a protective shell in the shape of a head and body. Man and the other creatures represent a cooperative activity of ideas and matter. Incidentally light and other forms of energy are also degraded forms of ideas of less intensive activity and they occupy and intermediate place between ideas and matter.

**9. Some Special Expressions**

Some of the expression used in the Veda have been misunderstood leading to wrong interpretations. Hence we give below some of the expressions and what they truly indicate.

(1) Head : This is refereed to as heaven, the rock, hill, assembly and ocean.
(2) Body : cow, corpse, buffalo, earth, land, prison.
(3) Brain : hṛdaya, broth, porridge, sky
(4) Brain cells: stars, Viśvedevas, drops, corn
(5) Nerves : grass, hair, thread, snakes, reeds, cobwebs.
(6) Spinal cord: snake, pillar, ahi, crossbeam, tree.
(7) Skull : pipru
(8) Prāṇa : aśva (horse), trita; trita āptaya means activity moving in all three states.
(9) Yajña, yaja, Soma yajña : life-activity.

**10. Misconception about S.V. and Y.V. Originating from R.V.**

The current belief among scholars is that the Ṛg Veda is the oldest Veda and that the other two Vedas have borrowed to a very great extent from it. Except for 75 mantras in S.V. and about 220 in Y.V. all the rest are ascribed to R.V. How wrong, these notions are can be seen from the following considerations.

(1) We have already shown that the S.V. and Y.V. spring from inter-glacial times whereas R.V. is of the period of solar and lunar dynasty kings say about 5,000 to 4,000 B.C. which separates them by 5,000 years.
(2) The two older Vedas are of Arctic origin and vested with the Devas and Asuras who were of a different race from the patriarchs and their descendants in whom the R.V. was vested in Indian soil.
(3) While the whole of the Ṛg Veda has been ascribed to some 400 Ṛṣis, the S.V. and Y.V. claim to be of traditional origin and no ṛṣis are mentioned about them.
(4) The three Vedas have wholly different outlook and goals and approaches to life. Sāma Veda stresses only prayers for release to the original home in heaven and

had not conceived yajña. The Yajur Veda introduced the yajña ritual and believed in life on earth and prayed for return to this earth again and again. Both S.V. and Y.V. deal with evolution and the activities of the Devas in our brain and body. The S.V. deals more with perceptions whereas the Y.V. deals more with Mind. The Ṛg Veda comprises thought and aspirations of a more sophisticated age with different outlook on life and living. It deals with different paths for salvation such as bhakti, karma, mysticism, yoga and wisdom.

(5) The Ṛg Veda has adopted 1,443 mantras from Sāma Veda and 481 from Y.V. actually. In the Bhagavad Gītā Kṛṣṇa says "of the Vedas I am Sāma Veda". He did not cite Ṛg Veda. Some of the mantras of Sāma Veda have been adopted by more than one Ṛṣi.

| | | |
|---|---|---|
| (1) S.V. 1208 | R.V. IX.25.6 | Dṛḍahacyuta Āgastya |
| do | „ 50.4 | Ucathya Āṅgirasa |
| (2) S.V. 1,167 | VIII. 11.8 | Vatsa Kāṇva |
| do | „ 43.21 | Virūpa Āṅgirasa |
| (3) S.V. 76 | III.7.11 | Gādhino Viśvāmitra |
| do | do 15.7 | Utkīla Kātya |
| do | do 23.5 | Devaśravā Devavātaśea |
| (4) S.V. 169/682 | IV.31.1 | Vāmadeva Gautama |
| do | VII.32.23 | Maitrāvaruṇī Vaśiṣṭha |

## 11. Repetition of Mantras

There are 222 mantras as given in App. VII which are repeated. But in many cases the mantras are addressed to a different Deva, sometimes a different meaning is conveyed when so addressed.

12. In App. IX, we have grouped the mantras according to each Deva which are not presented in one block but scattered over the whole Veda indicating that mantras about every deva were added from time to time establishing a tradition. The number of mantras devoted to the various

Devas are follows:—

(1) Savitā 29, (2) Aśvins 31; (3) Consciousness/Uṣas 125; (4) Agni 328; (5) Activity/seven Ṛṣis 80; (6) Indra/prāṇa 658; (7) Soma/Mind 251; (8) Mitra 53; (9) Varuṇa 8; (10) Jīva 72; (11) Ṛta 10; (12) Devas/Maruts 36; (13) Soma Juice 36; (14) Tvaṣṭṛ 3; (15) Water 3; (16) Vṛtra 8; (17) Speech 12; (18) Nerves 31; (19) Head and body 39, Miscellaneous 60. Total 1,873.

## 12. An Earlier Race of Men

The Veda mentions having known a race of men in Mantra 322 who appear to be a super-human type from the brief description given. This contradicts the Western anthropologists' view of early man as a semi-savage brute. We may pause to consider what must have really taken place in the course of evolution. The first men from a descendant of a gorilla were more of god-like type rather than savage. We know from our own experience that a dunce be gets a genius and a genius be-gets a dunce. So, as the Veda says, the early man must have been a superman and his descendants degenerated to a savage state due to natural calamities as had been foretold in the Yajur Veda to the Devas and Asuras at the advent of glaciation in Tretā yuga. After all the same Intelligence pervades both the genius and the savage and how they come about depends on the creator and the environment.

## 13. The Brain

The Veda also admits of two halves of the brain, only one of which is in operation in normal waking hours. The other half affords a 100 per cent reserve. As we said earlier the left half of the brain is under the control of Indra and the right half under Viṣṇu. The left side of the brain holds only current life experiences while the right section holds both the current and the unfulfilled longings from the past life. External impulses arising from heaven or from the world of matter spilit into two and feed both halves of the brain. What is carried from previous life breaks out in a man's career suddenly when it is most propitious. This alone can explain sudden changes for the good or bad in every man's life time at some point of time. All repressed desires probably are also stored in the right half of the brain giving us a conception of a sub-conscious Mind. In dreams the right section of the brain comes into play bringing in experiences of earlier lives.

### 14. Translation of the Veda

There are no doubt a few translations of the Veda already in the field and some bhāṣyas (commentaries) in Sanskrit by Sāyaṇa and in Hindi by Bhagavadacharya and Satavalekar. The English translation is by R.T.H. Griffith who has largely been influenced by Sāyaṇa. There is also an English translation by Devichand which is re-translation from Ḫindi by Swami Dayanand Sarasvati, founder of the Arya Samaj. These English translations, do not convey much sense most often. They are abstruse, distorted in sense and often times absurd also. They do not present a consistent system of thought on which the Veda should have been based. They do not tell us definitely what the functions of the various Devas are. The Veda repeatedly affirms that the Davas are engaged in Yajña establishing the creatures and the worlds. Nowhere is this fact been brought out in these translations. Although this Veda has been acclaimed as the best among all the four books of knowledge, one cannot get this impression by reading these translations. We are struck with many absurdities in them. We, therefore, felt that the Veda should be rescued and restored to its proper preeminent place by a fresh translation. In whatever other ways a number of mantras could be translated, for which the Veda easily lends itself, both by reason of brevity of expression and improper transcription from chanting to writing, they would be valueless unless they jointly present a consistent picture. Our claim is that the Veda lends itself to be correctly translated as we have done which establishes the aims of the Veda unmistakably namely about the yajña (life-activity) conducted by the Devas for manifestation of the creatures and maintaining them. Our guiding light has been the belief in the wisdom of the ancients who desired to preserve their thoughts for future generations having been convinced of their eternal value.

### 15. The Destiny of Man

The Sāma Veda conceives of man's destiny differently from the Upaniṣads and later śāstras. These latter hold, what is to a large extent accepted by the Hindus even now, that man, after endless births and experiences secures wisdom and extinction by merging with the creator. If this is to be his destiny then why should the creator have taken the trouble to evolve him? At the same time it is argued by them that the individual self is at all times on with the Supreme Self, which remains unknown until wisdom dawns. This means only that there never is an individual soul, then who is to merge?

The Sāma Veda presents two different concepts namely: (1) that all that exists and that may come in the future too are nought by the Puruṣa known as Savitā or Viṣṇu. All activity belongs to him and he manifests himself as all creatures and the worlds. (2) He creates man in his own image as a subtle being endowed with all seven principles of activity,. who degenerates to lower forms by shedding one activity after another in the subtle world until he is devoid of all seven activities and reduced to the state of inanimate matter. Then the universal Devas pull him up through low forms of life rising higher and higher in the scale of existence reaching the stage of man finally. In this state he undergoes many trials and tribulations and longs to go back to his original heavily home. He prays for it continually and finally gets back. After a time he is seized with a desire to return to earth and is born again as a human being and undergoes the fortunes of earthly existence. He does no merge with the creator at any time. This second view may be considered as identical with the first if it is taken that the conception of a Jīva makes it easy to explain the processes of creation. Any way the sole purpose of the creator is to continue activity and unending existence and towards this end he has diversified the activity with increasing sense perceptions. Activity alone ensures existence.

### 16. Prayers

The sole means to be resorted to be man, according to Sāma Veda, is prayers. These prayers take the form of extolling the various universal Devas for their varied activities in establishing the creatures, evolving and maintaining them all impartially. The devotee prays for an unimpaired life of a hundred years, in welfare, keen in perceptions and sound of limbs and in understanding. The aim of prayers is to keep in touch with the creator continually. Whether one prays or not the activities are always of the creator but by ever-recurring renewal of contacts with him life's burden can be borne lightly.

**First Grand Division.—Books I.-VII.**

Seven books of short hymns (433) of miscellaneous subjects

## 1. Book the first

1. For the retention of sacred learning
2. Against injury and disease: with a reed
3. Against obstruction of urine: with a reed
4. To the waters: for blessing
5. To the waters: for blessings
6. To the waters: for blessings
7. To Agni: for the discovery of sorcerers
8. To Agni and other gods: for the discovery of sorcerers
9. For some one's advancement and success
10. For some one's release from Varuṇa's wrath
11. For successful childbirth
12. Against various ailments (as results of lightning?)
13. Deterrent homage to lightning
14. Imprecation of spinsterhood on a woman
15. With an oblation: for confluence of wealth
16. Against demons: with an amulet of lead
17. To stop the vessels of the body
18. Against unlucky marks
19. Against enemies
20. Against enemies and their weapons
21. Against enemies
22. Against yellowness (jaundice)
23. Against leprosy: with a healing herb
24. Against leprosy
25. Against fever (takmán)
26. For protection from the wrath of the gods
27. Against various evils
28. Against sorcerers and witches
29. For a chief's success: with an amulet
30. For protection: to all the gods
31. To the divine guardians of the quarters
32. Cosmogonic
33. To the waters: for blessings
34. A love-spell: with a sweet herb

35. For long life etc.: with a gold amulet

**II. Book the second**

1. Mystic
2. To Gandharvas and Apsarases
3. For relief from Flux: with a certain remedy
4. Against various evils: with a *jañgiḍā* amulet
5. Praise and prayer to Indra
6. Praise and prayer to Agni
7. Against curses and cursers: with a plant
8. Against the disease *kṣetriyā:* with a plant
9. Against possession by demons: with an amulet
10. For release from evils, and for welfare
11. To counteract witchcraft: with an amulet
12. [Against such as would thwart my incantations]
13. For welfare and long life of an infant
14. Against *sadānvās*
15. Against fear
16. For protection
17. For various gifts
18. For release from demons and foes
19. Against enemies: to Agni (fire)
20. The same: to Vāyu (wind)
21. The same: to Sūrya (sun)
22. The same: to the moon
23. The same: to water
24. Against *kimīdins,* male and female
25. Against *kāṇvas:* with a plant
26. For safety and increase of kine
27. For victory in disputation: with a plant
28. For long life for a certain person (child?)
29. For some one's long life and other blessings
30. To secure a woman's love
31. Against worms
32. Against worms
33. For expulsion of *yākṣma* from all parts of the body
34. Accompanying the sacrifice of an animal
35. To expiate errors in the sacrifice: to Viśvakarman

36. To get a husband for a woman

### III. Book the third

1. Against enemies
2. Against enemies
3. For the restoration of a king
4. To establish a king
5. For prosperity: with a *parṇá*-amulet
6. Against enemies: with *açvatthá*
7. Against the disease *kṣetriyá*
8. For authority
9. Against *vīṣkandha* and other evils
10. To the *ekāṣṭká*(day of moon's last quarter)
11. For relief from disease, and for long life
12. Accompanying the building of a house
13. To the waters
14. A blessing on the kine
15. For success in trade
16. Morning in vocation to various gods, especially Bhaga
17. For successful agriculture
18. Against a rival wife: with a plant
19. To help friends against enemies
20. To Agni and other gods: for various blessings
21. With oblation to the various forms of fire or Agni
22. To the gods: for splendor *(várcas)*
23. For fecundity
24. For abundance of grain
25. To command a woman's love
26. Homage to the gods of the quarters etc. [snake charms?]
27. The same: with imprecation on enemies
28. To avert the ill omen of a twinning animal
29. With the offering of a white-footed sheep
30. For concord
31. For welfare and long life

### IV. Book the fourth

1. Mystic
2. To the unknown god

3. Against wild beasts and thieves
4. For recovery of virility: with a plant
5. An incantation to put to sleep
6. Against the poison of a poisoned arrow
7. Against poison
8. Accompanying the consecration of a king
9. For protection etc: with a certain ointment
10. Against evils: with a pearl-shell amulet
11. In praise of the draft-ox
12. To heal serious wounds: with an herb
13. For healing
14. With the sacrifice of a goat
15. For abundant rain
16. The power of the gods
17. Against various evils: with a plant
18. Against witchcraft: with a plant
19. Against enemies: with a plant
20. To discover sorcerers: with an herb
21. Praise of the kine
22. For the success and prosperity of a king
23. Praise and prayer to Agni
24. Praise and prayer to Indra
25. Praise and prayer to Vāyu and Savita
26. Praise and prayer to heaven and earth
27. Praise and prayer to the Maruts
28. Praise and prayer to Bhava and Çarva
29. Praise and prayer to Mitra and Varuṇa
30. Self-laudation of Speech (?)
31. Praise and prayer to fury *(manyu)*
32. Praise and prayer to fury (*manyu*)
33. To Agni: for release from evil
34. Extolling a certain rice-mess offering
35. Extolling a rice-mess offering
36. Against demons and other enemies
37. Against various superhuman foes: with an herb
38. For luck in gambling: by aid of an Apsaras
39. For various blessings
40. Against enemies from the different quarters

**V. Book the fifth**

1. Mystic
2. Mystic

3. To various gods: for protection and blessings
4. To the plant *kúṣṭha: against takmán* [fever]
5. To a healing plant, *lākṣá*
6. ? [Disconnected verses]
7. Against neggardliness and its effects
8. Against enemies: to Indra and other gods
9. For protection: to various gods
10. For defense from all quarters
11. [Dialogue between] Varuṇa and Atharvan
12. Āprí-hymn: to various divinities
13. Against snakes' poison
14. Against witchcraft: with a plant
15. For exorcism: to a plant
16. Exorcism
17. The Brahman's wife
18. The Brahman's cow
19. The Brahman's cow
20. To the war-drum
21. To the war-drum
22. Against fever (*takmán*)
23. Against worms
24. To various gods as overlords
25. For successful conception
26. Accompanying a sacrifice
27. Āprí-hymn: to various divinities
28. With an amulet of three metals: for safety etc.
29. To Agni: against demons
30. To lengthen out some one's life
31. Against witchcraft

### VI. Book the sixth

1. Praise to Savitar
2. Praise and prayer to Indra
3. To various divinities: for protection
4. To various divinities: for protection
5. For some one's exaltation
6. Against enemies
7. For blessing
8. To win a woman's love
9. To win a woman's love

10. Greeting to divinities etc. of the three spheres
11. For birth of sons
12. Against the poison of snakes
13. To the instruments and ministers of death
14. Against the *balása*
15. For superiority
16. To various plants (?)
17. Against premature birth
18. Against jealousy
19. For ceremonial purification
20. Against fever (*takmán)*
21. To healing plants
22. To the Maruts
23. To the waters: for blessings
24. To the waters: for blessings
25. For relief from pains (?) in neck and shoulders
26. Against evil
27. Against birds of ill omen
28. Against birds of ill omen etc.
29. Against birds of ill omen
30. To the *çamí* plant: for benefit to the hair
31. At rising of the sun (or moon)
32. Against demons
33. Praise to Indra
34. Praise and prayer to Agni
35. Prayer to Agni Váiçvánara
36. In praise of Agni
37. Against curses
38. For brilliance
39. For glory
40. For freedom from fear
41. To various divinities
42. To remove wrath
43. To assuage wrath
44. For cessation of a disease
45. In atonement of offenses
46. Against evil dreams
47. For blessings: at the three daily libations
48. To the deities of the three daily libations
49. To Agni etc.
50. Against petty destroyers of grain

51. For various blessings
52. For deliverance from unseen pests
53. For protection: to various gods
54. To secure and increase some one's superiority
55. For various blessings
56. For protection from serpents
57. With a certain remedy against disease
58. For glory
59. For protection to cattle
60. For winning a spouse
61. Prayer and boasts
62. Váiçvánara etc.: for purification
63. For some one's release from perdition (*nirṛti*)
64. For concord
65. For success against enemies
66. For success against enemies
67. For success against enemies
68. To accompany the act of shaving
69. For glory etc.
70. To attach a cow to her calf
71. Against harm from improper food
72. For Virile power
73. To assure supremacy
74. For harmony
75. To eject a rival
76. For a *kṣatriya's* security from death
77. For recovery and retention of what is lost
78. For matrimonial happiness
79. For abundance at home
80. The heavenly dog and the *kālakāñjás*
81. For successful pregnancy: with an amulet
82. To obtain a wife
83. To remove *apacíts*
84. For release from perdition
85. For relief from *yákṣma*
86. For supremacy
87. To establish some one in sovereignty
88. To establish a sovereign
89. To win affection
90. For safety from Rudra's arrow
91. For remedy from disease

92. For success of a horse
93. For protection: to many gods
94. For harmony
95. For relief from diseases: with *kúṣṭha*
96. For relief from sin and distress
97. For victory
98. To Indra: for victory
99. For safety: to Indra
100. Against poison
101. For virile power
102. To win a woman
103. To tie up enemies
104. Against enemies
105. To get rid of cough
106. Against fire in the house
107. For protection: to various divinities
108. For wisdom
109. For healing: with *pippali*
110. For a child born at an unlucky time
111. For relief from insanity
112. For expiation of overslaughing
113. For release from seizure (*grahi)*
114. Against disability in sacrifice
115. For relief from sin
116. For relief from guilt
117. For relief from guilt or debt
118. For relief from guilt
119. For relief from guilt or obligation
120. To reach heaven
121. For release from evil
122. With an offering for offspring
123. For the success of an offering
124. Against evil influence of a sky-drop
125. To the war-chariot: for its success
126. To the drum: for success against the foe
127. Against various diseases: with a wooden amulet
128. For auspicious time: with dung-smoke
129. For good-fortune: with a *çiṅçápā* amulet
130. To win a man's love
131. To win a man's love
132. To compel a man's love

133. To a girdle: for long life etc.
134. To crush an enemy with a thunderbolt
135. To crush an enemy
136. To fasten and increase the hair
137. To fasten and increase the hair
138. To make a certain man importent
139. To compel a woman's love
140. With the first two upper teeth of a child
141. With marking of cattle's ears
142. For increase of barley

### VII. Book the seventh

1. Mystic
2. Of Atharvan
3. Mystic
4. To the wind-god with his steeds
5. Mystic: on the offering or sacrifice
6. Praise of Aditi
7. Praise of the Ādityas
8. For some one's success
9. Praise and prayer to Púshan
10. To Sarasvatī
11. Against injury to the grain by lightning
12. For success in the assembly
13. Against one's foes
14. Prayer and praise to Savitar
15. Prayer to Savitar
16. Prayer to Savitar (or Brihaspati)
17. Prayer to Dhátar for blessings
18. For rain, etc.
19. For progeny, etc.
20. Praise and prayer to Anumati
21. In praise of the sun
22. To the sun (?)
23. Against ill conditions and beings
24. To various gods
25. Praise to Vishṇu and Varuṇa
26. Praise and prayer to Vishṇu
27. Prayer and praise to Iḍā
28. Of the instruments of offering
29. To Agni and Vishṇu

30. For successful anointing
31. To Indra: for aid
32. Homage to Soma (?)
33. For blessings: to various gods
34. To Agni: against enemies
35. Against a rival (woman)
36. Husband and wife to one another
37. The wife to the husband
38. To win and fix a man's love: with a plant
39. In praise of Sarasvant (?)
40. Prayer and praise to Sarasvant
41. To the heavenly falcon (the sun)
42. To Soma and Rudra
43. Of speech (?)
44. Extolling Indra and Vishṇu
45. To cure jealousy
46. To Sinīvālī (goddess of the new moon)
47. To Kuhū (goddess of the new moon)
48. To Rākā (goddess of the full moon)
49. To the spouses of the gods
50. For success with dice
51. For protection by Brihaspati and Indra
52. For harmony
53. For some one's health and long life
54. Extolling verse and chant
55. To Indra (?)
56. Against poison of snakes and insects
57. Prayer to Sarasvatī etc.
58. Invitation to Indra and Varuṇa
59. Against cursers
60. To the home: on returning or leaving
61. For success of penance
62. To Agni: against enemies
63. To Agni: for aid
64. Against evil in fuence of a black bird
65. To the plant *apāmārgá:* for cleansing
66. For recovery of sacred knowledge (*brahmaṇa*)
67. For recovery of sense, etc.
68. Praise and prayer to Sarasvatī
69. Prayer for good fortune
70. Against an enemy's sacrifice

71. To Agni: for protection
72. With an oblation to Indra
73. With a heated offering to the Açvins
74. Against *apacīts:* against jealousy: to Agni
75. Praise and prayer to the kine
76. Against *apacits* and *jāyanya:* etc.
77. To the Maruts
78. To Agni: in favor of some one
79. To Amāvāsyā (night or goddess of new moon)
80. To the night or goddess of full moon (*pāurṇamāsi*)
81. To the sun and moon
82. Praise and prayer to Agni
83. For release from Varuṇa's fetters
84. To Agni: and to Indra
85. Invocation of Tārkshya
86. Invocation of Indra
87. Homage to Rudra
88. Against poison
89. To Agni and the waters
90. To destroy some one's virile power
91. To Indra: for aid
92. To Indra: for aid
93. For Indra's aid
94. For Indra's help to unanimity
95. A spell against some one
96. For quite kidneys (?)
97. Accompanying an offering
98. With an oblation to Indra
99. When bestrewing the *Védi*
100. Against bad dreams
101. As to food enjoyed in a dream
102. Accompanying self-relief
103. For betterment
104. Concerning Atharvan's cow
105. An exhortation to holy life
106. Deprecation for offenses
107. To relieve a stinging pain
108. Against enemies: to Ani
109. [For success with the dice]
110. To Indra and Agni: for help

111. To a soma-vessel
112. For release from guilt and distress
113. Against a (woman) rival: with a plant
114. Against enemies
115. Against ill luck
116. Against intermittent fever
117. Invitation to Indra
118. When arming a warrior

**Second Grand Division.—Books VIII.-XII.**

Five books of long hymns (45) of miscellaneous subjects

### VIII. Book the eighth

1. For some one's continued life
2. To prolong some one's life
3. To Agni: against sorcerers and demons
4. Against sorcerers and demons: to Indra and Soma
5. Against wichhcraft etc.: with an amulet
6. To guard a pregnant woman from demons
7. To the plants: for some one's restoration to health
8. To conquer enemies
9. Mystic: extolling the *viraj*
10. Extolling the *viraj* (first *parāya*-hymn, with 6 *prayāyas*)

### IX. Book the ninth

1. To the honey-whip etc.
2. To Kāma: for various blessings
3. To accompany the releasing of a house
4. Accompanying the gift of a bull
5. With the offering of a goat and five rice-dishes
6. Exalting the entertainment of guests (second *paryāya*-hymn, with 6 *prayāyas* )
7. Extolling the ox (third *paryāya*-hymn, with I *prayāya*)
8. Against various diseases
9. Mystic
10. Mystic

### X. Book the tenth

1. Against witchcraft and its practisers
2. The wonderful structure of man
3. With an amulet of *varaṇd*
4. Against snakes and their poison
5. Preparation and use of water-thunderbolts (largely prose)
6. With an amulet

7. Mystic: on the *skambhá* or frame of creation
8. Mystic
9. With the offering of a cow and a hundred rice-dishes
10. Extolling the cow (*vaçá*)

**XI. Book the eleventh**

1. Accompanying a rice-dish offering
2. To Rudra, especially as Bhava and Çarva
3. Extolling the rice-dish (*odaná*) (fourth *paryāya*-hymn, with 3 *paryāyas*)
4. Extolling the breath (*prāṇá*)
5. Extolling the Vedic student (*brahmacārīn*)
6. To many different gods: for relief
7. Extolling the remnant (*úcchiṣṭa*) of the offering
8. Mystic: especially on the constitution of man
9. To conquer enemies: to Arbudi
10. To conquer enemies: to Trishandhi

**XII. Book the twelfth**

1. To the earth
2. The flesh-eating and the householder's fires
3. Cremation as a sacrifice
4. The cow (*vaça)* as belonging exclusively to the Brahmans
5. The Brahman's cow (fifth *paryāya*-hymn, with 7 *paryāyas*)

**Third Grand Division.—Books XIII.-XVIII.**

Six books of long hymns (15), the books showing unity of subject

**Book XIII.—Hymns to the Ruddy Sun or Rohita. Seer: Brahman**

1. To Rohita (the sun, as ruddy one)
2. To the sun
3. To the sun (with imprecation on the evil-doer)
4. Extolling the sun (*prayāya*-hymn, with 6 *paryāyas*)

**Book XIV.—Wedding Verses, Seer: Sāvitrī Sūryā**

1. Marriage ceremonies
2. Marriage ceremonies (continued)

**Book XV.—The Vrātya. Seer:—**

| | | |
|---|---|---|
| 1. | Paryāya the first | or xv. 1.1 |
| | Paryāya the second | or xv. 1.2 |
| | Paryāya the third | or xv. 1.3 |
| | Paryāya the fourth | or xv. 1.4 |
| | Paryāya the fifth | or xv. 1.5 |
| | Paryāya the sixth | or xv. 1.6 |
| | Paryāya the seventh | or xv. 1.7 |
| 2. | Paryāya the eighth | or xv. 2.1 |
| | Paryāya the ninth | or xv. 2.2 |
| | Paryāya the tenth | or xv. 2.3 |
| | Paryāya the eleventh | or xv. 2.4 |
| | Paryāya the twelfth | or xv. 2.5 |
| | Paryāya the thirteenth | or xv. 2.6 |
| | Paryāya the fourteenth | or xv. 2.7 |
| | Paryāya the fifteenth | or xv. 2.8 |
| | Paryāya the sixteenth | or xv. 2.9 |
| | Paryāya the seventeenth | or xv. 2.10 |
| | Paryāya the eighteenth | or xv. 2.11 |

**Book XVI.—Paritta. Seer: Prajāpati [?]**

| | | |
|---|---|---|
| 1. | Paryāya the first | or xvi. 1.1 |
| | Paryāya the second | or xvi. 1.2 |
| | Paryāya the third | or xvi. 1.3 |
| | Paryāya the fourth | or xvi. 1.4 |
| 2. | Paryāya the fifth | or xvi. 2.1 |
| | Paryāya the sixth | or xvi. 2.2 |
| | Paryāya the seventh | or xvi. 2.3 |
| | Paryāya the eighth | or xvi. 2.4 |
| | Paryāya the ninth | or xvi. 2.5 |

**Book XVII.—Prayer to the Sun as Indra and Vishṇu. Seer: Brahman**

1. Prayer and praise to Indra and the Sun

**Book XVIII.—Funeral Verses. Seer: Atharvan**

1. [Funeral verses]
2. [Funeral verses]
3. [Funeral verses]
4. [Funeral verses]

Supplement.—Book XIX.

After-gleanings (72 hymns), chiefly from the traditional sources of division I.

**Book XIX.—Supplementary Hymns**

1. With an oblation for confluence
2. Praise and prayer to the waters
3. Praise to Agni
4. To various divinities
5. Praise and prayer to Indra
6. Purusha and his sacrifice
7. To the lunar asterisms: for blessings
8. For well-being: to the asterisms etc.
9. For appeasement and weal: to various divinities
10. For well-being
11. For well-being
12. For success and long life
13. For success in war: [Apratirath hymn]
14. For safety
15. For safety and success
16. For safety and protection
17. For protection: to various gods
18. For protection: to various gods
19. For protection by various gods
20. For protection by various gods
21. The meters
22. Homage to parts of the Atharva-Veda
23. Homage to parts of the Atharva-Veda
24. For prosperity: with a certain garment
25. To a horse
26. For long life etc.: with something golden
27. For protection etc.: with something golden
28. For various blessings: with an amulet of *darbhá*
29. Continuation of the foregoing
30. For protection etc.: with an amulet of *darbhá*

31. For various blessings: with an amulet of *udumbára*
32. For long life etc.: with an amulet of *darbhá*
33. For various blessings: with an amulet of *darbhá*
34. With a *jañgiḍá* amulet: for protection etc.
35. The same
36. With a *çatávāra* amulet: for protection etc.
37. With an amulet: for various blessings
38. With *gúggulu:*against disease
39. With *kúṣṭha*: against diseases
40. To various divinities: for various blessings
41. For some one's welfare
42. Extolling the *bráhman* etc.
43. To various gods: for attaining heaven
44. With an ointment: against diseases etc.
45. With an ointment etc.: for various objects
46. With and to an amulet called *ástṛta* 'unsubdued'
47. To night: for protection
48. To night: for protection
49. Praise and prayer to night
50. To night: for protection
51. Accompanying acceptance (?)
52. Of an to desire (*kāma*)
53. Praise of time (*kālá*)
54. Praise of time
55. To Agni
56. To sleep (or dream)
57. Against evil-dreaming
58. For various blessings
59. For successful sacrifice
60. For physical abilities
61. For length of life etc.
62. For popularity
63. To Brihaspati: for sundry blessings
64. To Agni: with fuel
65. Praise of the sun
66. To Agni: for aid
67. For long life and prosperity
68. With ceremonial performance
69. To the waters: for long life
70. For long life

71. For various blessings
72. For the favor of the gods

# six

## INTRODUCTION TO THE ATHARVA-VEDA

### The Meaning of the World Atharvaveda

The word *Atharvaveda* means the Veda of the Atharvan—the fire-priest. In the Avesta, the also word signifies a priest. Dr. Winternitz says, 'The Atharvans or fire-people of the Avesta correspond to the Indian Atharvans. The fire-cult played no less part in the daily life of the ancient Indians than that of the ancient Persians, soften designated as fire-worshippers, the priests of the very ancient fire-cult, however, were still like the Shamans of Northern Asia and the Medicinemen of the American Indians, 'priests of magic' that is "priest and wizard combined in one person, as in the world 'Magi'—as the Atharvans in Medea were called—the ideas of the wizard and priest are merged together."

This Veda is also known by the composite term—'Atharvāṅgirasaḥ' that is which combines both holy magic as well as hostile magic. The former part—Atharvan means a priest dealing with medicine for diseases while the latter part—Aṅgiras stand for curses directed against enemies. This designation occurs in both recensions of the *Atharvaveda* in the following verses:

यस्यादृचो अपातक्षन् यजुर्यस्मादपाकषन्।
सामानि यस्य लोमान्यथर्वाडि॒गरसो मुखं स्कम्भं तं ब्रूहि कतमः स्विदेव सः॥
(*AVŚ*. X.7.20)

येन पूता अथर्वाङ्गिरसो देवताः सह येन पूताः।
तेना सहस्रधारेण पवमानः पुनातु माम् ॥ (*AVP.* IX.23.11)

अथर्वाङ्गिरसो ब्रह्म सर्पपुण्यजनाश्च ये।
उच्छिष्टाज् जज्ञिरे सर्वे दिवि देवा दिवि श्रिताः॥ (*AVP.* XVI.84.7)

Dr. Weber holds that Aṅgirasaḥ belonged to Indo-Iranian period. Agni is often designated as 'Aṅgiras'[1]. They are connected with 'Yama'. In the *Ṛgveda* (II.23.18) Bṛhaspati is invoked as Aṅgiras.

(h) Upon the crest gems of the queens appeared footprints marked with wheels, conchs and lotuses.

(i) The chauries of the slave women slipped suddenly from their hands.

(j) On the elephants' cheeks were parted the honey symposia of the bees.

(k) As if sniffing the scent of Yama's buffalo, the panting steeds refused to eat the green grass.

(l) In the courtyards the sluggish peacocks would not dance, though coaxed by girls clapping music accompanied by the sound of tossing bracelets.

(m) Near the gateways troops of dogs howled at night with upturned faces.

(n) Shaking her forefingers as if to count the dead, a naked woman—Koṭavī, wandered all day in the parks.[2] As a comparative evidence this nude woman is seen depicted in the clay figurines of Ahicchatra. This finds support in the *Śāṅkhāyana Gṛhya Sūtram* (V, 10, 1-3) 'If the bees make honey in his house, let him fast and sacrifice a hundred and eight pieces of Udumbara wood which are besmeared with curds, honey, and ghee, with the two verses 'No harm to us in our offspring'. (*RV.*I.I 14.8-9).[3]

**The Word Therapy echoes Atharvan Bhaiṣajya-Karma**

Buddist Philosophy unlike that of the Jain did not believe in physical torture of body for the attainment of Nirvāṇa.

It had, however, evolved a philosophy of a balanced approach in life. Buddha himself adopted the middle path as the way for his salvation called—Madhyama Mārga. This was also called the Aryan eightfold path—right beliefs, right aspiration, right speech, right conduct, right mode of livelihood, right effort, right-mindedness and right rapture.[4] Life succeeds if a person develops himself along the above said lines. He is a conqueror. This vibrant conviction has turned a noble saying. 'Not even a god can change into defeat or victory of a man who has vanquished himself.'

By adopting the Middle Course Buddha saved his waning body from sure early death by accepting the curds and milk offered by Sujātā, as he set under a Pīpala tree at Uruvelā, who took him to be a god. Thus nourished, he sat cross-legged in meditation resolved not to rise from his seat until he had attained enlightenment. Thereafter he adopted a missionary's life with all its attendant dangers of poverty, unpopularity and opposition. First he converted five disciples who had kept his company during the years of asceticism and in the deer park, at what is now called Sāranātha, he preached his first sermon. Soon more disciples: 'gathered around him, including the beloved Ānanda, who remained the companion of all his wanderings. One day he told his disciples: 'Go now and wander for the gain of many, for the welfare of many, out of compassion for the world, for the good, for the gain and for the welfare of gods and men. Let not two of you go the same way. Preach the doctrine which is glorious in the end, in the spirit and in the letter: proclaim a consummate, perfect and pure life of happiness!'[5]

As medicine plays an important part in alleviating the sufferings of beings Buddha's followers were well adept in this branch of learning. This finds an unmistakable evidence through a discovery of an ancient Sanskrit manuscript containing seven texts in Kucha, Chinese Turkistan in 1890 buried in a Buddhist relic-mound. Palueographists have dated it about 350 A.D. Three of the seven texts are medical. Caraka, the great authority on medicine was, according to the Chinese translation of the Buddhist Tripiṭaka, the official physician of King Kaniṣka in the first century A.D.

Not only this. Devānāṁ Priyadarśī Aśoka declared his state policy, consonant with the teachings of Dharma to see to the welfare of all peoples of other lands beyond the borders of his Empire. His welfare scheme included the happiness of men as well as animals. His Government provided for the medical treatment of men and animals, arranged medical roots and herbs to the foreign countries. He was one of the most remarkable Emperors in the annalas of the world who changed the course of history from bloody and brutal violence to non-violence through thought, word and deed. His second Rock Edict at Girnar contains his immortal world which eloquently express his missionary spirit.

To quote text of the edict:

1. सर्वत विजितम्हि देवानं प्रियस प्रियदसिनो राञो
   (सर्वत्र विजिते देवानां प्रियस्य प्रियदर्शिनः राज्ञः)

2. एवमपि प्रचंतेसु यथा चोडा पाडा सतियपुतो केरलपुतो आतंब
   (एवमपि प्रत्यन्तेषु यथा चोलाः पाण्डयाः सतियपुत्रः, केरलपुत्र आताम्र-)

3. पंणी अंतियको योनराजा ये वापि तस अंतियकस सामीपा
   (पार्णि अन्तियकः योनराजः ये वा अपि तस्य अन्तियकस्य सामीपाः)

4. राजानो सर्वत्र देवानंप्रियस प्रियदसिनों राञे द्वे
   (राजानः-सर्वत्र देवानांप्रियस्य प्रियदर्शिनः राज्ञः द्वे)

5. मनुसचिकीछा च पसुचिकीछा च ओसुढानि च यानि
   (मनुष्य-चिकित्सा च पशुचिकित्सा च। ओषधानिः च यानि)

6. पसोपगानि च यत-यत नास्ति सर्वत्रा हारापितानि च
   (पशुपगा च यत्र-यत्र न सन्ति सर्वत्र हारितानि च)
   रोपापितानि च (रोपितानि च)

7. मूलानि च फलानि च यत्र-यत्र नास्ति सर्वत्र हारापितानि च
   (मूलानि च फलानि च यत्र-यत्र न सन्ति सर्वत्र हारितानि च)

रोपापितानि च (रोपितानि च)

8. पथेसू कूपा च खानापिता ब्रछा च रोपापिता परिभोगाय
(पथिषु कूपा च खानिताः, वृक्षाः च रोपिताः परिभोगाय)
पसुमनुसानं (पशु-मनुष्याणाम्)

Before the birth of Islam, Arabs had developed their contacts with India. Buddhist monks and already propagated the teachings of Buddha among Arabs. History has recorded that there was a medical institution in Senna of Southern Arabia. Dr. Lassen, a German scholar, has proved the fact that Harith-bin-Kaladah was the director of this institution who had received his education in India. With the conquest of Sindha, the doors of India were open to the people of Arabia. There was a regular communication between these two parts of the world. At the time of Harun-Al-Rashid Buddhist monks had occupied the highest positions in his Court. There were Indian Vaidyas enjoying fame for their expert knowledge in medicine. There was one Saleh bin-Bhela son of Bhela teacher who had successfully cured one Ebrahim, a relative of Harun. He was declared dead by Greek physician-Gabriel.

Among Sanskrit classics on medicine translated into Arabic were *Caraka, Suśruta, Aṣṭāṅgahṛidaya, Mādhavanidāna*[6] etc. A Hindu lady Rusa was an author of a booklet on the diseases of women. Arbas medicine was considered authoritative for Europe. Arabs were, thus, retailers of Indian medical lore for European countries.[6]

The travel-accounts of I-tsing (700 A.D.) who visited India after his fellow travellers has stated eight divisions of ever progressive medical science which are as follows: (a) sores—inward and outward (b) diseases above the neck (c) below the neck (d) demoniac diseases due to attack of evil spirits (e) antidote to poisons (f) diseases of children embryo stage to the sixteen year (g) the means of lengthening life and (h) the method of invigorating the legs and body.

The same Chinese traveller has recorded that Buddhists showed partiality for the study of medicine. Among celebrated authorities on medicine are Nāgārjuna, and Vāgbhaṭṭa. These holy men have left indelible impact on various countries where their mark thrives on customs, myths, traditions, scriptures, architecture and literature like the immortal splendour that of ten shines between the lines of a great poem.[7]

Recently some revealing facts have been unfolded by the excavations in *Boghaz Koi* in Iraq known as Mesopotamia in ancient times which dealt with the treaties between the king of Hittites and the king of Mitani at the inception of 14th of century B.C. The gods of both kingdoms were invoked as guardians of the treaties. It included the names of Mitra, Varuṇa, Indra, Aśvini Kumāras, Dasra and Nāsatyau. There is a reference to Aśvini Kumāras' myth that they taught Āyurveda to Indra. He disseminated it to Bṛgu, Atri, Vasiṣṭha, Kaśyapa and Agastya.

The history of certain words also supports the thesis that Āyurveda was very popular in the neighbouring countries like Gandhāra, Central Asia, Iran, and Burma etc. The Sanskrit words Bhisak and Bhesaja are the same though phonetically changed into Bijisk—doctor, and Beshaj in Pahalvi language of Persia. The same words migrated to Armenia and are known as Bhijisk and Bheshaj respectively. Dr. Baden is of the view that many words of the seals excavated in Sumeria are from Sanskrit. For instance, Bhṛgu, Bhrāgava, Garga and Janaka are changed to Vrigu, Vargava, Gurgu and Hanaka respectively.

As already referred to, the disciples of Lord Buddha preached their Dhamma in countries like Egypt, Mesopotamia and Assyria. First they tended the weak and the sick. Such monks residing in Egypt were known as theraputes. This word was adopted as a term, therapeutics in the west.

Recent researches have also demonstrated the fact that about 250 texts of Āyurveda have been found in Bali-an island of Indonesia. The Medical system of Tibet is drawn form Āyurveda. It migrated to Mongolia and North-Eastern Siberia. The Kumbum Monastery of Sinkiang was the leading centre for the propagation of Āyurveda. The Students from Tibet, Mongolia and around Volga river were drawn to this dynamic place of medical education.

It is most astonishing that the sage Ghora Aṅgirasa, who was dreadful and used terrible spells for the destruction of enemies became an exponent of healing art. He was the teacher of Kṛṣṇa, the greatest incarnation of Hinduism. The sage taught him to recite the following three mantras at the time of final departure from this world:

(i) अक्षितमसि Thou art indestructible.
(ii) अच्युतमसि Thou art unshakable.
(iii) प्राणसंशितमसि Thou art the subtlemost essence of life.[8]

In short, the world 'Therapy' speaks of Hindu ethos. Buddhist monks are called in Pali 'Thera' drawn from Sanskrit word 'Sthavira'. If ideas are great forces, infinite, too, is the power of personality. A union of the two always makes history. 'Therapy' is a shining example of this principle. Buddhist monks practised the art of healing. In Greece the same word of India was accepted in their language called—'Therapeutic' and to-day it is used in compound with other words.

These Buddhist Bhikhus, no doubt, resurrected the ideals of the sages of the *Atharvaveda* who proclaimed values of non-violence, love and friendship through their sublimest prayers:

यदिह घोरं यदिह क्रूरं यदिह पापम्।
तच्छान्तं तच्छिवं सर्वमेव शमस्तु नः।।

'What there is terrible, what there is cruel, what here is evil, be that appeased, be that propitious, be everything also well-being for us. (*AV.* XIX. 9.14).

## Foot Notes

1. Compare the note in वैप 1. p. 281 : गतिसमास, उत्तरपदस्य करणे घञि पूर्वपदस्य दीर्घत्वं थाथादि-स्वरश्च (यथाक्रमं पा 3, 3, 121; 6, 3, 122; 6, 2, 144).
2. ततश्च तथा कृतप्रतिज्ञे प्रयाणं विजयाय दिशां समादिशति देवे हर्षे गतायुषां प्रतिसामन्तानामुदवसितेषु बहुरूपाण्युपलिङ्गलि वितेनिरे। तथा ह्याविप्रकृष्टाः काल-दूत-दृष्टय इवेतस्ततश्चेरुचटुलाः कृष्ण-शारश्रेणयः। प्रचलित-लक्ष्मीनूपुर-प्रणाद-प्रतिमा मधुसर-घातझंकारा जह्लादिरे। चिर विवृत-विकृत-वदन-विवर-विनिःसृत- वह्निविसरा वासरेऽपि वि-रसं विरेसुश् चिरमशिवार्थमशिवाः शिवाः। शव-पिशित-प्ररूढ-प्रसरा इव कपिपोतकपोल कपिलपक्षतयः काननकपोताः पेतुः। आमन्त्रयमाणा इव दधुर् अकाल-कुसुमानि सममुपवनतरवः। तरल-कर-कल-प्रहार-प्रहत-पयोधरा रुरुदुः प्रसमं सभाशालभञ्जिकाःददृशुर् आसन्न-कच-ग्रह-भयोद्-भ्रन्तोत्तमाङ्गमि वाऽऽत्मानं कबन्धमादर्शोदरेषु योधाः। चूडापाणिषु चक्र-शङ्ख-कमल-लक्ष्मणः प्रादुरभंवन् पादन्यासा राजमहिषीणाम्। चेटी-चामराण्य् अकस्माद् अधावन्त पाणिपल्लवात् (पृ. 347-8)।
3. Edited by S.R. Sehgal, New Delhi, 1960. also 'Omens and Portents in Vedic Literature', *All India Oriental Conference,* Nagpur, 1946, pp. 65-71.
4. Compare

   युक्ताऽऽहार-विहारस्य युक्त-चेष्टस्य कर्मसु।
   युक्त-स्वप्राऽवबोधस्य योगो भवति दुःख-हा।। (गीता 6, 17)
   इज्याऽध्ययन-दानानि तपः सत्यं क्षमा दया।
   अलोभ इति मार्गोऽयं धर्मस्याऽष्टविधिः स्मृतः।। (महाभारत 3, 2, 75)
5. चरथ भिक्खवे, चारिकं बहुजनहिताय बहुतनसुखाय लोकानुकम्पाय अत्थाय हिताय सुचाय देवमनुस्सानं।....अहं पि भिक्खवे, येन उरुवेला येन सेनानिगमो तेनुपसङ्कमिस्ससामि धम्मदेसनाया इति। (महावग्गो 1, 2, 5, 1)
6. The effect of Hindu Medical Science upon the Arabs after about 700 A.D. was considerable, for the Khalifs of Bagadad caused several books on the subject to the translated. The works of Caraka and Suśruta probably not later than the fourth century A.D. were rendered into Arabic at the close of the eight century, and are quoted as authorities by the celebrated Arabic physician Al-Razi, who died in 932 A.D. Arabic medicine in its turn became the chief authority, down to the seventeenth century, of European physicians. By the latter Indian medical authors must have been thought highly of, for Caraka is repeatedly mentioned in the Latin translations of the Arab writers Ibn Sina, Al-Razi, and Ibn Sarafyun. In modern days European surgery has borrowed the operation or rhinoplasty,

or formation of artificial noses, from India, when Englishmen became acquainted with the art in the last century. (Macdonell's *History of Sanskrit Literature*, pp. 426-27).

7. The University of Nālandā was not confined to Buddhism alone. The Brahminical subjects were also taught. For example, the sacred and secular study of the Vedas and the Atharvaveda, Śabdavidyā (grammar and philology, Cikitsāvidyā (medicine) Sāṅkhya. Nyāya Yoga-Śastra under Chancellor Śilabhadra-the highest authority on the subject. Nālandā was the ideal university which provided full freedom in learning and kept its doors open to all shades of thinking and not a sectarian denominational school. (Mookerji's, *Harṣa*, p. 132).

8. तद् धैतद् घोर आङ्गिरसः कृष्णाय देवकीपुत्रायोक्त्वोवाचाऽपिपास एव स बभूव।
   सोऽन्तवेलायामेतत् त्रयं प्रपद्येत-अक्षितमसि, अच्युतमसि, प्राणसंशितमसीति।
   (छान्दोग्योपनिषद् 3, 17, 6)

# seven

## INTRODUCTION TO THE YAJUR-VEDA

"The history of the Yajur Veda differs in so far from that of the other Vedas, as it is marked by a dissension between its own schools, far more important than the differences which separated the schools of each other Veda. It is known by the distinction between a Yajur Veda, called the *Black-*, and another, called the *White-Yajur Veda*. Tradition, especially that of the Puránas, records a legend to account for it. Vaiśampáyana, it says, the disciple of Vyása, who had received from him the Yajur Veda, once having committed an offence, desired his disciples to assist him in the performing of some expiatory act. One of these, however, *Yájñavalkya*, proposed that he should alone perform the whole rite; upon which, Vaiśampáyana, enraged at what he considered to be the arrogance of Yájñavalkya, uttered a curse on him, the effect of which was, that Yájñavalkya disgorged all the Yajus texts he had learned from Vaiśampáyana. The other disciples, having meanwhile been transformed into partridges (tittiri), picked up these tainted texts, and retained them. Hence these texts are called *Taittiríyas*. But Yájñavalkya, desirous of obtaining other Yajus texts, devoutly prayed to the Sun, and had granted to him his wish—'to possess such texts as were not known to his teacher.' And because the Sun on that occasion appeared to Yájnavalkya in the shape of a horse (*vája*), those who studied these texts were called. *Vájins*. That part of this legend was invented merely to account for the name of the *Taittiríyas*, after whom a Sanhitá and Bráhmana of the Black *Yajur Veda*, and for that of the *Vájasaneyins*, after whom the Sanhitá of the White *Yajur Veda* is named is clear enough. Nor is greater faith to be placed on it when it implies that the origin of this dissension ascended to the very oldest period of the Yajur Veda; for there is strong reason to assume that the division took place even after the time of the grammarian Páṇiní, (q.v.). But so much in it is consistent with truth—that the Black Yajur Veda is the older of the two; that the White Yajur Veda contains texts which are not in the Black; and that, compared to the motley character of the former, it looks 'white,' or orderly. This motley character of the Black Yajur Veda, however, arises from the circumstance, that the distinction between a Mantra and Bráhmaṇa portion, is not so clearly established in it as the other Vedas; hymns and matter properly belonging to the Bráhmaṇas there being intermixed. This defect is remedied in the White *Yajur Veda*; and it points, therefore, to a period when the material of the old Yajus was brought into a system consonant with prevalent theories, literary and ritual.

The contents of both divisions of the Yajur Veda are similar in many respects. Two of the principal sacrifices of which they treat are the Darṣapúrṇamása, or the sacrifice to be performed at new and full moon, and the Aṣwamedha, or the horse-sacrifice, at the performance of which 609 animals of various descriptions, domestic and wild, were tied to 21 sacrificial posts. A *Purushamedha*, or man-sacrifice, unknown to the other Vedas, is also mentioned in it; its character, however, is symbolical.

The text of the Black *Yajur Veda* is extant in the recension of two schools—that of *Apastamba*, to which the *Taittiríya Sanhitá* belongs, and that of *Charaka*. The former, which is in course of publication—the first volume and part of the second having been already published, with the commentary of Mádhaváchárya (Sáyaṇa), by Dr. E. Roer and E. B. Cowell in the *Bibliotheca Indica* (Kolkata, 1860—1864)—consists of seven Káṇḍa, or books, which comprise 44 Prapáṭhaka, or chapters sub-divided into 651 Anuváka, or sections, and containing 2,198 Káṇḍikás, or portions.

The *Vájasaneyi-Sanhitá*, or the Sanhitá of the White *Yajur Veda*, exists in the recension of the *Mádhyandina* and Káṇva School. In the former—the text of which, apparently also with the commentary of *Mahídkara*, has been edited by Professor A. Weber (Berlin, 1852)—this Sanhitá has 40 *Adhyáyas*, or books, sub-divided into 303 *Anuvákas*, with 1,975 Káṇḍikás.

The principal Bráhmaṇa of the Black *Yajur Veda* is the *Taittiríya-Bráhmaṇa*, which, with the commentary of (Mádhava) Sáyaṇa, is in the course of publication by Baboo Rajendralála Mitra—the first volume and part of the second having already appeared in print (Kolkata, 1860-1865) in the *Bibliotheca Indica* (q.v.). That of the White *Yajur Veda* is the *Śatapatha-Brahmána*, the most complete and systematic of all Bráhmaṇas. Its text, with a semblance of the commentary of Sáyaṇa, has been edited by Professor A. Weber (Berlin, 1855).—*Chambers' Encyclopaedia*, Vol. IX, p. 727.

## THE SAṂHITĀS OF THE YAJURVEDA

Just as the Sāmaveda-Saṃhitā is the textbook of songs for the Udgātar, so also the Yajurveda-Saṃhitās are the prayer-books for the Adhvaryu-priest. The grammarian Patañjali[1] speaks of "101 schools of the Veda of the Adhvaryu" and it is understandable that there are many schools of just this particular Veda; because with respect to the individual sacrificial acts as the Adhvaryu had to perform them and to accompany them with his prayers, easily differences of opinion and sectarian variations were caused which led to the creation of their own handbooks and prayer-books. The slightest divergence in ceremony or liturgy was enough for the foundation of a new Vedic school. We know till today the following five Saṃhitās and schools of the Yajurveda:

1. The Kāṭhaka, the Yajurveda-Saṃhitā in the recension of the Kaṭha-school, which was known for a long time only as a manuscript in the Berlin library, but is now published by L. von Schroeder.[2]

2. The Kapiṣṭhala-Kaṭha-Saṃhitā which is preserved in only few fragment of manuscripts.[3]

3. The Maitrāyaṇī-Saṃhitā i.e. the Yajurveda-Saṃhitā in the recension of the Maitrāyaṇīya-school, which L. von Schroeder has edited.[4]

4. The Taittirīya-Saṃhitā i.e the Yajurveda-Saṃhitā in the recension of the Taittirīya-school, according to the Āpastamba-school, one of the main schools in which this text was taught, also called "Āpastamba-Saṃhitā". The same was edited by A. Weber.[5]

These four recensions are closely related to one another and are described as belonging to the "black Yajurveda". Different from these is—

5. The Vājasaneyī-Saṃhitā or the Saṃhitā of the "white Yajurveda" which derives its name from Yājñavalkya Vājasaneya, the principal teacher of this Veda. Of this Vājasaneyī-Saṃhitā there are two recensions, that of the Kāṇva school and that of the Mādhyandina school, which however differ from each other in minor aspects. This Saṃhitā also was edited by A. Weber.[6]

The main difference between the Saṃhitās of the "black" and the "white" Yajurveda lies in this that the Vājasaneyī-Saṃhitā contains only the mantras, i.e. the prayers and sacrificial formulas which the Adhvaryu priest has to say, while the Saṃhitās of the black Yajurveda contain, in addition to the Mantras, also a description of the sacrificial rites together with discussions on them. Thus there is, in the Saṃhitās of the black Yajurveda that which is called "Brāhmaṇa" or "theological discussion" and which constitutes the contents of the Brāhmaṇas to be discussed in the next chapter, mixed with the Mantras. It is therefore easy to understand that in the prayer books meant for the use of the Adhvaryus the sacrificial performances were also discussed because these priests had to perform especially the individual sacrificial acts, and the murmuring of prayers and formulas in intimate relationship with these acts constituted only a small part of their duties. It can therefore be scarcely doubted that the Saṃhitās of the black Yajurveda are older than the Vājasaneyī Saṃhitā. Only later systemastisers among the Yajurveda theologians perhaps felt the need to have analogous to the other Vedas, a Saṃhitā consisting of only Mantras by the side of a Brāhmaṇa devoid of them.[7]

However significant the differences between the individual Saṃhitās of the Yajurveda might be for the priests and theologians of ancient India, for us they are quite insignificant; and even chronologically the various Saṃhitās of the black and white Yajurveda might not be wide apart from each other. If I now give hereunder a short description of the contents of the Vājasaneyī-Saṃhitā, it is entirely sufficient to give to the reader an idea of the content and character of the Saṃhitās of the Yajurvaveda in general.

The Vājasaneyī-Saṃhitā consists of 40 chapters, of which however the last 15 (perhaps even the last 25) chapters are of a later date. The first 25 chapters contain the prayers for the most important big sacrifices. And the first two chapters give the prayers for the New-moon and Fullmoon-sacrifices (Darśa-pūrṇamāsa) with their connected sacrifices for the names (piṇḍapitṛyajña). Then follow in the third chapter the prayers for the daily fire-cult, for the inception of fire and for the fire-offerings (Agnihotra) to be made every morning and evening and for the seasonal-sacrifices (Cāturmāsya) performed once every four months. The prayers for the Soma-sacrifice[8] in general including the animal sacrifice connected with it are found in chapters IV to VIII. Among the Soma-sacrifices there are some which last for one day and some which last for many days. Among the one-day sacrifices is the Vājapeya or "contest drink", a sacrifice which was performed originally perhaps only by warriors and kings which was connected with a chariot-race and in the course of which, part from the Soma, brandy (surā)[9] which was normally forbidden according to brahminical law, was drunk. The sacrifice at a king's coronation or "Rājasūya" a sacrificial festival connected with some sorts of popular customs—with a symbolic battle march, with the play at dice and with all sorts of magic rites. The prayers for these two kinds of Soma sacrifices are found in the chapters IX and X. Then follow in chapters XI to XVIII numerous prayers and sacrificial formulas for the Agnicayana or the "Fire-altar-laying", a ceremony which extends over one whole year and to which a profound mystic symbolic significance is attributed in the Brāhmaṇas. The fire altar is nothing but "Agni" and is considered as identical with the god of fire. It is built with 10800 bricks in the shape of a big bird with its wings stretched out. In the lowest layer of the altar the heads of five sacrificial animals are immured and the bodies of the animals are thrown into the water out of which the mud is taken for making the bricks and the fire-bowl. The shaping and baking of the fire-bowl and of the individual bricks, of which many have special names and their own special significance, takes place with great ceremony and under incessant chanting of charms and prayer formulas. The chapters XIX to XXI following that give the prayers for the Sautrāmaṇī ceremony, a peculiar sacrificial ceremony during which brandy is used instead of the Soma drink and is offered to the Aśvins and to goddess Sarasvatī and to Indra. The ceremony is recommended to one who has drunk too much Soma or who cannot endure it—and this might be the original purpose of it—but also for a Brahmin who desires success, for a banished king who wants to regain his throne, for a warrior who wants to gain victory and a Vaiśya who wants to attain great wealth. The texts connected with this sacrifice make many references to the saga of Indra who had qualms of conscience due to excessive enjoyment of Soma and who had to be cured by the Aśvins and Sarasavatī.[10] Finally chapters XXII to XXV with which the old part of the Vājasaneyī-Saṃhitā ends, contain the prayers for the great horse sacrifice (Aśvamedha), which only a powerful king, a mighty conqueror or "world-ruler" was permitted to perform. Old sagas and epic poems give reports of kings of prehistoric times who performed this sacrifice and it is considered as the highest fame for a ruler if it can be said of him: "He has performed the horse-sacrifice". The purpose of this great sacrifice is given out very beautifully in the prayer Vāj. Saṃh. XXII, 22:

> "O Brahman ! May in this kingdom the Brahmin be born who shines by holy knowledge ! May the warrior who is a hero, an excellent archer, of perfect aim and a great chariot-fighter ! Also the cow that yields good milk, the ox that pulls well, the swift horse, the honourable housewife! May to this sacrificer a heroic son be born, who is victorious, an excellent chariot-fighter and eloquent

in assembly. May Parjanya send us rain as we desire ! May our fruit-bearing plants ripen ! May we have luck and prosperity !"

That the last 15 chapters are of later origin is not doubtful. The chapters XXVI to XXXV are termed even by Indian tradition as "khilas" i.e. "addition", "supplements". Actually XXVI to XXIX contain only additions to the prayers of the preceding chapters. The XXX chapter proves itself to be a supplement even by the fact that it does not contain any prayers but only an enumeration of people who shall be sacrificed at the Pruṣamedha or human sacrifice to the most díverse divine beings and powers or to those that have been elevated to the status of deities for the moment. Not less than 184 persons should be butchered during this Puruṣamedha; and that as follows—for example: a Brahmin is sacrificed to priestly honour, a warrior to royal honour, a Vaiśya to the Maruts, a Śūdra to an ascetic, a thief to darkness, a murderer to hell, a eunuch to evil, a whore to pleasure, a singer to noise, a bard to dance, an actor to song, a hunter to death, a gambler to the dice, a blindman to sleep, a deafman to injustice, an incendiary to lustre, a washerwoman to the sacrifice, a dyer-woman to greed, a barren woman to Yama, a Vīnā-player to the joy of ceremony, a flute-player to shouting, a cripple to the earth, a bald-headed man to the heaven etc. It is certainly not likely that all these kinds of people were brought together and should have been killed. This is perhaps only a symbolic act which represents a sort of "human sacrifice" by which the great horse sacrifice must be surpassed which however existed only as a constituent of the sacrificial-mystic and sacrificial theory, but which in reality hardly ever happened.[11] Moreover it is also true that the XXXI chapter contains a version of the Puruṣasūkta known to us from the Ṛgveda—i.e. of the hymn RV, X 90 in which the birth of the world is explained as by sacrificing the Puruṣa and the identification of the world with the Purusa, and thereby Puruṣa, "the man" is at the same time considered as the highest being—and this that chapter which the Brahman should recite at the Puruṣamedha is also described as Upaniṣad i.e. secret teaching. The XXXII chapter is also, in form and content, nothing but an Upaniṣad: The Creator Prajāpati is equated here with the Puruśa and the Brahman. The first six verses of the XXXIV chapter are similarly classified as Upaniṣads—and are given the title Śivasaṃkalps-Upaniṣad.[12] The texts of chapters XXXII to XXXIV are to be used during the so-called Sarvamedha or "All-sacrifice". This is the highest sacrifice that exists and it ends with the sacrificer giving away all his movable and immovable property as sacrifical reward to priests and then retiring as a hermit to the forest to spend the rest of his life there. There XXXV chapter contains some verses for funeral cremonies which are taken from the Ṛgveda. Chapters XXXVI to XXXIX contain the prayers for a ceremony called Pravargya in which a drum is heated to glow on the sacrificial fire to represent the sun symbolically; in this drum milk is then boiled and offered to the Aśvins. The whole ceremony is considered as a great mystery. At the end the sacrificial implements are put up in such a way that they represent a man: The milk pots are the lead, on which a bundle of holy grass represents the locks of hair; two milking tubs represent the ears, two small gold leaves the eyes, two shells the ankles, the flour strewn all over the body the marrow, a mixture of milk and honey the blood etc. To the mysterious ceremonies correspond naturally also the prayers and formulas.[13] The XL and the last chapter of the Vājasaneyī Saṃhitā contains once again an Upaniṣad, and indeed one that is found in all collections of Upaniṣads, very important Īśa-Upaniṣadd, about which we have to speak once again in the chapter on the Upaniṣads.

If it is clear even from the contents of the last chapters that they are of a later origin, it is still further testified by the fact that the prayers contained in the Saṃhitās of the Black Yajurveda correspond only to those of the first half of the Vājasaneyī-Saṃhitā.[14]

As regards the prayers and sacrificial formulas themselves, which form the main content of the Yajurveda-Saṃhitā, they consist partly of verses (ṛc) and partly of prose texts. It is the latter that the termed as "Yajus" and from which the Yajurveda gets its name. The prose of these texts is sometimes also a measured one and is even elevated here and there to a rhythmic swing.[15] The verses that occur here are also found for the most part in the Ṛgveda-Saṃhitá. The divergent readings however, which the Yajurveda often offers, are not in any way older than the text found in the Ṛgveda, but they are mostly changes intentionallly made in order to connect the verses more closely with the sacrificial acts. Only rarely have whole hymns of the Ṛgveda been included in the Yajurveda-Saṃhitās; mostly they are simply individual verses, isolated from the context which appeared to be suitable for some sacrificial ceremony and were hence included in the Veda of prayers. Therefore we have less interest in these verses as well. What is characteristic of the Yajurveda are the prose formulas and prayers.[16]

The simplest prayer that we can imagine, is the dedication of an offering with just mentioning the name of the deity to whom it is offered. Formulas of this kind are very numerous in the Yajurveda. "you for Agni", "you for Indra" or "this for Agni", or even simply "Hail Agni" or "Hail Indra" etc.—which such words the offerings were placed or thrown in the sacred fire. And we can hardly imagine a shorter and simpler hymn of praise to god than the words with which every morning and evening the fire-offering (Agnihotra consisting of milk is offered: "Agni is light, light is Agni, hail ! (in the evening) and "Sūrya is light, light is Sūrya, hail !" (in the morning). In just as short words the purpose of a sacred act is also often hinted at, when for example the sacrificial priest cuts the branch with which the calves are driven from the cows and says then: "you to sap, you to power !" Or the object serving a holy act is shortly named and a wish is added, when for example the wooden splinter with which the sacrificial fire is to be lit, is consecrated with the words: "This, Agni, is your igniter; through this you shall grow and prosper. May we too grow and prosper !" If there is fear of evil or of a harmful spell, then a short text is used for protection against the same. Thus to the halter with which the sacrificial animal is tied to the post the following words are addressed: "Do not become a snake, do not become a viper !" To the razor with which the sacrificer is shaved of his beard when he is consecrated for the sacrifice, the priest says: "O razor, do not wound him !" During the coronation the king looks down to earth and prays: "Mother earth, may you not wound me, nor I you !"[17]

The deities are not always invoked or praised in these sacrificial formulas, but sacrificial implements and sacrificial acts are made to associate with deities in the most diverse ways. Thus for instance the priest ties a string round the girdle of the sacrificer's wife participating in the sacrifice with the words: "A gridle you are Aditi". At the consecration to the Soma-sacrifice the sacrificer ties round his girdle a belt made of hemp and reed-grass with the words: "You are the power of Aṅgiras,[18] soft like wool; lend me power !" Then he binds a knot in his underclothing and says: "you are the knot of Soma". Thereupon he covers his head with a turban (or with his upper cloth) while murmuring the words: "You are Viṣṇu's umbrella, the umbrella of the sacrificer". And to the horn of a black antelope which he wraps in the hem of his garment he says: "You are Indra's womb". He takes the sacrificial food from the carriage with the words: "You are the body of Agni, you to Ani. You are the body of Soma, you to Viṣṇu". When the priest takes any sacrificial implement in his hand he does it with the oft repeated formula: "Induced by God Savitar I take you up with the arms of the Aśvins, with the arms of Pūṣan."[19]

The holy sacrificial fire must be churned according to

the primitive method with a fire-borer;[20] and the production of fire is compared, even in Ṛgveda with the process of reproduction, by considering the lower plank as the mother, the upper churn-staff as the father of the child Agni (fire).[21] Thus the formulas are explained with which the fire-churning at a Soma-sacrifice is done, in which the two rubbing pieces of wood as the pair of lovers Purūravas and Urvaśī producing Āyu are addressed.[22] The priest takes the lower piece of wood with the words: "You are Agni's birth-place", lays two stalks of sacred grass on it and says: "You are the two semen-pourers (testicles)". Then he lays the plank with the words: "You are Urvaśī", touches the frying pan with the churning staff while saying: "You are Āyu", and with the words, "You are Purūravas" inserts the churning staff into the lower pieces of wood. Then he churns with the texts: "I churn you with the Gāyatrī metre, I churn you with the Triṣṭubh-meter, I churn you with the Jagatī metre".[23]

We should not seek any profound symbolical significance in the mention of the above metres. They are words, nothing but words, which fulfil their purpose just like any other words would do. And formal usages of the kind which have little or no sense are quite numerous in the Yajurveda. Only relatively seldom do we come across long prose texts in which the sacrificer announces his wishes to the deity as in the prayer already mentioned above which has been spoken at the horse-sacrifice. More frequent are of course the formal prayers like the following ones which nevertheless convey a good sense.

> "You, Agni, are the protector of the bodies; protect my body ! you Agni, are the giver of life, give me life ! You, Agni, are the giver of power; give me power ! You Agni, make perfect, what is imperfect in my body". (Vāj. III, 17) "May life flourish through sacrifice ! May the breath flourish through sacrifice ! May the eye flourish through sacrifice. May the ear flourish through sacrifice ! May the back flourish through sacrifice !

May sacrifice flourish through sacrifice !" (Vāj. IX, 21)

But even more frequently do we find end less texts in which the meaning is of more secondary importance, for example:

> "Agni has won the breath with the monosyllabic (word); may I win him ! The Aśvins have won the two-footed man with the two syllabic (word) ! Viṣṇu has won the three worlds with the three-syllabic (word), may I win them ! Soma has won the four-footed cattle with the four-syllabic; may I win it !" (Vāj. IX, 31-34).

But what specially contributes to the fact that these prayers and sacrificial formulas appear to us only as a senseless heaping up of words, is the favourite equating and combining of things in the Yajurveda which have nothing to do with one another. A cooking pot for example is placed on fire with the following words:

> "You are the heaven, you are the earth, you are the drum of the Mātariśvan".[24] (Vāj. I, 2).

Or the cow, with which the *Soma* is brought, the priest addresses with the following words:

> "You are the thought, you are the mind, you are the intellect, you are the sacrificial reward, you are suitable for mastery, you are suitable for sacrifice, you are the double-headed Aditi". (Vāj. IV, 19).

To the fire that is taken round in the pan at the time of laying the fire altar the following prayer is addressed: You are the beautifully-winged bird, the hymn of praise Trivṛt is your head, the Gāyatrī-melody is your eye, the two melodies Bṛhat and Rathantara are your wings, the hymn of praise is your soul, the metres are your limbs, the Yajus-formulas your name, the Vāmadevya-melody your body, the Yajñayagñīya-melody your tail, the fire-places are your hoofs, you are the beautifully-winged bird, go to heaven, fly to light!" (Vāj XII,4).

Then the priest takes three steps with the fire pan and speaks:

> "You are Viṣṇu's step destroying the rivals in love; mount the Gāyatrī metre, march along the earth ! You are Viṣṇu's step destroying persecutors; mount the Triṣṭubh-metre march along the air ! You are Viṣṇu's step distorting the malicious ones; mount the *Jagati* metre, march along the heaven! You are Viṣṇu's step destroying the inimical ones; mount the Anuṣṭubh metre, march along the parts of the world!" (Vāj. XII, 5).

Referring to this kind of prayers, Leopold von Schroeder says: "One should often even doubt that one finds here people who are still intelligent, and it is in this respect quite interesting to observe, that in the written records of persons in the stage of imbecility the tedious and monotonous variations of one and the same idea ar especially characteristic". He then gives some of the recordings preserved by psychiatrists about lunatics and these recordings show a striking similarity to many of the prayers of the Yajurveda.[25] We must not however forget that we do not have here very ancient popular magic formulas as in the Atharvaveda or partly also in the Yajurveda, but we have here only very clumsy works of priests, who had to provide the innumerable sacrifical rites ingeniously thought out by them with similarly innumerable texts and formulas.

Many a prayer formula of the Yajurveda is however nothing but magic charms in prose. Even exorcisms and curses quite similar to those which we have come across in the Atharvaveda, we find also in the prayers of the Yajurveda. For there are also sacrificial acts through which one can do harm to an enemy. Thus the priest says to the yoke of the chariot carrying the sacrificial implements: "A yoke you are, subjugate him whom we subjugate". (Vāj. I, 8).[26] The following examples of such sacrificial prayers are given by L. von Schroeder[27] from the Maitrāyaṇī Saṃhitā:

> "Which man is hostile to us and which one hates us, which one wants to abuse and harm us, all of them you shall crush into dust!"

> "O Agni with your incandescence glow off against him who hates us and whom we hate ! O Agni with you flame burn off against him who hates us and whom we hate ! O Agni, with your radiance radiate against him who hates us and whom we hate ! O Agni, with your pouncing power pounce him who hates us and whom we hate" !

> "The god of death, devastation shall seize the rivals in love".

Just as these exorcisms have in themselves something primeval and popular, we find also among the riddles that are preserved in the Yajurveda in addition to truly theological riddles, which certainly deserve the technical name "Brahmodya",[28] because they presuppose an acquaintance with the Brahman or the holy knowledge, also some old popular riddles. We have already got acquainted with this very old kind of literature in the Ṛgveda and the Atharvaveda. In the Yajurveda we also get to know the occasions when the games of riddles were common and indeed even formed a part of the cult. Thus we find in the Vājasaneyī-Saṃhitā in the XXIII chapter[29] a number of riddles with which the priests entertained themselves during the famous horses-sacrifice. Some of them remind us of our children's riddles, whereas the others refer to the sacrificial mysticism of the Brāhmaṇas and the philosophy of the Upaniṣads. As example the riddles of Vāj. XXIII—45-48, 51 ff. may be quoted:

The Hotar: "Who wanders lonely on his way?
Who is born always anew?
What is the cure for cold?
What is the great corn-container called?"

The Adhvaryu: "The Sun wanders lonely on his way
The moon is always born ane.v
The fire is the cure for cold
The earth is the great corn-container".

The Adhvaryu: "What is the light equal to the sun?
What the name of the flood equal to the sea?
And what is greater than the earth?
What is that which is immeasurable?"

The Hotar: "The Brahman[30] is the light equal to the sun
The heaven is the flood equal to the sea,
And greater than the earth is god Indra
And it is the cow of which no one knows the measure".

The Udgātar: "In what things is the Puruṣa permeated?
And what things are in Pruruṣa contained?
The riddle, Brahman, I give you to solve;
What have you to say now in reply?"

The Brahman: "The five it is in which the Puruṣa is permeated,
And these too are in Puruṣa contained[31]
That is it, what I have thought out as reply
In the miraculous power of knowledge you can't excel me".

These games with riddles are as important constituents of the veneration of gods as the prayers and sacrificial formulas. Of course the words "veneration of gods" express only inadequately the purpose of the prayers and formulas and even of the sacrifice themselves. The majority of the sacrificial ceremonies like the Yajus-formulas do not have the object of "venerating" the gods but of influencing them, of forcing them, in order that they may fulfil the desires of the sacrificer. And even the gods love *panem et circenses,* they too do not want merely to be fed but also to be entertained; that however the gods find a peculiar pleasure in what is mysterious, obscure, and only hinted at, is made clear to us very often by the Vedic texts.[32]

In the Yajurveda we also find already a sort of influencing the gods which later on gained the upper hand to a very great extent. This consists in showering on a god as many names and attributes as possible and to show reverence to him under all his names in this way in order to win some favour from him. Thus we find in later literature texts, which enumerate a thousand names of Viṣṇu,of thousand names of Śiva, and whose recitation is considered as a very effective and meritorious act of worship. The earliest beginnings of this kind of prayers are found in the Śatarudrīya, the enumeration of the hundred names of the god Rudra, in the XVI chapter of the Vājasaneyī-Saṃhitā and in the Taittirīya-Saṃhitā IV, 5.

Finally—there is another sort of "prayers"—as we must of course call them—which we come across even in the Yajurveda and with which in later times a lot of mischief was played. These are the individual syllables or words which do not have any sense or whose sense has been lost, which are pronounced in the most ceremonious way at particular occasions of the sacrificial performance and which are held to be extremely holy. There is firstly the sacrificial invocation "svāhā", which we usually translate with "hail", with which every offering for the gods is thrown into the fire whereas the invocation "svadhā" is used in the case of sacrificial offerings for the manes. Other quite understandable exclamations of this kind are vaṣat, vet, vat and above all the most sacred syllable om. This syllable, originally nothing but a consent,[33] was considered by the Hindus over many thousands of years and is considered even to the present day as extremely holy and full of mystical significiance. In the Upaniṣads it is equated with the Brahman the world-soul and recommended to the wise as the highest object of meditation, the Kaṭha-Upaniṣad (II, 16) says about it: "This syllable is indeed the Brahman, this syllable is the highest, for he who knows this syllable, for him, all the desires will be fulfilled." And this syllable om is joined by the three "great words" (mahāvyāhṛti), namely bhūr, bhuvaḥ, saver (explained by the Indians as "earth, air, heaven, which however is doubtful) of which it is said in a text:[34] "This indeed is the Brahman, this the truth, this the law; without this there is no sacrifice !".

Centuries later, in the Tantras, the religious books of later Indian sects, the use of such mystic syllables and words gained the upper hand in such a manner that often for pages at a stretch we find nothing but unarticulated sounds like "um, am, hrīm, um, em, krom, phaṭ, aḥ etc. It is also characteristic that the word "mantra" which originally meant the verses and prayers (ṛc and yajus) of the vedic saṃhitās, later on had only the meaning of a magic formula". Even in the Yajurveda we can very well follow this transition from prayer to magic formula these were both never strictly separate from each other.

And however tedious, uninteresting and unedifying the Yajurveda-Saṃhitās may be, if one wants to read them as literary works, still they are of very great importance and indeed of interest of the investigator of religion who studies them as source-books not only for the Indian but also for general theology. Whoever wants to delve deep into the origin, development and theological significance of prayer—and this is one of the most interesting chapters of theology—should in no case fail to get acquainted with the prayers of the Yajurvaeda.

Further, these Saṃhitās are also indispensable for understanding the whole religious and philosophic literature of the Indians in later times. Without the Yajurveda we cannot understand the Brāhmaṇas and without these, the Upaniṣads.

**Foot Notes:**

1. In the introduction to his "Mahābhāṣya".
2. Edited by L. v. Schroeder, Leipzig, 1990-1910, *Index Verborum* by R. Simon, 1912. For the contents of the Kāṭhaka see A. Weber, *Ind. Stud.* 3, 451 ff.; for the text and its interpretation see Keith, *JRAS,* 1910, 517 ff; 1912, 1095 ff.; Caland, *ZDMG,* 72, 1918, 12 ff.
3. See L. v. Schroeder, *WZKM,* 12, 362 f.
4. Leipzing 1881-1886. Numerous quotations from this Saṃhitā in German translation are found in L. von Schroeder: *Indiens Literatur und Kunst.* (Leipzig, 1887) p. 110-162. See also Schroeder, *ZDMG* 33, 1879, 177 ff; Caland, *ZDMG,* 72, 1918, 6 ff.
5. Ed. by A. Weber in the 11th and 12th volumes of his *Indische Studien,* 1871 and 1872; with Sāyaṇa's commentary in *Bibl. Ind.,* 1860-1899, and in *Ān. SS* Nr. 42; translated into English by A. B. Keith, *HOS,* vols. 18, 19, 1914.
6. The White Yajurveda, Part I, The Vājasaneyī-Saṃhitā ... with the commentary of Mahidhara, Berlin-London 1852. An English translation of the same is available by R. T. H. Griffith (*The text of the White Yajurveda,* translated with a popular commentary, Benaras 1899).
7. It is usually presumed that the name "white" Yajurveda means "clear, (ordered) arranged" Yajurveda and indicates the pure distinction between sacrificial text and ritual commentary in the same, whereas "black" Yajurveda signifies "unarranged" Yajurveda. This explanation which can be traced back even to Indian commentators, appears to me, to be highly improbable. But even Śatap. Br. XIV, 9, 4, 33 (of IV, 4, 5, 19) are called "the white sacrificial texts" (Śuklāni yajūṃṣi) as Ādityāni, "revealed by the sun"; and also the *Purāṇas* narrate that Yajñavalkya received new sacrificial texts from the sun (Viṣṇu-Purāṇa, III, 5) I believe that "white Yajurveda" owes its name to this connection with the sun. As against this the older Yajurveda was called "black". It is most probable "that the Saṃhitā of the white Yajurveda is most closely related to the original form of the Veda of the Adhvaryu," as Pischel thinks, *KG,* 172. Cf. Keith, *HOS,* Vol. 18 pp. lxxxv ff, on the mutual relationship of the Saṃhitās of the Yajurveda.

8. The sacrifices of ancient Indians fall into two broad categories: Food-sacrifices (during which chiefly milk, butter, cakes, stewed fruit, and corns are sacrificed) and Soma-sacrifices (whose main constituents are the Soma-libations). The individual sacrifices fall into one or the other of these two categories. The animal sacrifice is connected with sacrifice of the first category as well as with those of the second. Connected with all these kinds of sacrifices is the fire-cult, which is, in a certain way, the prerequisite for every kind of worship of gods.
9. According to the law books the drinking of brandy is a sin as great as the murder of a Brahmin.
10. Cf. page 72 above.
11. So also Oldenberg, *Religion des Veda,* 2nd Ed., pp. 362 f. and Keith, *HOS.,* Vol. 18, pp. cxxxvii, who says: "There can be no doubt that the ritual is a mere priestly invention to fill up the apparent gap in the sacrificial system which provided no place for man." Hillebrandt (Ritualliteratur, *Grundirss* III, 2, pp. 153), however, considers the Puruṣamedha to be a real human sacrifice. There can be no doubt that human sacrifices occurred in ancient India, though not in the Brahmanical cult—only survivals of it can be traced in the rite of building the brick-altar for the fire, and in the Śunaḥsepa legend—, just as cruel-human sacrifices occurred even in modern times among certain sects. But this does not prove the Puruṣamedha was such a sacrifice.
12. Vāj. Saṃh. 34, 1-6 is found as an Upaniṣad in the *Oupnekhat* of Duperron, and translated by Deussen, *Sechzig Upanishads des Veda,* p. 837. See above pp. 16-17.
13. More about all these sacrifices and festivals is found in A. Hillebrandt's "Ritual Literature, Vedische Ofer und Zauber" (Grundriss III, 2) p. 97-166, H. Oldenberg, *Religion des Veda* (2nd-Ed. p. 437-474),E. Hardy, *Die Vedisch-brahmanische Periode der Religion des alten Indiens,* Münster i.W. 1893, p. 154 ff. and Keith, HOS, Vol. 18, pp. ciii ff.
14. Only the first 18 Adhyāyas of the Vājasaneyī Saṃhitā are completely presented word for word and explained in the Śatapatha Brāhmaṇa belonging to the White Yajurveda.
15. See Keith, *HOS.,* Vol. 18, pp. cxl ff., and H. Oldenberg,

Zur Geschichte der altindischen Prosa-(*AGGW.* N. F. Bd. 16, Berlin, 1917), pp. 2 ff. On the language of the Yajus.

16. Also the Brāhmaṇa-like theological discussions which the Saṃhitās of the Black Yajurveda contain in addition to the prayers and formulas, are here left out of consideration. For, what will be said in the following chapter about the Brāhmaṇas applies to them as well.
17. Vāj. IV, 1, VI, 12; II, 14; I, 1; III, 9; X, 23.
18. The old fire and magic priests thought of as semi-divine beings.
19. Vāj. I, 30; IV, 10; V, 1; VI, 30.
20. It consists of two "Araṇis" or rubbing pieces of wood, of which one is a plank and the other a staff with a sharp pointed tip, which is turned round until a flame ensues. This fire producing device still in use with many primitive races like the Eskimos, is certainly one of the most primitive implements of mankind.
21. The Malays in Indonesia even today call the wooden board in which the fire staff is turned round, the "mother" or "woman" while they call the churning staff itself "man". Ancient Arabs also had two pieces of wood for producing fire and of these two they considered one as feminine and the other as masculine.
22. See above p. 87 f.
23. Vāj V, 2. Śatapath-Brāhmaṇa III, 4, 1, 20 ff. Cf. Śatapath Br. VIII, 5, 2, 1; Weber, *Ind. Stud.*, 8, 1863, pp. 8 ff., 28 ff., and above p. 59 f.
24. Mātariśvan is here the wind-god; therefore "the drum of Mātariśvan means "Space".
25. L. von Schroeder, *Indiens Literatur und Kultur,* p. 113f.
26. Also an example for the alliteration so fondly used in the Yajus formulas. The text runs: dhūr asi, dhūrva dhūrvantam, dhūrva tam yo 'smān dhūrvati, tam dhūrva yam dhūrvāmaḥ.
27. *Indiens Literature und Kultur,* p. 122.
28. On the Brahmodays see Ludwig, *Der Rigveda.* Koegel, III, 390 ff. Rud Koegel, *Geschichte der deutschen Litterature,* I, 1, 1894, pp. 5, 64 ff. includes the Brahmodyas, with which he compares the Old Germanic riddle poetry in the poetic heritage of the Indo-European period.

29. Similarly also in Taittirīya-Saṃhitā, VII, 4, 18.
30. This word with multifarious meanings signifies here probably "the priesthood", perhaps "the sacred knowledge".
31. Puruṣa means "man", "person" and also "spirit", "world-spirit". "The five" are the five senses, which are contained in the Puruṣa, i.e. "in the man" and permeated by the Puruṣa i.e. by "the world-spirit".
32. "The gods love what is hinted at, what is mysterious," is a sentence, again and again repeated in the *Brāhmaṇas,* for example in the Śatapatha Brāhmaṇa VI, 1,1, 2; 11; 2, 3, 7, 1, 23; VII, 4, 1, 10 etc. Bṛhadāraṇyaka Upaniṣad IV, 2, 2: "The gods love what is secretively hinted at and hate what is directly said."
33. According to the Aitareya-Brāhmaṇa VII, 18 Om means in the language used for the gods the same thing as what is expressed among men by "tathā" (so may it be), "yes". Similarly it is said in the Chāndogya-Upaniṣad I, 1, 8: "This syllable Om expresses consent for when one consents to some-thing he says: "Om". With the Hebrew "amen" the syllable *om* coincides only purely accidentally somewhat in its meaning and in its pronunciation.
34. Maitrāyaṇi-Saṃhitā I, 8, 5.

# eight

## VEDIC RISHIS

Chapter that certain pious and learned families obtained pre-eminence in the Vedic Period by their knowledge of performing religious sacrifices and their gift of composing hymns; that kings delighted to honour and reward these families; and that it is to them that the Aryan world is indebted for handing down the Vedic hymns from generation to generation. Modern Hindus take a pride in tracing their descent from these ancient families, and their names are a household word in modern Hindu society. Some account of these ancient Rishis—the revered pioneers of the Hindu religion,—will therefore not be unwelcome to Hindu readers.

Pre-eminent among the Vedic Rishis, or rather Rishi families, stand the Visvamitras and the Vasishthas. The learned and industrious scholar Dr. Muir has, in the first volume of his "Sanscrit Texts," collected many legend about these Rishis from later Sanscrit literature; but there is no Hindu who has not heard from his boyhood innumerable legends of this kind, connected with those revered names.

The Vasishthas and the Visvamitras were both honoured by the powerful conqueror, Sadas. The hymns of the third Mandala are ascribed to the Visvamitras, and in the 53rd hymn we find the following passage:—"The great god-born, god-commissioned Rishi, the beholder of men, has stayed the watery current. When Visvamitra sacrificed for

Sudas, then Indra was propitiated through the Kausikas." Again, the hymns of the seventh Mandala are ascribed to the Vasishthas, and in the 33rd hymn we find the following passage:—"The Vasishthas in white robes, with their hair knots on the right, devoted to sacred rites, have gladdened me. Rising up, I call the people round the sacrificial grass. Let not the Vasishthas depart from my door."

There was naturally some jealousy between these two priestly houses, and hard words were exchanged. The following verses in III, 53, are said to contain an imprecation against the Vasishthas:—

21. "Indra, approach us to-day with many excellent succour: be propitious to us. May he who hates us fall low; and let the breath of life forsake him whom we hate."

22. "As the tree suffers from the axe, as the Simbala flower is broken, as the cauldron boiling over casts forth form, so may the enemy, O Indra."

23. "The might of the destroyer is not perceived. Men lead away the Rishi as if he were a beast. The wise do not condescend to ridicule the fool. They do not lead the ass before the horse."

24. "These Bharatas have learnt to turn away from, not to associate with (the Vasishthas). They urge the horse against them as against a foe. They bear about the bow in battle."

Vasishtha is supposed to have hurled back the imprecation in the following verses of VII, 104.

13. "Soma does not bless the wicked nor the ruler who abuses his power. He slays the demon; he slays the untruthful man; both are bound by the fetters of Indra."

14. "If I had worshipped false gods, or if I had called upon the gods in vain,—but why art thou angry with

me, O Jatavedas? May vain talkers fall into thy destruction."

15. "May I die at once if I be a Yatudhana, or if I hurt the life of any man. But may he be cut of from his ten friends who falsely called me a Yātudhana."

16. "He who called me a Yātudhana, when I am not so, or who said I am a bright devil,—may Indra strike him down with his great weapon, may he fall the lowest of all beings."

So far the jealousy of the two angry priests is intelligible and even natural, however unbecoming of their great learning and sanctity. But when we proceed from the Rig Veda to later Sanscrit literature, incident which are human and natural become lost in a cloud of miraculous and monstrous legends.

It is assumed from the commencement in these later legends that Vasishtha was a Brahman and Visvamitra was a Kshatriya, although the Rig Veda justifies no such assumption and knows no Brahmans and Kshatriyas as castes. On the contrary, Visvamitra is the composer of some of the finest hymns cherished by later Brahmans, including the sacred Gayatri, the morning prayer of modern Brahmans.

Having assumed that Visvamitra was born a Kshatriya, the Mahabharata, the Harivansa, the Vishnu Purana, and other later works repeat an amusing story to account for the sage's attaining Brahmanhood. Satyavati, a Kshatriya girl, had been married to Richika, a Brahman. Richika prepared a dish for his wife, which would make her conceive a son with the qualities of a Brahman, and another dish for his mother-in-law (a Kshatriya's wife), which would make her conceive a son with the qualities of a Kshatriya. The two ladies, however, exchanged dishes; and so the Kshatriya's wife conceived and bore Visvamitra with the qualities of a

Brahman, and the Brabman's wife Satyavati bore Jamadagni, whose son, the fiery Parasurama, though a Brahman, became a renowned and destructive warrior! Such were the childish stories which the later writers had to invent to remove the difficulty they had created for themselves by assuming that Vedic Rishis belonged to particular castes!

In the celebrated legend of Harischandra, Visvamitra appears as a rapacious Brahman. He not only made the king give up his whole empire. but compelled him to sell his queen, his boy, and himself as slaves to pay the inevorable Brahman's fee! If such stories are invented to teach respect and duty due to Brahmans, they fail in their object and inspire other sentiments. The bereaved Harischandra was, however, rewarded in the end, and Visvamitra anointed his son as king, and Harischandra went to heaven. Vasishtha became angry and cursed Visvamitra to be a Vaka or crane, and Visvamitra, too, transformed Vasishtha into an Ari bird! The two birds began a furious contest which shook the whole world, until Brahmā had to interpose, and restored the saints to their own forms, and reconciled them!

In the legend of Trisanku, we are told that that prince wished to go bodily to heaven. Vasishtha declared the thing impossible, and in return for the king's angry words changed him to a Chandala. The fiery Visvamitra how appeared on the scene. He declared the thing quite possible, and began a great sacrifice and proceeded with it in spite of Vasishtha's absence. Trisanku ascended to heaven, but Indra refused to receive him, and threw the intruder, head downwards, towards the earth. The irrepressible Visvamitra, however, threatened to create another heaven with Indra and gods and Stars! The gods had to give in, and Trisanku ascended to heaven,—and shone like a star beyond the sun's course, but in a somewhat uncomfortable position, with his head still downwards!

In various other legends, which have almost become

household stories for Hindu boys and girls, these two sages continually appear, in defiance of chronology and cate, and are always at enmity with each other. The rival priests appear in courts of kings, twenty, thirty, or fifty generations removed from each over, and there is hardly a classical composition of note about a royal house or a semi-divine hero in which we do not find mention of Vasishtha and Visvamitra, eternally the rivals of each other. Thus the Vishnu Purana makes Vasishtha the priest of Ikshvaku's son Nimi, as well as the priest of Sagara, who was thirty-seventh in descent from Ikshvaku; and the Ramayana makes Vasishtha the priest of Ra ma, who was sixty-first in descent from Ikshvaku! Such is the use which later romancers have made of the simple materials furnished by the Rig Veda, and such is the manner in which they have piled story upon story, and myth upon myth in connection with incidents which in the ancient Veda are simple, natural, and—human. Not only the Rishis of the Veda, but every deity, and we may almost say every simile or allegory in the Rig Veda about a natural phenomenon, have received such treatment in the hands of the later imaginative Hindus.

But while a hundred wild stories were invented in later days to account for Visvamitra's attaining Brahmanhood, there was no thought of denying that accepted fact. Every legend, every learned disquisition, every childish tale, every great work, from the Mahabharata to Manu and the Puranas,—admit that Visvamitra was a Kshatriya and a Brahman. Yudhisthira in the Anusasana Parva (section 3) of the Mahābhārata inquires of Bhishma how Visvamitra had not only become a Brahman but had established the great and wise family of the Kusikas, *which included Brahmans and hundreds of Brahman Rishis."* The question would be a difficult one to answer in the Puranic Age in which the Mahabharata received its last touches. The question would not be difficult of solution in the Epic Age when the caste system was still a pliable institution. And the question would not arise at all in the Age of Visvamitra himself *i.e.,* in the Vedic Age, when caste as such did not exist.

From the legends of the Visvamitras and the Vasishthas, let us now turn to the scarcely less renowned houses of the Angirases, the Vamadevas, the Bharadvajas, and the Bhrigus. All these were families of Vedic Rishis, composers of vedic hymns; and later writers therefore feel somewhat uncertain about their caste. They are some-times called Brahmans with the character of Kshatriyas, sometimes Kshatriyas with the character of Brahmans; and occasionally the bold truth is conjectured that these Rishis lived before the institution of caste was formed.

The Angirases are the reputed authors of the ninth Mandala of the Rig Veda. About the Angirases, the Vishnu Purana (IV, 2, 2) has the following:—"The son of Nabhaga was Nabhaga; his son was Ambarisha; his son was Virupa; from him sprang Prishadasva, and from him Rathinara. On this subject there is this verse. These persons *descended from a Kshatriya stock and afterwards known as Angirases* were the chief of the Tathinaras, *Brahmans possessing also the character of Kshatriyas."*

Vamadeva and Bharadvaja are reputed to be the authors of the four ti' and sixth Mandalas of the Rig Veda. The Matsya Purana includes them (section 132) among the Angirases of whom we have spoken before.

To the Gritsamadas are attributed the hymns of the second Mandala of the Rig Veda. The commentator Sayana says of him that he was formerly of the Angiras race, but he afterwards became Gritsamada, of the Bhrigu race. This somewhat mystic legend is elaborated in the Mahabharata, Anusasana Parva (section 30), in which we are told that Vitahavya, a Kshatriya king, had taken shelter with Bhrigu, and Bhrigu, in order to save the fugitive from his pursue; stated there is no Kshatriya here, all these are Brahmans."

The word of Bhrigu could not prove untrue, and the fugitive Kshatriya Vitahavya forthwith bloomed into Brahmanhood and became Gritsamada! It must be allowed that this was an easier process than the penance of thousands of years which Visvamitra is said to have performed,—not to mention that his mother had exchanged dishes with a Brahman's wife!

But the story of Gritsamada's change of caste not universally accepted. The Visnu Purana and the Vayu Purana conjecture the bold truth that Gritsamada lived before the caste institution was formed. "From Gritsamada was descended Saunaka, *who originated the four caste*" (*Vish. Pur.*, IV, 8).

Lastly, let us turn to the Kanvas and the Atris. The Kanvas are the authors of the eighth Mandala of the Rig Veda, and we find the same uncertainty about their caste. The Vishnu Purana (IV, 19), and the Bhagavata Purana (IX, 20, 6, 7), maintain that Kanva was a descendant of Puru, a Kshatriya. Nevertheless the Kanvas were regarded as Brahmans. "From Ajamidha sprang Kanva, and from him Medatithi, *from whom were descended the Kanvanaya Brahmanas*" (*Vish. Pur.*, IV, 19).

The Atris are the reputed authors of the fifth Mandala of the Rig Veda, and we find the same uncertainty about their caste also. Thus the Vishnu Purana (IV, 6), calls Atri the grandfather of Pururavas, *who belonged to the Kshatriya race.*

These extracts are enough. They are made from works composed or revised two or three thousand years after the time of the Vedic Rishis, but those extracts enable us to comprehend the status and position of the Vedic religious leaders and warriors, and are therefore not out of place in an account of the Vedic Period. Writing at such a long distance of time from the Vedic Age the modern authors often misapprehended ancient facts and traditions. But nevertheless, the unswerving loyalty to the past which has ever characterised Hindu writers prevented them from tampering with such traditions. Those traditions pointed to a state of society which had long passed away, and which had become almost unintelligible. Puranic waters could scarcely comprehend that priests and warriors could spring from the same race, that a Rishi could be a warrior, or that a warrior could be a priest. The tried to explain such traditions by a hundred different theories and legends, but nevertheless they have faithfully and piously handed down the traditions unchanged and unaltered. Thus, to make only one more extract, the Matsya Purana enumerates 91 Vedic Rishis, and concludes with the following suggestive passage, (section 132):—"Thus 91 persons have been declared, by whom the hymns have been given forth. *They were Brahmans, Kshatriyas, and Vaisyas,* all sons of Rishis. They were the offspring of the Rishikas, sons of Rishis, Vedic Rishis."

Thus the Purana faithfully preserves the ancient tradition that the Vedic hymns were the common property of the entire Aryan population. And when the writer tells us that the composers of these hymns were Brahmans, Kshatriyas, and Vaisyas, we have little difficulty in discovering in that statement a dim recollection of the truth that the hymns were composed by the *undivided ancestors of those castes.*

Modern writers have classed Rishis under three classes, *viz.,* Devarshis, or saintly gods like Narada; Brahmarshis, or saintly Brahmans like Kanva of the Sakuntala drama; and Rajarsh is, or saintly Kshatriyas like Janaka, king of the Videhas. The ancient Vedic Rishis did not answer to any of these classes, did not belong exclusively to any of these categories, and were therefore a standing puzzle to modern writer. Hence the numerous legends to account for what was unaccountable; and often in the midst of these wild conjectures, the modern writer made a bold guess after the truth, and maintained that the Vedic Rishis must have lived before caste was originated. We do not wonder at the theories and legends which were multiplied in such profusion; we admire the bold-ness with which the truth was sometimes conjectured.

For the rest, these invaluable traditions—that priests and warriors were descended from the same races, and that the same Rishis were often both priests and warriors,—enable us to comprehend the true position of Vedic Rishis. For, divested of their miraculous—and legendary character, what do these traditions indicate? They indicate that the venerable families of the olden times,—like those of the Vasishthas, the Visvamitras, the Angi-rases, and the Kanvas,—furnished renowned warriors and eminent priests at the same time. A Percy or a Douglas might be an ambitious priest or a fiery warrior, and so might a Kanva or an Angiras. To be sure, the Hindu houses were pre-eminently priestly as the European houses were military, but *caste* was as unknown to the one as to the other. Many a baron of Medieval Europe, whose name is still preserved in the history of the crusades, had his father or uncle, son or nephew, immured in the solitude of holy monasteries; and many a Vasishtha or Visvamitra, whose religious hymns we still cherish and rever; had his son or nephew engaged in the wars of the Vedic Period, in the unending centests against the aborigines of the soil. These facts are proved by the texts of the Rig Veda itself which we have quoted in a previous chapter; and they are confirmed by the legends and traditions which we have quoted in this chapter from later Sanscrit literature. The Vedic Rishis composed their hymns, fought their wars, and ploughed their fields; but were neither Brahmans, nor Kshatriyas, nor Vaisyas. The great Rishi houses of the Vedic Age furnished priests and soldiers, but were no more Brahmans or Kshatriyas than the Percies or Douglases of Mediaeval Europe were Brahmans or Kshatriyas.

# nine

## VEDIC CIVILIZATION

### Cross-Cultural Traces Of Vedic Civilization

The ancient Greek writer Aratos tells the following story about the constellation Virgo, or the virgin. Virgo, he says, may have belonged to the star race, the forefathers of the ancient stars. In primeval times, in the golden age, she lived among mankind as Justice personified and would exhort people to adhere to the truth. At this time people lived peacefully, without hypocrisy or quarrel. Later, in the age of silver, she hid herself in the mountains, but occasionally she came down to berate people for their evil ways.

Finally the age of bronze came. People invented the sword, and "they tasted the meat of cows, the first who did it." At this point Virgo "flew away to the sphere"; that is, she departed for the celestial realm.[1]

The Vedic literature of India gives an elaborate description of the universe as a cosmos—a harmonious, ordered system created according to an intelligent plan as a habitation for living beings. The modern view of the universe is so different from the Vedic view that the latter is presently difficult to comprehend. In ancient times, however, cosmogonies similar to the Vedic system were widespread among people all over the world. Educated people of today tend to immediately dismiss these systems of thought as mythology, pointing to their diversity and their strange ideas as proof that they are all simply products of the imagination.

If we do this, however, we may be overlooking important information that could shed light on the vast forgotten period that precedes the brief span of recorded human history. There is certainly much evidence of independent storytelling in the traditions of various cultures, but there are also many common themes. Some of these themes are found in highly developed form in the Vedic literature. Their presence in cultures throughout the world is consistent with the idea that in the distant past, Vedic culture exerted worldwide influence.

In this article we will give some examples of Vedic ideas concerning time and human longevity that appear repeatedly in different traditions. First we will examine some of these ideas, and then we will discuss some questions about what they imply and how they should be interpreted.

In the Vedic literature time is regarded as a manifestation of Kṛṣṇa, the Supreme Being. As such, time is a controlling force that regulates the lives of living beings in accordance with a cosmic plan. This plan involves repeating cycles of creation and destruction of varying durations. The smallest and most important of these repeating cycles consists of four yugas, or ages, called Satyā, Treta, Dvāpara, and Kāli. In these successive ages mankind gradually descends from a high spiritual platform to a degenerated state. Then, with the beginning of a new Satya-yuga, the original state of purity is restored, and the cycle begins again.

The story of Virgo illustrates that in the ancient Mediterranean world there was widespread belief in a similar succession of four ages, known there as the ages of gold, silver, bronze, and iron. In this system humanity also starts out in the first age in an advanced state of consciousness and gradually becomes degraded. Here also, the progressive developments in human society are not simply evolving by physical processes, but are superintended by a higher controlling intelligence.

It is noteworthy that Aratos' story specifies the eating of cows as a sinful act that cut mankind off from direct contact with celestial beings. This detail fits in nicely with the ancient Indian traditions of cow protection, but it is unexpected in the context of Greek or European culture.

One explanation for similarities between ideas found in different cultures is that people everywhere have essentially the same psychological makeup, and so they tend to come up independently with similar notions. However, details such as the point about cow-killing suggest that we are dealing here with common traditions rather than independent inventions.

Another example of similarities between cultures can be found among the natives of North America. The Sioux Indians say that their ancestors were visited by a celestial woman who gave them their system of religion. She pointed out to them that there are four ages, and that there is a sacred buffalo that loses one leg during each age. At present we are in the last age, an age of degradation, and the buffalo has one leg.[2]

This story is a close parallel to the account in the Srimad Bhagavatam of the encounter between Maharaja Pariksit and the bull of Dharma. There, Dharma is said to lose one leg with each successive yuga, leaving it with one leg in the present Age of Kāli.

According to the Vedic system, the lengths of the Satya, Treta, Dvapara, and Kāli yugas are 4, 3, 2, and 1 times an interval of 432,000 years. Within these immense periods of time the human life span decreases from 100,000 years in the Satya-yuga to 10,000 years in the Treta-yuga, 1,000 years in the Dvapara-yuga, and finally 100 years in the

Kāli-yuga.

Of course, this idea is strongly at odds with the modern evolutionary view of the past.

In the ancient Mediterranean world, however, it was widely believed that human history had extended over extremely long periods of time. For example, according to old historical records, Porphyry (c. 300 A.D.) said that Callisthenes, a companion of Alexander in the Persian war, dispatched to Aristotle Babylonian records of eclipses and that these records covered 31,000 years. Likewise, Iamblicus (fourth century) said on the authority of the ancient Greek astronomer Hipparchus that the Assyrians had made observations for 270,000 years and had kept records of the return of all seven planets to the same position.[3] Finally, the Babylonian historian Berosus assigned 432,000 years to the total span of the reigns of the Babylonian kings before the Flood.[4]

We do not wish to suggest that these statements are true (or that they are false). The point here is that people in the old Mediterranean civilization evidently had a much different view of the past than the dominant view today. And this view was broadly consistent with Vedic chronology.

Although the Bible is well known for advocating a very short time-span for human history, it is interesting to note that it contains information indicating that people at one time lived for about 1,000 years. In the Old Testament the following ages are listed for people living before the Biblical Flood: Adam, 930; Seth, 912; Enos, 905; Kenan, 910; Mahaleel, 895; Jared, 962; Enoch, 365; Methusaleh,969; Lamech, 777; and Noah, 950. If we exclude Enoch (who was said to have been taken up to heaven in his own body), these persons lived an average of 912 years.[5]

After the Flood, however, the following ages were recorded: Shem, 600; Arphachshad, 438; Selah, 433; Eber,

464; Peleg, 239; Reu, 239; Serug, 230; Nahor, 148; Terah, 205; Abraham, 175; Issac, 180; Job, 210; Jacob, 147; Levi, 137; Kohath, 133; Amaram, 137; Moses, 120; and Joshua, 110. These ages show a gradual decline to about 100 years, similar to what must have happened after the beginning of Kali-yuga, according to the Vedic system.

Here we should mention in passing that the Biblical Flood is traditionally said to have taken place in the second or third millenium B.C., and the traditional date in India for the beginning of Kāli-yuga is February 18, 3102 B.C. This very date is cited as the time of the Flood in various Persian, Islamic, and European writings from the sixth to the fourteenth centuries A.D.[6] How did the middle-eastern Flood come to be associated with the start of Kali-yuga? The only comment we can make is that this story shows how little we really know about the past.

In support of the Biblical story of very long human lifespans in ancient times, the Roman historian Flavius Josephus cited many historical works that were available in his time: Now when Noah had lived 350 years after the Flood, and all that time happily, he died, having the number of 950 years, but let no one, upon comparing the lives of the ancients with our lives...make the shortness of our lives at present an argument that neither did they attain so long a duration of life...

Now I have for witnesses to what I have said all those that have written Antiquities, both among the Greeks and barbarians, for even Manetho, who wrote the Egyptian history, and Berosus, who collected the Chaldean monuments, and Mochus, and Hestiaeus, and beside these, Hiernonymous the Egyptian, and those who composed the Phoenician history, agree with what I here say: Hesiod also, and Hecataeus, Hellanicaus, and Acuzilaus, and besides Ephorus and Nicolaus relate that the ancients lived a thousand years: but as to these matters, let everyone look upon them as he sees fit.[7]

Unfortunately, practically none of the works referred to by Josephus are still existing, and this again shows how little we know of the past. But in existing Norse sagas it is said that people in ancient times lived for many centuries. In addition, the Norse sagas describe a progression of ages, including an age of peace, an age when different social orders were introduced, an age of increasing violence, and a degraded "knife-age and axe-age with cloven shields."[8] The latter is followed by a period of annihilation, called Ragnarok, after which the world is restored to goodness.

The Norse Ragnarok involves the destruction of the earth and the abodes of the Norse demigods (called Asgard), and thus it corresponds in Vedic chronology to the annihilation of the three worlds that follows 1,000 yuga cycles, or one day of Brahma. It is said that during Ragnarok the world is destroyed with flames by a being called Surt, who lives beneath the lower world (appropriately called Hell) and was involved in the world's creation. By comparison, the Srimad Bhagavatam (3.11.30) states that at the end of Brahma's day, "the devastation takes place due to the fire emanating from the mouth of Sankarsana." Sankarsana is a plenary expansion of Kṛṣṇa who is "seated at the bottom of the universe" (Srimad Bhagavatam 3.8.3), beneath the lower planetary systems.

There are many similarities between the Norse and Vedic cosmologies, but there are also great differences.

One key difference is that in the Srimad Bhagavatam, all beings and phenomena within the universe are clearly understood as part of the divine plan of Kṛṣṇa, the Supreme Personality of Godhead. In contrast, in the Norse mythology God is conspicuously absent, and the origin and purpose of the major players in the cosmic drama are very obscure. Surt, in particular, is a "fire giant" whose origins and motives are unclear even to experts in the Norse literature.[9]

One might ask, If Vedic themes appear in many different societies, how can one conclude that they derive from an ancient Vedic civilization? Perhaps they were created in many places independently, or perhaps they descend from an unknown culture that is also ancestral to what we call Vedic culture. Thus parallels between the accounts of Surt and Sankarsana may be coincidental, or perhaps the Vedic account derives from a story similar to that of Surt.

Our answer to this question is that available empirical evidence will not be sufficient to prove the hypothesis of descent from an ancient Vedic culture, for all empirical evidence is imperfect and subject to various interpretations. But we can decide whether or not the evidence is consistent this hypothesis.

If there was an ancient Vedic world civilization, we would expect to find traces of it in many cultures around the world. We do seem to find such traces, and many agree with Vedic accounts in specific details (such as the location of Surt's abode or the sacred buffalo's loss of one leg per world age). Since this civilization began to lose its influence thousands of years ago, at the beginning of Kali-yuga, we would expect many of these traces to be fragmentary and overlain by many later additions, and this we also see. Thus the available evidence seems to be consistent with the hypothesis of a Vedic origin.

**Foot Notes**

1. E. C. Sachau, trans., *Alberuni's India* (Delhi 1964), pp. 383-4.
2. J. E. Brown, ed., *The Sacred Pipe* (Baltimore 1971), p. 9.
3. D. Neugebauer, *History of Ancient Mathematical Astronomy* (Berlin 1975), pp. 608-9.
4. J. D. North, "*Chronology & the Age of the World*," in Cosmology, History & Theology, eds. Wolfgang Yourgrau and A. D. Breck (N.Y. 1977), p. 315.
5. D. W. Patten and P. A. Patten, "*A Comprehensive Theory on Aging, Gigantism & Longevity*," Catastrophism & Ancient History, Vol. 2, Part 1 (Aug. 1979), p. 24.
6. J. D. North, *Ibid*., p. 316-7.
7. D. W. Patten, *Ibid*., p. 29.
8. V. Rydberg, *Teutonic Mythology*, R. B. Anderson, trans. (London 1889), pp. 88,94.
9. *Ibid*., pp. 448-9.

# ten

## THE AGE OF THE VEDA

We have pursued the whole Vedic literature up to its final offshoots and addenda and cannot avoid any more the question of the age of this great literature. If it were possible to state—even to within a few centuries—how far back into the past the oldest hymns of the Ṛgveda and of the Atharvaveda would reach, then it would be unnecessary to devote a special chapter to this question. It would suffice to give the approximate date in a few words. But unfortunately it is a fact,—and it is particularly regrettable to have to admit this fact—and the opinions of the best researchers in the matter of the age of the Ṛgveda differ not by a few centuries, but a few thousands of years, that some put the lower limit for the Ṛgvedic hymns at the year 1000 B.C., whereas others put it somewhere between 3000 and 2500 B.C. Where the opinions of experts are at such great divergence from one another, it is not enough, even in a hand-book meant for laymen, to give some approximate date, but even the layman must have an idea as to what is the basis for the divergent opinions on the age of the Veda. It is so much the more necessary as the question of the age of the oldest Indian literature is linked with the question of the beginnings of the Indo-Aryan culture, a question which is of great importance for every historian, researcher of archaeology and philologist. For, only when we can fix chronologically the oldest testimonies of Aryan culture in India can we draw conclusions about the period of the development of Indo-Iranian and further of the Indo-Germanic culture. But even for the historian who is concerned with the history of the ancient world and wants to pursue the multifarious relations among the cultured peoples of the ancient world, it is of importance to know that was the relationship of India with reference to the beginnings of its oldest cultural epoch to the three other great cultural centres of the orient—Babylon, Egypt and China.

Under such circumstances it seems to be unavoidably necessary to tender even to the layman an account of the question and, as far as it is possible, to show the limits and to substantiate our ignorance or our knowledge.

When Indian literature became known to the world for the first time, one was inclined to attribute an exceedingly old age to all works of Indian literature. Friedrich Schlegel expected from India, as we all know, nothing less than "information about the history of the ancient world that is so dark till now.[1] As late as in 1852 A. Weber wrote in his *History of Indian Literature,* "The Indian Literature is generally considered as the oldest literature, of which we possess written documents, and this justly so," and added only in 1876 in the second edition, "as long as there are no objections raised against this by the monumental writings and papyrus-rolls of Egypt or perhaps even by the Assyrian literature discovered most recently." The grounds on which, according to Weber, "The Indian literature has to be considered as the oldest literature of which extensive written documents are handed down to us," would be partly geographical ones and partly based on the history of religion. In the older parts of the Ṛgveda the Indian folk appears to us as settled in the Punjab. The gradual spread from there to the east over Hindustan towards the Ganges can be pursued in the later parts of the Vedic literature. Then the epic literature shows us further the spread of Brahminism towards the south. It must have taken some centuries before such a vast stretch of lands "inhabited by wild, mighty tribes of men" could be Brahminised. It must have also taken many centuries for the development in the history of religion from the simple nature-worship of the Ṛgveda hymns upto the theosophical-philosophical speculations of the Upaniṣads and again to those phases of belief in gods and cults as was found by Megasthenes about 300 B.C. in India. A more exact determination of the age of the Veda was not at all attempted by Weber; he even declares expressly every such attempt to be entirely futile.[2]

The first one who made this attempt and tried to put up a sort of chronology of the oldest Indian literature was Max Müller in his *History of Ancient Sanskrit Literature* which appeared in 1859. Starting from the less reliable clues which we possess for the Indian chronology, the attack of Alexander and the appearance of Buddhism[3] he drew further conclusions in the following manner: Buddhism is nothing but a reaction against Brahminism and it presupposes the existence of the whole Veda, i.e. of the literature consisting of the hymns, the Brāhmaṇas, Āraṇyakas and Upaniṣads. This entire literature must have originated before Buddhism i.e. before 500 B.C. The Vedāṅga or Sūtra literature might be almost simultaneous with the birth and the early propagation of Buddhism. These Sūtras-works, whose origin falls into the period between 600 and 200 B.C.—with the propounding of these purely arbitrary dates begins the untenable element of the Max Müller calculations—are so conceived that the Brahmaṇa-literature must have necessarily preceded them. But the Brāhmaṇas of which there are older and younger ones, in which are contained long lists of teachers, which older Brāhmaṇas handed down, cannot be possibly accommodated in less than 200 years. Hence in the opinion of Max Müller, one will have to accept as the period of birth of these prose works the period between 800 and 600 B.C. But the Brāhmaṇas in their turn again presuppose the existence of the Vedic Saṃhitās. But at least 200 years were necessary to compile these collections of songs and prayers, hence the space of approximately 1000 to 800 B.C. might have to be considered as the period on which these collections were made. But prior to the origin of these compilations, which were already considered as sacred sacrificial poetry and authorised prayer books, there must have been a period in which the songs and prayers contained in them have originated as popular or religious poetry. This period, Max Müller concluded, must be anterior to 1000 B.C. And as he had already presumed 200 years once for the "mantra period" so named by him, therefore he presumed also—however not lying much emphais on this number 200 years for the birth of this poetry and arrived thus at 1200 to 1000 B.C. as the initial period of Vedic poetry.

Now it is clear that the presumption of 200 years for each of the various literary epoques in the birth of the Veda is purely arbitrary. And Max Müller himself did not want to say anything more than this, that at *least* such as interval must be presumed and that at *least* by 1000 B.C. our Ṛgveda-Saṃhitā must have been already completed. He has looked upon his dating of 1200 to 1000 B.C. always only as *terminus ad quem,* and in his lectures on "Physical Religion" which appeared in 1890 he said expressly, that we must not hope to propose a *terminus a quo.* "No power on earth will be able to determine"[4] he says, "whether the Vedic hymns were composed in 1000 or 1500 or 2000 or 3000 before Christ." But it is remarkable, how strong the power of suggestion is even in science. The purely hypothetical and actually quite arbitrary chronological fixation of the Vedic epoques by Max Müller received, without the addition of any new arguments or actual proofs, in course of time more and more the recognition and character of a scientifically proved fact. One formed the habit—and even W. D. Whitney[5] reprimanded this habit—of saying, Max Müller has proved 1200 to 1000 B.C. to be the date of the Ṛgveda. Only with hesitation did some researchers like L. von Schroeder[6] dare to go beyond, upto 1500 or even upto 2000 B.C. And when a few years ago, by reason of astronomical calculations H. Jacobi tried to push back the vedic literature into the 3rd millenium before Christ, a hue and cry was raised by the scholars against such a heretic step, and even today most researchers cannot comprehend that Jacobi could put forth such a crazy view on the age of the Veda. It was strangely forgotten on how weak a footing "the prevailing view" actually stood which they tried to defend so vigorously.

The idea of drawing conclusions about the chronology of the oldest Indian literature from the history of the starry sky with the help of astronomical data is nothing new. Even A. Ludwig has made such an attempt[7] based on solar eclipses. The priests of ancient India who had to determine the times of sacrifices were, just like the pontifices in ancient Rome, at the same time also calendar-makers. They had to observe the starry sky to regulate and determine in advance the times of the sacrifices. And so we find also numerous data on astronomy and calendars in the Brāhamaṇas and the Sūtras. In them the so-called nakṣatras or "Moonhouses" play an important role. The ancient Indians have naturally noticed, that the moon needs for sidereal revolution approximately 27 day nights and spends every night of the sidereal month in a different constellation. These stars or constellations, all of which lie not far from the ecliptic, were combined into a kind of zodiac, a series of 27 nakṣatras encircling the sphere; and this lunar zodiac was used for the purpose of giving out the position of the moon at a particular time.[8] So there are many texts in the Vedic literature which say that a particular sacrificial act must take place "under such and such Nakṣatra" *i.e.* "when the moon is in conjunction with that Nakṣatra." Still more numerous are the texts in which the Nakṣatras are brought in relation to full moon and new moon. And even in the more early literature very often only 12 of the 27 nakṣatras appear connected with the full moon, by which we can explain the names of the months derived from the 12 Nakṣatras. These names of the months were originally applied only to lunar months but were extended later also to the twelfth part of the solar year. As even in the Vedic times the solar and lunars years were somehow tried to be made to correspond to each other, the question arises, whether from the combination of particular full-moon Nakṣatras with the seasons and the beginning of the year it is not possible to draw inferences about the time from which the concerned calendar-data originate. Such inferences, which led to surprising results, have been sought to be made in 1899 simultaneously and independent of each other by H. Jacobi in Bonn and the Indian Bal Gangadhar Tilak in Bombay.[9] Following different ways, both researchers have come to the opinion that during the time of the Brāhmaṇas the Pleiades (Kṛttikās) which formed in those days the starting point of the Nakṣatra-series, coincided with the spring-equinox, but also in the Vedic texts there are also traces of an older calendar in which the spring-equinox fell in the Orion (Mṛgasira). From a calculation of the value of the precision it follows however that by about 2500 B.C. the spring-equinox lay in the Pleiades and by about 4500 in the Orion. But whereas Tilak goes so far as to trace back some Vedic texts upto the year 6000 B.C. Jacobi is contented with pushing back to about 4500 B.C. "the beginning of the cultural-period, as whose ripe, perhaps even late product the songs of the Ṛgveda have come down to us." This period of culture stretched according to him approximately from 4500 to 2500 B.C. and he is inclined to ascribe "the collection of hymns preserved to our present day to the second half of this period.[10] In this view Jacobi was strengthened further by a second astronomical observation. The Gṛhya-sūtras tell us about a marriage-custom in ancient India which consisted in the following—After arriving in the new house the bridegroom and the bride and to sit still on an ox-skin, until the stars became visible, whereupon the bridegroom showed to his bride the Pole star—called "Dhruva" "the firm"—and said a sentence then as for example, "Be firm, flourshing with me", whereupon she replied: "Firm you, firm I may be in the house of my husband". Of great importance is the name 'Dhruva' "the firm" under which this star appears in the marriage-rite, and the whole ceremony during which the star appears especially as a symbol of firmness, of unchangeable loyalty, is based on this that the pole star was considered to be immovable or one did not notice its movement. This description as well as the ceremony can therefore originate at a time in which a bright star was so close to the celestial pole that it appeared to stand still to the observer of that time. Now it is again a result of the precision that along with the gradual change of the celestial equator its north pole also moves and it evidently describes in approximately 26000 years a circle of 23-½ degree radius around the fixed pole of the ecliptic. By this slowly one star after another moves nearer and becomes Northern star or Pole Star, but only sometimes does a bright star approach the pole so much that for all practical purposes it can be considered as "a firm one" "Dhruva". At present the star of 2nd magnitude in the Little Bear is the Polestar on the northern hemisphere. Obviously this star cannot be meant when the Polestar of the Vedic times is referred to, because it was, 2000 years ago still so far away from the pole that it could not have been possible called "firm". But only in 2780 B.C. do we come across another Polestar that deserves this name. At that time Alpha Dracoins stood for over half a millenium so close to the pole that it had to appear as immovable when observed with the naked eye. Therefore we must put the origin of the name Dhruva as well as of the custom of showing the 'fixed' star to the bride as a symbol of firmness in the wedding night, in a period in which Alpha Dracoins was the Polestar, i.e., in the first half of the third millenium B.C. In the marriage texts of the Ṛgveda there is no mention of this custom yet, and this is the reason why Jacobi considers it probable "that the use of Dhruva in the marriage ceremonies belongs not to the time of the Ṛgveda but to the following period, and that therefore the Ṛgvedic period of culture lies anterior to the third pre-Christian millenium."[11]

As has been said, the assertions of Jacobi and Tilak met with violent opposition. The most serious objection to the argument about the Pleiades was that the Indians of the most ancient times were concerned only with the position of the Nakṣatras in relation to the moon and not to the sun, and that there is not a single trace of any observation of the equinoxes to be found in the most ancient times. The passage[12] in which we read that the Pleiades "do not swerve from the East" should probably not be interpreted as meaning that they rose "due east" (which would have been the case in the third millenary B.C., and would point to a knowledge of the vernal equinox): the correct interpretation is more likely that they remain visible in the eastern region which was the case about 1100 B.C.[13] Coming to the argument of the New Year in various millenia, it is most difficult to decide these questions, primarily because in our texts the year sometimes begins with spring, some-times with winter, and sometimes with the rainy season, and moreover the number of seasons varies between three, five and six.[14] The argument of the Pole Star, too, provoked serious objections. We cannot deny the possibility of one of the lesser stars in the Little Bear having been visible (about 1250 B.C. and even later still) as the Pole Star in the clear Indian firmament.[15] At any rate it is not permissible to draw any conclusion from the non-mention of this custom in the Ṛgveda: for by no means all of the marriage-customs are mentioned in the marriage-hymn of the Ṛgveda. So there is no reason why this custom should have been singled out for mention in preference to another.

Though the astronomical arguments of Tilak and Jacobi did not succeed in proving what was to be proved, they have stimulated the enquiry whether there are no other grounds for assuming a greater antiquity of Vedic culture. From the point of view of Indian history there is no argument against the presumption that the Vedic literature reached as far back as the third millenium and ancient Indian culture upto the fourth millenium, whereas the suggestion of 1200 or even 1500 made by Max Müller for the beginning of the Vedic period is not compatible any more with the present state of our knowledge about the political history as well as the literary and religious history of ancient India. This has been convincingly proved in my opinion by G. Būhler[16] in particular.

Inscriptions show that in the third century B.C. South India was conquered by Aryan Indians and overrun by Brahminic culture. But the fact that some Vedic schools as those of the Baudhāyana and Āpastamba have originated in the south, makes it probable that the conquest of the south by the Aryans has taken place already much earlier—perhaps already in the 7th or 8th century B.C. For immediately after the conquest the whole country cannot have been so completely colonised and Brahminised, that Vedic schools could come into being in the distant south. But we cannot at all reconcile with the conquest of southern India about 700 or 600 B.C.[17] the presumption that the Indo-Aryans were still settled in the north western corner of India or in eastern Afghanistan around 1200 or even around 1500 B.C. Bühler says, "the idea that the Indo-Aryan race of the Vedic age with its numerous divisions into clans and the continuous battles should have conquered the 1,23,000 sq. miles of actual India (excliding Punjab, Assam and Burma), within 5, 6 or even 8 centuries, should have founded states and should have organised as per one and the same pattern, appears simply ridiculous; especially when one considers that this areas was inhabited not by forest tribes but partly by races which possessed a culture which was not much inferior to those of the conquerors.

Now, one could say,—and it has been said by Oldenberg—700 years are a good span of time in which much can happen. "one need only to consider," says Oldenberg,[18] "what 400 years have meant for the vast areas of northern and southern America." This is however a wrong comparison. The races and cultures which came into collision in America, were quite different from those, with which we are concerned in India. As regards the political conditions of ancient India, we learn from some songs of the Ṛgveda and from the epics that just exactly as the later history of India shows us, in early and in the earliest times the individual Aryan clans were continuously fighting among themselves. Under such circumstances the conquest of India could take place only very slowly, only step by step. In fact we also see, when we compare the two oldest layers of the Indian literature with each other, that the advancement of the Aryans towards east and south progressed only very slowly. In the hymns of the Ṛgveda we find the Indo-Aryan folk still settled exclusively in the extreme north-west of India and in eastern Afghanistan. And yet the periods in which the hymns of the Ṛgveda have originated must have extended over centuries. This is proved by the numerous different layers of earlier and later components which we find in this hymns. This is proved by the Anukramaṇis but also in the Brāhmaṇas as "Seers" or authors of hymns, are considered in the hymns themselves as seers of a preceding age[19] And the authors of the hymns speak also rather too often of "old songs", of "songs composed as per old melody" as if this poetry had been practised since times immemorial.[20] M. Bloomfield[21] has shown that, of the approximately 40,000 lines of the Ṛgveda, nearly 5,000 lines are repetitions. This proves that, at the time when the Ṛgveda was composed, the more modern poets would frequently borrow lines and expressions from older ones, and that there was actually in existence a large number of floating lines of verse, which any singer could incorporate in his song if he so fancied. But in this chapter we have seen repeatedly how backward the Ṛgveda is behind all other literary works belonging to the Veda. Even the language of the hymns is much older than that of the Vedic prose works. The religious views and the cultural conditions are quite different. The Brāhmaṇas, Āraṇyakas, and the Upaniṣads presuppose not only the hymns of the Ṛgveda but also the sentences and prayers of the remaining Saṃhitās as primeval holy texts. Indeed these old hymns and sentences were mostly not understood any more. The old legends had fallen into oblivion. Let us remember only the gap that separates the Śunaḥśepa-legend of the Aitareya-Brāhmaṇa from the hymns of the Ṛgveda.[22]

The oral tradition presupposes still longer intervals, than when these texts would have been written down. Generations of pupils and teachers must have passed, before all the existing and the numerous lost texts and acquired a fixed form in the Vedic schools.[23] On linguistic, literary and cultural-historical grounds we must therefore presume that between the time of the oldest hymns and the final combination of the hymns to a Saṃhitā or "collection"—for the Ṛgveda Saṃhitā describes evidently only the close of a long preceding period.[24]—and many centuries have again lapsed between Ṛgveda Saṃhitā and the Brāhmaṇas. But the Brāhmaṇas themselves with their numerous schools and ramifications of schools, with their endless lists of teachers and the numerous indications regarding teachers of the earlier times require a period of many centuries for their formation.[25] Both these literature and the propagation of Brahmanic culture, of theological knowledge and last but not least important of priestly supremacy which goes hand in hand with it, must have taken centuries. And when we come to the Upaniṣads, we see that they too belong to different periods of time, that they too presuppose generations of teachers and a long tradition.[26] Both these literature and the propagation of Brahmanic culture, of theological knowledge and last but not least important of priestly supremacy which goes hand in hand with it, must have taken centuries. And when we come to the Upaniṣads, we see that they too belong to different periods of time, that they too presuppose generations of teachers and a long tradition.[26] And yet we see that during the whole of this period, which has lasted from the first beginnings up to the last off-shoots of the Vedic literature, the Indo-Aryan race has conquered only the relatively small stretch of land from the Indus to the Ganges, the actual Hindostan. If even this advancement from the extreme north-west upto the eastern Gangetic land has taken such a long time, how many centuries must the conquest of the whole Central and South India have taken! When we consider this, 700 years will not appear to us as a long period any more.

There are other considerations besides this. It is indisputably to the credit of Max Müller to have shown that Buddhism at about 500 B.C. absolutely presupposes the existence of the whole of Vedic literature. In refutation of the view, held by some scholar,[27] that the earliest Upaniṣads should not be placed prior to the 6th century B.C., Oldenberg[28] has shown that centuries must have elapsed between the earliest Upaniṣads and the earliest Buddhist literature. Buddhist literature, however, presupposes not only the Veda, but the Vedāṅgas also,[29] and indeepd brahmanical literature and science in a highly developed state. Today, too, more light has been thrown on the religious conditions of ancient Indian than was the case in Max Müller's day, when it was thought possible to squeeze the whole development of the religious history of India up to the appearance of Buddhism within the limit of 700 years. Even before the appearance of Buddhism, there were sects in India, as Bühler has pointed out, which denied the sanctity of the Veda. The tradition of one of thesè sects, the Jainas, has in other respects proved so reliable as to chronology, that we may regard with some confidence a report which places the life of the first founder of this sect about 750 B.C. Bühler also thought he could prove that other sects antagonistic to the Veda and to Brahmanism went back to a much more hoary antiquity than had hitherto been supposed.[30] Unfortunately he did not live to demonstrate this proof.

The discoveries made by Hugo Winckler in Boghazköi

in Asia Minor in the year 1907, gave an impetus to more recent discussions on the question of the age of the Ṛgveda and of Vedic culture.[31] The clay tablets from the archives of the capital of the ancient Hittite kingdom, which were found in Boghazköi, included records of treaties concluded by the king of the Hittites and the king of Mitani at the beginning of the 14th century B.C. The gods of both kingdoms are invoked as guardians of the treaties, and in the list of gods there appear, beside numerous Babylonian and Hittite deities, the names of Mitra, Varuṇa, Indra and Nāsatyau among the gods of Mitani.[32] How did the names of these deities reach the Mitanis in Asia Minor? Scholars diverge greatly in their reply to this question. The historian Ed. Meyer ascribes these gods to the Aryan period, i.e., the period when the Indians and Iranians as yet formed an undivided nation in language and religion[33] and assumes that, at the same time as these "Aryans" appeared in western Mesopotamia and Syria, the separate development of the Aryans in the north-western India had already begun: the Vedic hymns, the earliest of which arose "probably not later than about 1500 B.C." bearing witness to this development. A similar opinion has been expressed by P. Giles. Oldenberg[34] thinks it more likely "that these are the gods of some western Aryan tribe akin to the Indians, inherted from some common past, as the Indians on their part had inherited them from the same source." He leaves the question open whether these were Iranians before Zoroaster's time, or whether a third branch of the Aryans is meant, and takes the view that this discovery does not justify us in assuming greater antiquity for the veda.

It is a fact, however, that this particular grouping of the gods Varuṇa and Mitra, Indra and Nāsatyau, with these forms of their names, can be traced *only in the Veda*. For this reason I agree with Jacobi, Konow and Hillebrandt in considering these gods to be Indian, vedic deities and that there is no possible justification for any other view. We shall have to assume that, just as there were Aryan immigrations into India from the west, there must have been isolated migrations back to the west. We may think either of warlike adventurers or of connections by marriage. Nor should we forget that, at the time of the Ṛgveda, the Aryan Indians were as yet much nearer the west from the geographical point of view.[35] As regards chronology, however, all that we can glean from the inscriptions at Boghazköi is that, about the middle of the second millenium B.C., Aryan tribes which worshipped Vedic gods must already have been established in north-western India for a very considerable time, as several of these tribes had migrated far back to the west as early as about 1400 B.C.[36] This small but important fact would be supported still further, if it should prove to be true that also traces of Indian numerals are to be found in the Boghazköi text.[37]

The idea of so early a date as the third millenium B.C. for the Veda would certainly be out of the question, if it were proved that the individual Indo-European peoples had not yet separated from the primitive Indo-Europeans in the third millenium[38] This view which is very unlikely and has not been satisfactorily proved, is welcomed by those who wish to assign as low a date as possible to the Ṛgveda and to the beginnings of Indian culture. Thus J. Hertel[39] promises to demonstrate that the Ṛgveda originated, not in north-western India but in Iran, and at a time not far distant from that of Zoroaster, who, according to Hertel, lived about 550 B.C., G. Hüsling[40] goes still further, and turns and twists certain of the names of kings occurring in the cuneiform inscriptions so long that they are metamorphosed into those of Indian kings. On the basis of these "facts," he then concludes that from about 1000 B.C. the Indians wandered from Armenia to Afghanistan, which was the scene of the Ṛgvedic period, and that it was only later that they were driven further towards India. Following a suggestion of H.Brunnhofer, he even assumes that the king Kānita

Pṛthuśravas[41] who is mentioned in the Ṛgveda is identical with a Scythian king Kānitas who is mentioned in a Greek inscription and on a coin, and who lived in the 2nd century B.C. This would mean that "the collection of these songs was not yet completed in the 2nd century B.C." This must surely be the very latest date every yet assumed as that of the Ṛgveda!

The strongest argument for a later dating of the Veda is undoubtedly the close relationship between the Veda and the Avesta with regard to language and religious views.[42] There are, however, very great differences to counteract the points of agreement in religion. Moreover the points of agreement can easily be explained, considering firstly that Indians and Iranians once formed one Aryan cultural unit at a pre-Vedic and pre-Avestic period, and secondly that they remained neighbours even after the separation. As regards the kinship of the languages, it is quite impossible to state definite chronological limits within which languages change. Some languages change very rapidly, others remain more or less unaltered for a long period.[43] It is true that hieratic languages, like those of the Vedic hymns and the Avesta, can remain unaltered much longer than spoken vernaculars.

Neverthelss, all that we know of the history of other languages and branches of languages compels us to say that languages do not remain unchanged for an indefinte number of millenia, let alone tens of thousands of years. For this reason, the fantastic figures of 16000 or even 25000 B.C.[44] as the date of the Veda, built up on the basis of astronomical or geological speculations, are absolutely impossible. Figures like this imply, too, that scarcely any cultural progress worthy of the name was made in the whole course of the overwhelmingly long aeon, which would be most surprising in the case of so talented a race as the Indians. These figures are impossible, too, because the continuity between the Vedic and the later brahmanical culture, which cannot be explained away especially as regards religion would then become utterly inexplicable. Moreover, classical Sanskrit, as fixed by Pāṇini in his Grammar more especially on the basis of the language of the Brāhmaṇas which still formed part of the Veda proper, and again the language of the inscriptions of King Aśoka in the third century B.C., show too close a relationship with the language of the Veda for it to be feasible that a stretch of so very many thousands of years lay between.

In summing up, we may say:

1. Attempts to determine the period of the Veda by the aid of *astronomy* come to grief owing to the fact that there are certain passages in the vedic texts which admit of various interpretations. However correct the astronomical calculations may be, they prove nothing unless the texts in question admit of an unambiguous interpretation.

2. The *historical* facts and hypotheses, such as the mention of Vedic gods in the cuneiform inscriptions, and the relationship of Vedic antiquity to the Āryan (Indo-Iranian) and Indo-European period, are so uncertain in themselves that the most divergent and contradictory conclusions have been drawn from them. Neverthless, we have now such likely evidence of relations between ancient India and western Asia penetrating as far west as Asia Minor in the second millenium B.C., that Vedic-culture can be traced back *at least* to the second millenium B.C.

3. The linguistic facts, the near relationship between the language of the Veda and that of the Avesta on the one hand, and between the Vedic language and classical Sanskrit on the other, do not yield any positive results;

4. They serve as a warning to us, however, to refrain from dating the Veda back to an inconceivable distant period on the strength of astronomical or *geological* speculations.

5. As all the external evidence fails, we are compelled to rely on *the evidence arising out of the history of Indian literature itself,* for the age of the Veda. The surest evidence in this respect is still the fact that Pārśva, Mahāvīra and Buddha pre-suppose the entire Veda as a literature to all intents and purposes completed, and this is a limit which we must not exceed. We cannot, however, explain the development of the whole of this great literature, if we assume as late a date as round about 1200 B.C. or 1500 B.C. as its starting-point. We shall probably have to date the beginning of this development about 2000 or 2500 B.C., and the end of it between 750 and 500 B.C. The more prudent course, however, is to steer clear of any fixed dates, and to guard against the extremes of a stupendously ancient period or a ludicrously modern epoch.

**Foot Notes:**

1.Cf. above p. 12
2.Weber: *Indische Literaturegeschichte,* p. 2, ff, 7.
3.Cf. above, p. 23 f.
4.*Physische Religion,* Gifford-Lectures delivered by F. Max Müller. Translated from English by R. O. Franke Leipzig, 1892 p. 86 f. English original *(Physical Religion)* pub. London, 1901, p. 91.
5.*Oriental and Linguistic Studies* First series, New York, 1872, p. 78.
6.*Indiens Literature und Kultur* p. 291 f.
7.Refer "Uber die Erwähnung von Sonnenfinsternissen im Ṛgveda". *(Sitzungsberichte der Königl. böhmischen Gesellschaft der Wessenschaften,* Prag 1885).
8. The lunar zodiac has remained in vogue in India till the present day beside the solar zodiac which has probably entered India only with the teachings of the Greek astronomers in the first century A.D. The question of the origin of this lunar zodiac and the relationship between the Indian nakṣatras, the Manāzil of the Arabs and the Sieou of the Chinese is still undecided. See especially A. Weber, Die vedischen Nachriachten von den Naxatra, 1, 2, *ABA* 1860, 1862; G. Thibaut, Astronomie (*Graundriss* III 9), pp., 12 ff; H. Oldenberg, Nakṣatra und sieou, *NGGW* 1909, 544 ff. Macdonell and Keith *Vedic Index,* I, 427 ff., plead for Babylonian origin, which F. Hommel (*ZDMG* 45, 1891, 592 ff) has tried to prove; but see B.V. Kamesvara Aiyar, *Ind. Ant.* 48, 1919, 95 ff.
9.A. Ludwig, *Der Rigveda* III, Prag, 1878, pp. 183 ff. and R. G. Bhandarkar, Report, 1883-1884, p. 39, have already pointed out the chronological significance of the Kṛttikās heading the list of the Nakṣatras in the Brāhmaṇas. But Bhandarkar places the Brāhmaṇas between 1200 and 900 B.C. Violent discussions were aroused by H. Jocobi's papers in *Festgruss an Rudolf von Roth,* Stuttgart, 1893, pp. 68-73, in *NGGW,* 1894, pp. 105-116, and in OC, X, Geneva, 1894, I, pp. 103-08, and the book of B.G. Tilak, *The Orion or Researches into the Antiquity of the Vedas,* Bombay, 1893. Cf. G. Bühler, *Ind. Ant.* 23, 1894, pp. 238 ff.; W. D. Whitney in *JAOS, Proceedings.* March

1894, (reprinted in *Ind. Ant.* 24, 1895, p. 361 ff.); G. Thibaut, *Ind. Ant. 24,* pp. 85 ff.; and Astronomie *(Grundriss* III, 9) pp. 18 f. A Barth, *JA* 1894, pp. 156 ff.; *Oeuvres* II, 248 ff.; A. Weber, *SBA* 1894, pp. 775 ff.; H. Oldenberg in *ZDMG* 48, 1894, pp. 629 ff.; 49, pp. 470 ff.; 50 pp. 450 ff.; Jacobi in *ZDMG* 49, pp. 218 ff.; 50 pp. 69 ff.; S. B. Dikshit in the *Ind. Anti.,* vol. 24, p. 245 f., E. W. Hopkins, *The Religions of India,* Boston and London, 1895, pp. 4 ff.; A. A. Macdonell, *History of Sanskrit Literature,* London, 1900, p.12.

10.*Festgruss an Roth,* p. 71 f.

11.*ZDMG.,* Vol. 50, p. 71.

12.Śat. Br. II, 1, 2, 3. See Oldenberg and Jacobi, *ZDMG.* 48, p. 631, note; 50, pp. 72 and 452. Sankar B. Dikshit (*Ind. Ant.* 24, 1895, pp. 245 f.), B. V. Kamesvara Aiyar (The Age of the Brāhmaṇas, in the *Quarterly Journal of the Mythis Society* 1922, and previously in *Proc, FOC* I, p. 1 ff., and Dhirendranath Mukhopadhyaya, The Hindu Nakṣatras, pp. 41 f. (Reprint from Vol. VI of the *Journal of the Department of Science,* Calcutta University, 1923), have concluded from this passage, that the Śatapatha-Brāhmana was written about 3000B.C.

13.This explanation is given by Professor A. Prey, the astronomer of the University of Calcutta, who informs that, in about 1100 B.C. the Pleiades rose approximately 13° to the north of the east point, approaching nearer and nearer the east line, and crossing it as late as 2 h 11 m after their rise, at a height of 29°, when seen from a place situated at 25° North latitude. They thus remain almost due east long enough to serve as a convenient basis for orientation. This interpretation of the passage is proved to be the correct one, by Baudhāyana-Śrautasūtra 27, 5 (cf. W. Caland, *Uber das rituelle Sūtra des Baudhāyana,* Leipzig, 1903, pp. 37 ff.), where it is prescribed that the porting beams of a hut on the place of sacrifice shall face the east, and that this direction shall be fixed after the Pleiades appear, as the latter "do not depart from the eastern region." It is true that, about 2100 B.C., or about 3100 B.C., the Pleiades touched the east line earlier, but they preceded southwards so rapidly that they were not suitable for orientation.

14. In the Śat. Br. XII, 8, 2, 35, it is said: "All seasons are the first, all are the intermediate, all the last."
15. Professor Prey believes that Groombridge 2001 and 2029, stars of the fifth to the sixth magnitude in Little Bear, the first of which approached the pole as far as 17' in about 1250 B.C., and the second of which approached the pole as far as 8' in 1500 B.C., are easily visible in view of the favourable atmospheric conditions of India.
16. *Indian Antiquary,* XXIII, 1894, p. 245 ff.
17. Bühler, *Ind. Ant.* 23, 1894, p. 247.
18. *ZDMG,* Vol. 49, p. 479.
19. Cf. above, p. 52 f.
20. Cf. Ludwig, *Der Rigveda,* III, p. 180 f.
21. The Vedic Concordance, *HOS,* Vol. 10, 1906; Rig-Veda Repetitions, *HOS,* Vols. 20 and 24, 1916; *JAOS* 29, 1908, p. 287 f.; 31, 1910, 49 ff.
22. Cf. above pp. 52, 54, 56 ff, 61 f, 67, 70 f, 95, 181 ff., 199.
23. That the texts have been written down, when one did not fully understand them any more and a break in the tradition had come, is explained to us also by the fact that such diverse pieces of varied content and of different times occur in all Vedic texts, that for example some Upaniṣads are found in the Saṃhitās and Brāhmaṇas. Cf. above p. 114,139 ff., 210.
24. Even the Aitareya Āraṇyaka presupposes the Ṛgveda-Saṃhitā with its division into ten books (Max Müller, *History of Sanskrit Literature,* P. 340 f.)
25. Cf. above p. 181.
26. Cf. above p. 218 ff.
27. Cf. Hopkins, *JAOS* 22, 336 n.; Rapson, *Ancient India,* p. 181.
28. *Die Lehre der Upanishaden und die Anfänge des Buddhismus,* pp. 288, 357.
29. It is noteworthy that the Buddhists, too, call their didactic texts "Sūtras", although these are by no means composed in the "Sūtra" style indicated above. They took "Sūtra" to mean "didactic text."
30. R. Garbe, too (*Beiträge zur indischen Kulturgeschichte,* pp. 27 ff.), is inclined to date the origin of the sect of the Bhāgavatas or Pañcarātras back to pre-Buddhist times.

31.Cf. ed. Meyer, *SBA* 1908, pp. 14 ff.; *Zeitschrift für vergleichende Sprachwissenschaft,* 42, 1909, pp. 1 ff.; *Geschichte des Altertums,* 2. Auflage, 1, 2, (1909) § 551, 574; H. Jacobi, *JRAS* 1909, 721 ff., 1910, 456 ff.; *Internal. Wochenschrifts,* 5, 1911, 387, A. B. Keith, *JRAS* 1909, 1100 ff.; 1910, 464 ff.; *Bhandarkar, Com, Vol.* pp. 81 ff. and *HOS.,* Vol. 18 Introd. (where the whole development of vedic literature is crammed in between 1200 and 350 B.C., see esp. pp. clxv f.); A. A. Macdonell in *Vedic Index* I, pp. viii f. and *ERE* 7, 1914, pp. 49 ff.: H. Oldenberg, *JRAS* 1909, 1095 ff.; 1910, pp. 846 ff.; L. De la Valleé Poussin, *Le Vedisme,* 3 iéme ed. Paris, 1909, pp. 29 f.; Winternitz, *Oesterreichische Monatschrift für den Orient,* 41, 1915 pp. 168 ff.; *Calcutta Review,* Nov., 1923. pp. 119 ff.; Sten Konow, *The Āryan Gods of the Mitani People* (Royal Frederik University Publications of the Indian Institute, Kristiania, 1921); F. E. Pargiter, *Ancient Indian Historical Tradition,* London, 1922, pp. 300 ff.; R. Giles, *Cambridge History of India,* I. pp. 72 f.

32.At least, nearly all scholars agree with Winckler (*Mitteilungen der Deutschen Orient-Gesellschaft* No. 35, 1907, p. 51, *s. Boghazköi-Studien* VIII Leipzig 1923, pp. 32 f., 54f.) that these names of gods have to be recognised in the following cuneiform text: ilani Mi-it-ra as-si-il ilfani U-ru-wa-na-as-si-e (inanother text: A-ru-na-as-si-il) In-dar (other text: In-da-ra) ilan Na-sa-at-ti-ya-as-na. Doubts against this identification have only been raise by J. Halevy in *Revue Semitique,* 16, 1908, pp. 247 ff.

33.H. Winckler (*Orientalist. Literaturzeitung,* 13, 1910, 289 ff.; *Mitteilunge der Vorderasiatischen Gesellschaft* 18, 1913, H. 4, pp. 75 ff.) even think that the Harri who in the inscriptions are mentioned as the ruling class Mitani are identical with these very "Āryans." But this is quite uncertain Cf. A. H. Sayce, *JRAS* 1909, pp. 1106 ff.

34.*NGGW,* Geschäftliche Mitteilungen, 1918, p. 91.

35.See A. Hillebrandt, *Aus Alt-und Neuindien,* Breslau, 1922, p. 1 ff and *ZII* 3, 1924, pp. 1ff who points out traces of relations to Western countries especially in the eighth Book of the Ṛgveda. For other views about the Aryan Indians in Asia Minor see R. G. Bhandarkar, *JBRAS* 25,

1918, pp. 76 ff., and E. Forster, Die Acht Sprachen der Boghazköi-Inschriften, *SBA* 1919, pp. 1036 f.

36. Konow suggests that the Nāsatyas are mentioned in the Mitani treaty on account of their playing a role in the ancient marriage-rites, because the treaty, following upon a war between the Hittite king Subbiluliuma and the Mitani king Mattiuza, was confirmed by a marriage of the later with the Hittite king's daughter. As this connection of the Aśvins with the marriage-ritual, however, occurs only in the late Sūrya sūkta, Konow concludes "that the extension of Indo-Āryan civilisation into Mesopotamia took place after the bulk of the Ṛgveda had come into existence" so that the oldest portions of the collection would "have to be considered as considerably older than the Mitani treaty." There is no force in this argument, as Indra and the Nāsatyau (Indranāsatyā) are invoked together in Rv. VIII, 26, 8, where they have nothing to do with marriage. K. Chattopadhyaya (*Calcutta Review,* May 1924, pp. 287 ff.) concludes from the mention of Vedic gods in the Boghazkōi treaties that between 2000 and 1500 B.C. there were several arrivals of Aryan peoples in Asia Minor at the same time when other Aryan tribes entered India from Central Asia and became known as Vrātyas. This chronological combination of the Vrātyas with the Indians in Asia Minor has no foundation in fact whatsoever, hence Mr. Chattopadhyaya's chronological conclusion (Brāhmaṇa period from 2000 B.C. to 1400 B.C., Yajurveda and Atharvaveda about 2000 B.C. and Ṛgveda before 3000 B.C.) are quite unfounded.

37. Cf. P. Jensen Indische Zahlwörter in Keilschrithittitischen Texten, *SBA* 1919, pp. 367 ff.

38. Gunther Ipsen (*Indogerman, Forschungen* 41, 1923, pp. 174 ff.; Stand und Aufgaben der Sprachwissenschaft, *Festschrift für W. Streiberg,* Heidelberg 1924, pp. 200 ff.), endeavours to prove that the Indo-European words for "copper", "cow", "star" were borrowed from the Sumerian, and not earlier than between 3000 and 2100 B.C. However, when we consider that the domestic cow and copper are among the most ancient of prehistoric finds, we shall hesitate to accept Ipsen's theory.

39. *Indogerman. Forschungen,* 41, 1923, p. 188; *Die Zeit*

*Zoroasters,* Leipzig, 1924; *Die Himmelstore im Veda und im Avesta,* Leipzig, 1924, pp. 7. f. A book by Hertel on the age and home of the Ṛgveda is announced, but has not yet been published. Zoroaster's date is still uncertain, but there are good reasons for placing him about 1000 B.C. See C. Clemen, *Die griechischen und lateinischen Nachrichten über die perisisiche Religion,* Giessen, 1920, pp. 11 ff.; H. Reichelt in *Festschrift für W. Streitberg,* pp. 282 f.

40. *Die Inder in Boghazköi, in Prace linguistycyzne ofiarowane Janowi Baudouinowi de Co urtenay* . . . Krakow 1921, pp. 151 ff.

41. Rv. VIII, 46, 21; 24. The story of this King Pṛthuśravas is one of the old tales which, like the Ākhyāna of Śunaḥśepa, were recited at the Puruṣa-medha, see Sānkhāyana-Śrautasūtra XVI, II, 23.

42. Thus A. A. Macdonell (*ERE.* Vol. 7, 1914, pp. 49 ff.) says, that "it seems impossible to avoid the conclusion that the Indians cannot have separated from the Iranians much earlier than about 1300 B.C."

43. Cf. A. C. Woolner (*Proc. FOC* I, pp. xvii.; II, p. 20 ff.) who rightly says "that as far as any philological estimates go, 2000 B.C. remains quite as possible as 1200 B.C. for the earliest Mantra." See also B. V. Kamesvara Aiyar, *Quarterly Journal of the Mythic Society* XII, 1, p. 4.

44. Refer also Abinas Chandra Das, *Rig-Vedic India,* I, Calcutta 1921 (see also *Calcutta Review,* March 1924, pp. 540 ff.) and D. N. Mukhopadhyaya, The Hindu Nakṣatras (reprinted from Vol. VI of *Journal of The Department of Science,* Calcutta University, 1923.)

# eleven

## THE VEDIC WORLD OF GODS AND DEMONS

### 1. Introductory

It is a commonplace of psychology that thinking is conducted under the pressure of practical needs[1]. Primitive man found himself in an environment partly helpful and partly untoward and perilous. There were all about him friendly objects and forces such as sunshine, rain, fire, dawn, rivers, etc. the very epithet 'friendly' applied above to 'objects' and 'forces' indicates incipient personification and shows the naturalness of the process. Then there were other forces which were hostile and perilous, such as drought, darkness and the mysterious causes of the blighting of crops, of disease, and of death. The friendly forces became gods and the hostile forces demons. All nature thus divided into friendly and hostile forces was regarded as an aggregate of animated entities[2]. This attitude of mind toward its environment began undoubtedly with the very first manifestation of the religious consciousness in the dim pre-historic past, and extended down far beyond the Vedic age. It is the well-known doctrine of animism, which has had such a wide sway in the early stags of manking, and forms in a sense the background of all our religions thinking. To ascribe life, will and agency to inanimate nature was just as natural for man in his childhood stage as it is for children to personify their play-things. Animism presented itself at the beginning as probably only a haunting sense of the mystery and potency of the world and its forces. This primitive attitude based on the experience of both harmful and helpful powers was made gradually more articulate through the interpretation of the powers of nature as animals (*theriomorphism*) or as men (*anthropomorphism*).

**2. Process of Personification**

The book which deals most fundamentally with this topic has already been mentioned[3]. Usener's main thesis is that the stage of 'personal gods' was preceded by that of 'special gods.' In the case of a 'special god'[4] the name of the thing is the name of the god, *e.g. dyaus* 'sky', *agni* 'fire', *Sūrya* 'sun', *Uṣas* 'dawn', *vata*, 'wind', etc. Furthermore, the province of a special god is limited to the sphere of activity indicated by his name, that is to say, Agni had to do originally only with fire, Vāta with wind, etc. The special god enjoyed only an incipient degree of personification. But "all the special god had the capacity of annexing the sphere activity of others"[5]. The more a special gods annexed the territory of his neighbours, and the more fully emancipated he became from his own 'primitive nature significance', the more completely personalized he was. Accordingly in the case, *e.g.* of Dyaus 'Heaven' and Pṛithivi 'Earth' the personification is very rudimentary, whereas *Varuṇa* and *Indra* are the most completely personalized gods of the Vedic pantheon. One reason was that the names Dyāus and Pṛithivi remained "transparent, meaning quite simply 'heaven' and 'earth'. Hence the personifying imagination was checked by their constant presence and obvious physical nature. It was not so with Varuṇa, Indra and the Aśvins, whole original physical basis had been almost or quite forgotten. In general, we may say, then, that the survival of the 'transparent' name of a god such as Agni 'god fire', Sūrya 'god sun', Uṣas 'goddess dawn', Vāta 'god wind', etc. prevents to a greater or less degree the full personification of the god. Even here, however, other influences work, so that the personification of Agni 'the priestly gods' *par excellence* is in some respects much more complete than that of Sūrya 'god sun'.

Usener's first stage is that of the 'special god'. The name of anything in nature or in culture which impressed primitive man as mysterious, haunting, potent for good or for ill, might be the starting point of a process of personification[6]. This tendency to ascribe specialization of function to the gods, a tendency which Usener finds amply illustrated in the Litu-Prussian and ancient Roman religions is regarded by Schrader[7] as a primitive Indo-European characteristic. It is a fruitful cause of the tendency to create what Hillebrandt aptly calls 'mythological synonyms'[8], a tendency which is well represented in the Ṛigveda. Just as verbal synonyms are words which have much the same significance, while each possesses its own special shade of meaning; so 'mythological synonyms' are gods which in general are in charge of the same department of nature or life, while each one has his own special physical basis, distinguishing characteristic and theopanic moment. Thus, according to the Ṛigveda, we have as gods of the sky, Dyaus and Varuṇa (?); as gods of the sun, Sūrya, Mitra (?), Savitar, Pūṣan, Viṣṇu, etc.; as gods of the lightning and the storm, Indra, Tṛita Aptya, Apām Napāt, Mātarisvan, Ahi Budhnya, Aja Ekapād, Rudra and the Maruts; as priestly, and sacrificial gods, Agni and Bṛihaspati. Usener[9] points out the minute 'division of labour' which existed in the same department (*e.g.* agriculture) among the Roman and the Lithuanian gods, and by the same analogy was later extended to the Lithuanian Church saints. According to Varro's account[10] every separate fact and process of agriculture, *e.g.* first, second and third ploughing, dragging, sowing, growth, blossoming, etc. was under the care of a special deity. So also with the Lithuanians *e.g.* in the matter of cattle raising. Even after Lithuanians were christianized the same primitive tendency asserted itself in the form of a minute specialization of the functions of their numerous parton saints; *e.g.* in the department of healing Apollonia curing toothache, Augustinus warts, Its headache, Deicolus cramps and Eutropius dropsy. A similar tendency may be invoked to help explain the 'mythological synonyms' of the Ṛigveda[11]. The sky is the home of light by day (*Dyaus*) and by day and night is all-encompassing (*Varuṇa*). The sun has many distinguishable aspects and functions. It is a bright orb (*Sūrya*), a light-giving friendly power of nature (*Mitra*), a great stimulator of life and activity (*Savitar*), a nourisher and protector of cattle, shepherding them and finding them when lost (*Pūsān*), wide-striding from earth through mid-air to zenith, 'he of the three steps' (*Viṣṇu*), and the one who at dawn shines in every dirction (*Vivasvant*). The function of the gods of the lightning and the storm are similarly differentiated. Thus the lightning fighting to release the cows of the sky manifests itself as an impetuous warrior (*Indra*); it is the third or aerial form of fire dwelling in the clouds (*Tṛita Aptya*); it is born of the heavenly waters (*Apam Napat*); it grows in the mother cloud and brings fire down from heaven to earth (*Matarisvan*); it looks like a serpent in the lower atmosphere (*Ahi Budhnya*); it leaps down from the cloud-mountains in a single streak of fire like a 'one-footed goat' (*Aja Ekapad*); it strikes the earth, shatters trees and kills animals and men (*Rudra*); accompanied by thunder, wind and rain, it manifests itself in numerous lightning flashes (*Maruts*)[12].

The formation of such 'special gods', each originally with delimited province and function, was not confined to the Indo-European or even the Indo-Iranian period. There were plenty of such creations in the Ṛigveda, as, *e.g.* (1) the abstract agent gods, *Savitar* 'stimulator', *Dhatar* 'creator', *Vidhatar* 'disposer', *Dhartar* 'supporter', *Trata*r 'protector', *Netar* 'leader', *Tvaṣṭar* 'artificer', and *Visvakarman* 'all-creating', (2) compounds in pati[13] 'lord', as *Prajapati* 'lord of creatures', *Bṛihaspati* 'lord of prayer', *Vastaspati*

(VV. 54) 'lord of the house', *Ksetrasya pati* 'lord of the field' (VII 57, 1), and perhaps some others, of the same formation[14]; (3) the abstract goddesses *Sraddha* 'faith', *Anumati* 'favour', *Aramati* 'devotion', *Sānṛita* 'bounty', *Asuniti* 'spirit-life' and *Nirritti* 'decease' or the goddess of death; probably also *Aditi* and *Diti*; (4) the wives of the great gods as *Indrani*, *Agnaya*, *Varunnani* and *Asviri*; (5) deified objects connected with the ritual, as *Gravan* 'press-stone for crushing the soma-plant', Apas 'sacrificial waters mixed with Soma, *Ghṛita* 'sacrificial oil' (IV. 58), *Barhis* 'the sacrificial litter' upon which the gods sit (I. 13, 5), *Yupa* (*Vanaspati*) 'the sacrificial post', to which the victim was bound (I. 13, 11), and Dakṣiṇa 'largess', the deified fee of the priest (I. 18, 5), etc., etc.; (6) the deified implements and objects of agriculture[15] such as *Laṇgala* 'plough' *Sunāsira* 'plough-share', *Urvara* 'plough-land', Sita 'furrow', etc.; and (7) the deified weapons of war, Bow, Arrows, Quiver, Car, etc. (VI. 75).

It is obvious that such gods whose designations are merely appellative, the name of the god being the name of the thing or concept, would in general be inconspicuous and shortlived, never attaining to the dignity of the 'great gods', unless they represented some dominant aspect of nature, as *Agni* 'fire', or were fundamentally important in the ritual of worship, as *Agni* and *Soma*, or were caught on the tide of a new and growing conception, as *Prajapati*. We have already quotes Schrader's statement that 'all the special gods had the capacity of annexing the sphere of activity of others' (ERE. 11. 35). When thus annexed, many 'special gods' undoubtedly became merely epithets of one or other of the great gods, their entire being having been absorbed[16]. Such annexation was doubtless furthered by the principle of congruity. In general, harmonious elements would attach themselves, *e.g.* to Varuṇa the 'holy' god, that is attributes corresponding to his nature; and in like manner Rudra in his development would attract to himself such semi-domonic qualities as were akin to his original character as probably the destructive aspect of lightning[17], such qualities for example as are celebrated in the *Satarudriya* litany[18], and such as have made him in the Yajurveda period the god of diseases[19], as well as of healing.

Doubtless other factors also co-operated in the making of the gods. The Aryan tribes brought with them from their earlier home beyond the Hindu Kush a fairly elaborate mythology and cult, as may be seen at a glance by referring to the table of Vedic-Avestan equivalents[20]. Probably, too, the Aryan tribes came in at different times covering a period possibly of centuries. At any rate, we know there were different tribes and different priestly families, each tribe and priestly family probably having its own special beliefs and rites in addition to the things held in common. These condition would naturally produce a multiplicity of gods and rites of worships, which would tend to become common property. As Hillebrandt[21] well puts it, Vedic mythology is not a system, but a conglomerate, a kind of mythological 'confusion of tongues', which arose through the coming together and fusion of the traditions of different clans.

With the changes geographical, climate and ethnological there would naturally be changes in the gods themselves, reflecting as they did the changing environment and experiences of the Aryan tribes. Accordingly, like earthly rulers, one god would increase his domain at the expense of another, or himself be despoiled of some or all of his attributes. Thus Varuṇa, the majestic god of the Ṛigveda, became later a night-god and finally only a god of lakes and pools, so completely did he lose his sublime attributes of holiness and sovereignty. After having been one of the most completely personalized gods of the Ṛv., he is gradually depersonalized and de-ethicised, until his final estate is like his first, that of a 'special god' in charge of a limited province of nature. This illustration brings out the fact that, like the sun, the Vedic gods have their times of rising and setting. They appear above the horizon, go on waxing until they reach the zenith of their influence, then begin to wane in importance, and finally reaching 'the twilight of the gods' pass away for ever. The gods of the Ṛigveda are all to be found somewhere within these various stages. Indra, Agni and Soma are at the Zenith. Varuṇa has just passed the zenith. Vivasvant and Tṛita are distinctly waning gods. Prajāpatri, the chief god of the Brahmaṇas, is just appearing above the horizon. Viṣṇu and Rudra (Siva), destined to such a distinguished career extending even to modern times, have not yet reached the zenith of their influence.

The Vedic gods, then, have varying degrees of personification, extending all the way from that, for example of *Śraddha*[22] 'faith', which at least in the Ṛv. is little more than a poetic symbol or at most a candidate for the honours of full apotheosis, on to that of Varuṇa and Indra, the most completely personalized of all the gods of the Ṛigveda. If, as already stated, the more a god enlarged the sphere of his activity and emancipated himself from the limitations of his original nature as a 'special god', the more completely personalised he became, then it follows logically that complete personification would be attained only in a condition of monotheism, when one God had taken to himself the attributes and functions of all gods[23].

The various stages of personification existed side by side. If some gods were waxing, others were waning. If some were passing below the horizon others were rising above the horizon. The 'special god' were capable creation at any time[24]. It was through the birth of new special gods that the loss through the passing of the old gods was made good.

### 3. Gods and Demons

The Vedic gods as we have seen, are equally true of the Vedic demons. The contrast between god and demon is not so much one of power, for the demons also are strong, as of benevolent; the demons, as a rule, malevolent and injurious. The psychology of this distinction is not difficult to discern. The activities of nature are partly helpful and partly noxious. A beneficial force or activity like fire or water or wind, when personified, becomes a god. Injurious activities or experiences such as drought, blasting of crops, darkness, illness, etc. are personified as demons. It was seen that the thunderstorm by producing a vast downpour of rain destroys the drought. What more natural than to think of a struggle between Indra the storm-god and Vṛitra the withholder of the rain. In the fight Indra pierces with his bolt *Vala*, the 'cave' where the cows of the sky are confined, and slays Vṛitra the 'obstructor', thus releasing the waters. The whole imagery is reminiscent of cattle-lifting. As thieves carried off cattle and hid them in the caverns of the mountains, so Vṛitra 'obstruction', then more concretely conceived as 'obstructor' carried off the cloud-cows and hid them in a cave. The 'cave' itself, *Vala*, becomes in time personified as a cave, demon. In a time of drought, when the heavens were as brass and no clouds were visible, the conclusion was that the cloud-cows had been stolen. This is but one example of how cosmic phenomena were interpreted after the analogy of, and in terms of, human experience.

Such is the most probably origin of gods and demons, at least in the Indo-European world. The concept 'gods' was distilled as it were, from the contemplation of the gracious and kindly powers of nature[25], and in the same way the concept 'demons', from the experience of nature's grim and hostile forces. The psychology of the whole process is found in the working of the principle of analogy. Man naturally gave an anthropomorphic interpretation to the physical powers and phenomena in the midst of which he was placed, by finding in his own nature as man the key to their interpretation. As there was a human race (*manusajana*) so over against and above it there was a heavenly or divine race (*daivyajana*), which was suggested by the human race. And as the human race for the Vedic Indians was divided into Aryans and Dasyus mutually hostile to each other, so the superhuman powers incarnate in sun, lightning, storm, dardness, drought, desease, death, etc., were divided by analogy into gods and demons. The correspondence between Dasyu and Demon was so close that the same term 'Dasyu' covered both human enemies and superhuman enemies, producing frequently considerable uncertainty in interpretation.

It has already been pointed out that there was a considerable development of demonlogy[26] in the Indo-Iranian period, together with corresponding magic practices. Words for 'ghost', 'demon' and 'evil spirit'[27] were in use before the breaking up of the Indo-Iranian unity. Hence the Aryans brought with them into India a belief in demons as well as in gods. The Ṛigveda as devoted to the worship of the higher gods gives relatively little attention to the demons, that is, the Ṛv. as contrasted with the Atharvaveda and the Brāhmanas. The great atmospheric demon is Vṛita[28] from whom comes indra's cult name *Vṛitrahan* 'slayer of Vṛitra'. There are other atmospheric demons such as *Susna*[29] 'scorcher' or 'hisser', *Sambara*, *Pipru Varçin*, etc., although some of these may have been aboriginal chiefs or aboriginal gods. In the Ṛigveda Indra as the powerful atmospheric god purges his own domain of the demons of the air. What is often described is the single combat between Indra and Vṛitra after the fashion of a Homeric struggle between two champions. The *Raksasas*, as earth demons, are driven off by Agni the fire-god of earth, whose cult name accordingly is *Raksohan* 'slayer of Raksas'. Thus Indra and Agni, gods respectively of lightning and fire, are the great antagonists of the demons of darkness. Of the three domains, heaven mid-air and earth, the demons are confined to the last two. They do not intrude upon the heavenly abode of the gods and the glorified 'fathers'. The demons are referred to by a variety of group names, as *Dasyus*, *Panis* 'niggards', *Raksasas* 'injurious' or 'to be guarded against', *Druhas* 'deceivers', *Aratis* 'illiberalities', *Yatus* 'demons', *Yatudhanas* 'sorcerers', and *Asuras*, the standing designation for the demons in the later Vedic literature. According to the Ṛv. the numerous demons are smitten either singly or collectively by some one or other of the great gods, who is always victorious. This way of stating the case seems to be a reflection of the successful and optimistic character of the Ṛigveda period. Later on it is no longer a conflict between single god and demon or demons, but between the collective Davas being often worsted in the fight. Does this reflect the more difficult climatic conditions and consequently more pessimistic outlook of life further cast in the Ganges valley?

4. **Specimen of Vedic Demonology.**—While, as already stated the Ṛigveda is chiefly concerned with the mythology and worship of the great gods, it nevertheless incidentally through many a vivid phrase as well as through two entire hymns throws light, all the stronger because undesigned, upon the demonology of the Vedic age. In order to bring forward the matter concretely, the hymn, VII. 104 is presented in a metrical version with now and then a phrase adopted from Griffith.[30]

**To Indra-Soma VII. 104 (AV. VIII. 4).**

1. O Indra Soma, burn, destroy the *Raksasas*.
Thrust down, ye strong ones, those that flourish in the dark,
Annihilate the fools, consume them utterly,
Smite, thrust and overthrow the greedy Atriṇas.

2. O Indra-Soma, 'gainst the sinner and his sin
Let heat boil up like kettle glowing with the flame;
Against prayer-hating raw flesh-eating dreadful-eyed
Kimdin, deep hostility, unceasingly.

3. O Indra-Soma, plunge the evil-doers down
Into the pit, the gloom profound and bottomless,

So that not one of them may ever thence emerge;
Such wrathful strength and might be yours to conquer them.

4. O Indra-Soma, Hurl your weapon from the sky
And earth, your weapon crushing the mailgnant one;
From the cloud-mountains forge a whizzing thunder bolts;
Wherewith ye may consume the waxing Raksas foe.

5. O Indra-Soma, shoot ye forth from out the sky,
With your fire-heated sling-stones, heavenly thunder bolts;
With glewing darts unfailing hurl the Atrinas
Down the abyass, and let them into silence sink.

6. On all sides, Indra-Soma, may this song of ours
Beset you both, as girth surrounds two mighty steeds,
Which song as offering I with wisdom send to you,
These prayers, O lords of men, do ye inspire and speed.

7. Remind yourselves in your effective manner,
Smite the *Druhas* and *Raksasas*, the tricky ones;
No, bliss be to the wicked, Indra-Soma,
Whoso at any time against us plots with guile.

8. Whoso accuses me of walking falsely,
With lying words, although my heart is guileless,
May such a liar come to naught, O Indra,
Like water which in shut hand seized escapeth.

9. Those who the good man's speech delight to slan der,
And those whose habit is to harm the righteous,
May Soma hand them over to serpent,
Or to the lap of Nirriti consign them.

10. Whatever one, O Agni, tries to injure
The substance of our food, steeds, kine or persons,
May such thief, robber, trickster go to ruin
Sink to destruction both himself and children.

11. May he be taken off himself and children,
Under all three earths let him lie imprisoned;
May his fair glory, gods dry up and wither,
He who by day or night desires to harm us.

12. Good wit is his who has discrimination
Truth and untruth, both words oppose each other;
Of these twain what is true and what is upright
That indeed Soma helps, untruth he smiteth.

13. Never aids Soma him whose ways are crooked,
Nor him who falsely claims the Ksatriya title;
He smites the Raksas, smites the falsehood – speaker,
Both lie entangled in the snare of Indra.

14. Is it that I to false gods was devoted,
Or held the gods as a delusion, Agni?
Why art thou angry with us, Jātaveḍas?
Deveivers shall experience thy destruction.

15. Let me at once die, if I practice witchcraft,
Or have oppressed the life of any mortal;
Likewise may he be severed from ten kinsmen,
The one who falsely calls me wichraft- monger.

16. Who calls me witch, me innocent of witchcraft,
Who claims he's pure, although himself a Rakṣas;
May Indra smite him with his mighty weapon,
May he fall down the lowest of all beings.

17. What owl-like creature cometh forth at night-time,
With trickery and guile herself concealing ,
May she plunge into bottomless abysses;
May press-stones with their clatter smite the de
mons.

18. Spread out and search among the clans, O Marut
host,
Seize ye the Rakṣaṣ and crush, them utterly
Who fly about at night-time in form of birds,
Or at the worship of the gods display their tricks.

19. Indra. hurt forth from heaven thy stony weapon,
Maghavan, sharpen it, made sharp by Soma;
In front, behind, and from above and under,
Smite thou the Rakṣasas with rocky missile.

20. These fly about in form of demon-dogs and seek,
Harm-lovers they, Indra to harm, whom none can hurt
Sakra mades sharp his weapon for the slanderers;
Now at the witchcraft-monger may he hurl his stone.

21. Indra is the destroyer of the Yātu-fiends,
Distrubers of the sacrifice with aim malign;
Now verily 'gainst the Rakaṣasas doth Sakra go
As axe against a wood, like vessels splitting them.

22. Smite the owl-fiend and owlet-fiend, O Indra,
Dog-fiend, or him who comes in guise of cuckoo,
The fiend in form of eagle or of vulture,
As with a mill-stone crush to every Rakśas.

23. Let not the demon of the sorcerers near us come,
With light may (Agni) drive *Kimidins* off in pairs;
Let earth protect us well from every earthly woe,
Mid-air deliver us from such as comes from heaven.

24. O Indra, buffet the male *Yātudhāna*,
The female also boasting of her magic;
Neck-broker, may the *Mūradevas* perish,
And see no more the sun as he arises.

25. Look straight ahead, look on each side,
Indra and Soma, watch ye both;
Your weapon hurl against the friends
Against the sorcerers your stone.

This hymn in addressed principally to Indra and Soma, to Indra as the great demon-slaying god of the atmoshphere, and to Soma as the deified sacrificial drink by which Indra was strengthened and exhilarated for his tasks. It is probably a late hymn, standing as it does at the end of Book

VII; quite likely, too, it is composed of several fragments originally distinct, which differ in metre and (a more important consideration) in thought. Very similar to it in spirit is X. 87[31].

**The following comments are made:**

(a) We may recall Hillebrandt's observation[32] that whatever excites the imagination and awakens fear or joy, and whatever moves the spirit in dream or waking hours, will or at least can become the starting point for a god or demon. Accordingly almost every Vedic demon can be traced back to the experience of something either hurtful or uncanny, that is, to the actual experience of cold, darkness, drought, disease, etc. or to the tendency to people the dark with ghostly and uncanny creatures and in general to find for every unhappy experience a demonic origin. As human troubles and calamities are multitudinous, so are the demons that cause them. As stated above, some demons are reflection of physical ills, while others are creatures of the imagination postulated as causes to account for mental ills. A Vedic demon was the embodiment, then, of every fear and dread, of every illness and calamity as well as of every physical evil such as cold, drought, etc. that bests mankind. A demon in the hymn under consideration is called in general *raksas*[33] or *yātu*[34].

(b) From rakṣas 'demon' there was formed raksas 'sorcerer' by shifting the accent to the last syllable. And from *yatu* were formed a number of words also meaning 'sorcerer[35]. Thus there was a close connection between demons and sorcerers. They were hand in glove with each other. The demon was apparently thought of as entering the sorcerer as a familiar spirit, and the sorcerer used the demon for his purposes[36]. Hence in some passages there is little or no distinction between the demon who dwells in the sorcerer and the sorcerer who is indwelt by the demon. The sorcerers were the 'sensitives' or 'mediums' of the Vedic age.

(c) The demon are described as 'devourers[37] eating raw flesh[38], the flesh of men[39] as well as of cattle and horses. They flourish in the dark (v. 1). They delight to injure the sacrifice[40]. Demons and sorcerers are alike in the ethical quality. They are fools[41], haters of prayer (v. 2), evil-doers (vv. 3, 7), tricky (v. 7; X. 87, 22), false accusers and slanderers[42] (vv. 8, 9, 20), thieves and robbers (v. 10), liars (vv. 8, 13, 14-16), and malicious[43]. Ethically this is a notable statement of the close relationship existing between evil sprits and evil men. The son of lying is specially emphasized.

(d) The demons are lovers of darkness and accordingly often appear in the form of night-birds such as owls, or in the form of dog, cuckoo, vulture, eagle, etc. creatures with strange uncanny cries; or even in the form of the roots of plants used for proposes of sorcery[44]: They are both male and female demons being much more prominent in the demon world than are goddesses in the aristocratic world of the great gods[45]. They are dreadful-eyed (v. 2) and cloven-hoofed[46]. The Kimidins go about in pairs[47], but in the two great hymns under consideration[48] the names for 'demon' and 'sorcerer' are usually in the plural.

(e) Agni, the sacrificial fire of earth and Indra the lightning fire of the mid-air, are the natural enemies of the demons of darkness. Hence with an ample use of synonyms they are besought to smite, crush, pierce, burn, destroy, annihilate, etc. their demon foes. Doubtless there is a reference to the cosmic conflict between light and darkness, but already in the two great 'demon' hymns of the Ṛv. there is mingles with the literal meaning of darkness the metaphorical meaning of evil and sin. The demon who roam about at night and seek to spoil the sacrifice and injure good people are lovers of darkness both literally and figuratively. As is their, nature so is their doom. Their place is the bottomless pit of darkness,[49] an abyss, a covert or hole having no end.[50] Into this they are hurled by the fiery bolts of Indra.[51] The imagery is Miltonic and reminds one of Paradise Lost. The demon go to their own place. By implication all who are akin to the demons in character go to the same place. There is here an implicit doctrine of hell.

(f) In both VII. 104 and X. 87 there is a distinctly ethical element. Good men take the side of Agni and Indra, the gods in whom is 'no darkness at all', against the demons of darkness and the evil men who are their confederates. The ethical antithesis between light and darkness, truth and untruth[52] is firmly drawn. And yet both hymns were used as spells or charms, certainly as incorporated in the Atharvaveda and possibly as originally very late hymns of the Ṛv. It shows the close connection that existed in Vedic India between the prayer that persuaded the gods and the magic that compelled them. The difference in the point of view of prayer and magic is somewhat uncertain and subjective. What for one was *brahman* 'prayer' might be for another *brahman* 'spell'. This ambiguity in the meaning of *brahman* 'sacred formula'[53] illustrates the subtle intermingling of both points of view in the hymns and ritual of Vedic age. What is certain is that the magical conception of brahman was on the increase, culminating finally in the magical theory of sacrifice as held in the Brāhmaṇa period, when the sacrifice in its potency was everything and the gods were little or nothing.

## 5. Father Dyaus and his Children the Devas

The conception of a heavenly clan with *Dyāus*[54] as head began, as we have seen[55], in the Indo-European period, extended through the Indo-Iranian period[56], and appears in a faded and vanishing form in the Vedic age. Dyāus 'Heaven' is celebrated in six hymns in conjunction with *Prithivi* 'Earth', the two appearing in the dual compound DyavapṚithivi 'Heaven and Earth'. Dyāus apart from PṚithivi has not a single hymn in his honour, in this respect falling behind the lady Earth, who is celebrated alone in one hymn. As specimens of Vedic thought concerning these oldest of the gods there are here presented metrical translation of Ṛv. VII. 53 and I. 160.

**To Dyàus-Prithivi, VII. 53**

1. With sacrifice devotedly I worship
   The Heave and Earth, adorable and mighty;
   For ancient sages praising them have given
   Pre-ominence to them, whose sons are *Devas*.
2. Bring these two parents ancient-born for worship,
   With newest praise-songs, to the seat of Ṛita.
   Come, Heaven and Earth, with all the heavenly people
   Hither to us, for great is your protection.
3. Full many are your treasures to be granted,
   O Heaven and Earth, to every liberal giver[57].
   To us may what you grant be not deficient;
   Ye gods, with welfare evermore preserve us.

**To Dyāus-Prithivi, I. 160.**

1. These two, indeed, the order-observing Heaven and Earth,
   To all beneficent, support the mid-air's sage;
   Between the fair-creating hemispheres divine
   Goes the resplendent sun according to fixed law.
2. The twain, far-reaching, mighty, inexhaustible,
   Father and mother like, all creatures guard and keep,
   Like two most proud fair women are the Heaven and Earth
   Because the Father has in beauty them arrayed.
3. Conductor, purifier, son of two parents, he,

The sage, by occult power all creatures purifies;
From out the speckled earth-cow and the heavenly bull,
The rich in seed, he always milks the shining fluid.

4. Of all the active gods most active is that one
On us, O Heaven and Earth, and lofty governance;
Such strength as worthy is of all praise brings to us,
Whereby o'er all the peoples we may ever spread.

Heaven and Earth bear exclusively the characteristic epithet *devaputre*, 'they whose sons are gods'[58], and they are bestought to some to 'the seat of *ṛita* or sacrifice along with their children, who constitute the heavenly clan[59]. They are parents[60] of Agni in his sun or lightning form[61]. In their majesty and beauty they are like two proud fair women. As parents they protect all creatures and bestow treasures, fame and dominion.

The conception of the parenthood of Heaven and Earth is very ancient and widespread, being found in the mythology of many peoples[62]. In the Ṛv. the picture which the hymns conjure up before us in that of Father Dyāus bending down in love over Mother Earth and bestowing his seed in the form of rain by which the earth is fertilized and made fruitful. In VI. 70, 1-5 rain is probably referred to under the figures of ghee, honey and mild.

Reference has already been made to the equation *Dyauspitar*[63] = A.D.=*Ζευ παιερ Jupiter*, as probing the existence of the conception of Father Heaven in the IE. period.[64] Zeus and Jupiter were the heads respectively of the Greek, and Roman pantheon. They were no mere 'departmental' deities, but were enriched and thoroughly personalized through the annexation of departments of activity which did not originally belong to them, especially that of the thunderstorm. They were no longer gods merely of the bright shining sky. Dyāus, as he is pictured to us in the Ṛv.

is very inadequately personalized. For one thing his name Dyāus 'sky' and 'day' was very transparent, perhaps somewhat more transparent than Zeus and Jupiter, and as regards gender Dyāus was both masculine and feminine. Then too, the most exalted moral attributers, as we shall see, had been appropriated by Varuṇa, while Indra and certain other gods almost monopolized the thunderstrom. Hence Dyāus and PṚithivi are in the Ṛv. little more than conventional figures, mythological fossils, as it were, which possibly bear witness to a time when the conception of Father sky was taken more seriously than it was in the Vedic age. The fact that the Vedic Dyaus is a waning god does not necessarily prove that he had never been in the ascendant.[65]

We have already noticed that the chief anthropomorphic trait of Dyaus is fatherhood. But even this characteristic of Dyāus is not take very seriously in the Ṛv. In 1. 160, 4, Heaven and Earth, the universal parents, are spoken of as themselves begotten or created, and the suggestion is thrown out that the one who begot them must have been the most active and skilful of all the active gods, and in v. 2 mention is made of the Father of heaven and earth who arrayed them in beauty. Hence, in the Ṛv. at least, fatherhood was little more than a 'fluid and shifting' conception which (within certain limits, of course) could be ascribed rather miscellaneously according to the fancy of the individual poet. Anything within the sphere of heaven and earth might be called their child. There were other relationships also which suggested fatherhood, such as antecedent in relation to consequent, head of a group in relation to the members of a group, etc.[66]

The IE. conception of Father Sky and his children the 'shining ones', after all necessary abatements have been made, remains still a very significant one. It means, as we have seen[67], that the heavenly powers and phenomena, such as sun, moon dawn, lightning, rain, etc., were already conceived anthropomophically after the analogy of an earthly family. Heaven and earth, which are always with us, and within whose sphere the various phenomena come and go, were very naturally conceived as father and mother. They are the primeval parents, the 'ancient-born,[68] since their existence, as we would say, is the presupposition of everything else. The phenomena which come and go within the sphere of heaven and earth are, with equal naturalness for the primitive mind, called children of heaven and earth. The significant thing in all this is the analogy which holds between earthly clan and heavenly clan. Bergaigne's[69] constructive principle in his study of Vedic religion is the analogy which he thinks holds between heavenly phenomena and the Vedic sacrifice, the latter being interpreted by him as an imitation of the former. Whether this principle be true or not, it is certain that the conception of Father Sky and his children the Devas is the reflection of human society. The devas are often refereed to in the Ṛv. as a heavenly clan, generation, tribe, nation, race[70], standing over against the human race[71]. The parallel is very complete. In most cases the singular or dual is used, but sometimes the plural is used of the gods as well as of men[72], thereby indicating perhaps that the gods as well as men are split up into groups.

The gods may be grouped according to several principles of division. As in Hebrew thought heaven and earth embrace the universe, so in Vedic thought they are the two world-halves[73] that comprehend everything. Within this scheme there are three levels, heaven, mid-air, and earth[74], for which there are thirty-three[75] gods, eleven apparently for each different level. This is the oldest classification, being found in the Ṛv. itself. The human race is bisected into males and females. By analogy the divine race will have the same division, and so there are goddesses as well as gods. The goddesses may be sub-divided into three groups: (a) those having a natural basis, as Uṣas 'Dawn', *Sarasvati* the deified 'Saravati', river, *Prithivi* 'Earth', *Ratrí* 'Night', *Prisni* the 'mottled' storm cloud and *Vac* 'Speech'[76] (b) abstract feminine nouns personified as goddesses, *e.g. Puramdhi* 'Plenty', *Ila* 'Nourishment', *Dhisana* 'abundance', etc.; (c) goddesses as wives of the great gods, as *Indrani, Varuṇani* and *Agnayi*. The great gods are furnished with wives in order to make the parallel between the human race and the divine race complete. No public functions are ascribed to them. They are 'house-wife' deities, Mistress Indra, Mistress Varuṇa, Mistress Agni. This detail may be taken as reflecting the attitude of the Ṛigvedic age as regards the proper sphere and function of marries women.

Again, the human race is broken up into small groups. By analogy the divine race will have similar groups, *e.g. Ādityas, Vasus, Rudras*, the semi-divine *Aṅgirasas*, and among the lower deities the *Ṛibhus, Apsarasas* and *Gandharvas*, and finally *Visvedevah* 'all-gods', a term designed to cover them all. As a tribal chieftain is represented as the head of his tribe, so Agni is the head of the *agnis* 'fires', Soma of the *somas* 'soma drops', Rudra of the rudras 'lightning flashes' (?) and Uṣas of the *Uṣasas* 'dawn gleams'.

The gods may be divided according to function. As in Vedic society there were priests, warriors and commons, so among the gods Agni and Bṛihaspati were priests, Indra and the Maruts warriors, Tvaṣṭar and the *Ribhus* artizans. The agricultural community, whether Vaisyas or Sūdras, had special agricultural deities such as *Kristrapati*[77] 'lord of the field', *Uravara* 'she of the ploughland', Sitā 'she of the furrow', and perhaps Pūṣan, the 'thirift'- god, guardian of flocks and herds.

We may also classify the gods according to certain great functions in which as groups, they share. There is the work of rain giving in which to a greater or less degree, Parjanya, Varuṇa, Indra, Dyaus, Rudra and the Maurts all participate. As gods of the lightning there are Indra, Tṛita Aptya, and so forth; as physician gods Rudra and ht Maurts, Varuṇa, Soma, Ašvins, Vāta and the Waters; as demon-slayers Agni and Indra and in general the gods of light; and as gods of song Bṛihaspati, the *Maruts* and the Aṅgirasas.

The so-called 'dual divinities, constitute the smallest groups of Vedic gods. The union of man and wife is the human analogy followed in the primeval conception of the marriage of Heaven and Earth. So compelling was this analogy that in harmony therewith the great Vedic gods had to be joined in wedlock, *e.g.* Indra with Indrani, Agni with Agnayi, Varuṇa with Varuṇani. There must also have been age. At any rate, after the analogy of *Dyaraprithivi* 'heaven and earth', a considerable number of male deities were joined together so as to form dual gods, *e.g. Mitra-Varuṇa* 'sunlight and sky', or possibly as Oldenberg and Hillebrandt think 'sun and moon', *Indra-Agni* 'lightning-flash and altar-fire', *Indra-Varuṇa* 'lightning flash and sky', *Indra-Vayu* 'lightning flash and storm-wind', *Indra-Soma* 'the drinking god and the drunken liquor', *Sarya-Masa* 'sun and moon', *Indra-Viṣṇu* 'lightning and sun', etc.; also one group of two female gods *Nakta-Uṣasa* 'night and dawn'. In the case of each dual divinity there is distinct contrast in the constitutive elements as well as close association of the same in sphere and function. The *Asvina* 'two horsemen' may also be mentioned here, since they are essentially dual gods, mening probably either 'morning star and evening star' or 'the twin-lights before dawn, half dark and half light[78]. In either case they are almost 'mythological synonyms' of 'night and dawn'.

Thus the whole 'clan of the devas' in conceived anthropomorphically after the analogy of human society. They wear ornaments of gold, ride in cars drawn by horses, and have house. They flight against the demons, as Aryans fight against the Dasyus. They are glorified Ksatriyas. Some gods are male, others are female. Indra, god of the lightning - flash and thunder-roll, is suitably represented as a man; Uṣas, the many-coloured dawn, as fair and richly-dressed woman. The gods are related together anthropomorphically. Examples of wedded gods have already been given. Some gods are represented as parents, *e.g. Dyāvā-Prithivi*, and others a children. Some are related as brothers and sister. Uṣas[79] is the daughter of Dyāus, the sister of Bhaga, the kinswoman of Varuṇa, and the wife (or mistress) or Sūrya. Night and Dawn are sisters. Agni[80] is the son of Dyāus and the brother of Indra. The principle of 'division of labour' exists among the gods. Each deity is in charge of some special aspects of nature or of life. While there is considerable overlapping of function, as explained in another place[81] yet on the whole the Vedic gods are 'departmental deities' although in some cases new and extensive function have been added in the course of time to their original tasks. As the members of a human clan act together and mutually support one another, so is it with the clan of the Devas. There is much mutual helpfulness and interchange of services among the gods, as is natural in a clan consisting of members related as husbands and wives, parents and children, brothers and sisters, etc., in general kinsmen, children of Heaven and Earth. Thus Varuṇa prepares a path for Sūrya (I. 24.8), and in turn Sūrya reports to Mitra and Varuṇa concerning the sinfulness of men (VII. 62, 2). Agni serves Indra, since Indra drinks Soma with the tongue of Agni (III. 35, 9-10) and Indra serves all the gods (includes Agni) by gaining the victory over Vṛitra and so giving freedom to the gods (III. 34, 7). Agni, too serves all the gods by acting as their messenger. The Maruts, who constitute the host of Indra, serve him as his soldiers (III. 35, 9). Tvaṣṭar fashioned the bolt of Indra and sharpened the metal axe of Bṛihaspati (V. 31, 4; X. 53, 9). Soma stimulates Indra to perform great cosmic deeds. Viṣṇu helps Indra in the fight with Vṛitra, etc., etc. The gods in general are thus conceived as living together in a state of harmony and mutual helpfulness. The only exception of importance is in the case of Indra, the violent and changeable weather god, the shift nature of whose tasks helps perhaps to excuse the note of discord which he sometimes introduces among the gods.

### 5. Common Characterstics of the Gods

As we have seen, the Vedic gods are a celestial folk, the clan of the shining ones. The members of the heavenly clan, as is natural, have a family resemblance one with another. Certain common features characterize them as a group. In the first place, they are all *Devas* 'bright heavenly ones', whose proper habitat is the sky[82] and proper nature light[83]. While the term *Asura* 'mysterious lord' is not explicitly applied to all the gods, yet in general it is not explicitly applied to all the gods, yet in general it is one of their epithets, emphasizing their 'mysterious' nature, which expresses itself through *maya* 'occult power'. In sharp contrast to mortal men the gods are described as '*immortal*'. As might be expected, brilliance is a common characteristic of the race of gods whole very nature is light. Since the Vedic gods in general preside over cosmical function, power is an attribute of them all. So with knowledge. Each god being in charge of special department must have knowledge and power adequate to his task. Beauty is commonly ascribed to the gods. As distinguished from the malevolent demons, the gods as a class are benevolent, and, on the whole, are unholders of moral order. The attributes of power, wisdom, beauty, benvolence and righteousness though possessed by all, are not possessed by all in same degree. Thus Uṣas, the lady 'Dawn', has more beauty than knowledge and strength; Indra, the warrior god, more strength than knowledge and righteousness. Of all the Vedic gods Varuṇa possess the best combination of physical and moral attibutes. Agni, as a priestly god, is well endowed with knowledge, Jatavedas 'knowing all generation' being his exclusive epithet.

The mutual relationship and mutual interchange of services that held among the Vedic gods have already been traced out with some detail. Every department of nature and of life is brought under the control of some deity. All the deities together function as a unity. The unity of the divine activity is not the unity of an individual will as in monotheism, but the unity formed by the collective will[84] of a clan, the clan of the devas. The multiplicity[85] of the Vedic gods reflects the multitudinous aspects of nature and of life; and the unity which, on the whole, pervades the diverse activities of the gods reflects, in like manner, the unity of nature, the fact that the universe is a cosmos, an ordered whole. One of the great conception of the Ṛigveda is that of *Ṛita* 'order, a conception which goes back to the Indo-Iranian period and the roots thereof to the IE. period. As the Greek and Roman gods are linked up with Fate (*Moira*, *Fatum*), so the Vedic gods are connected with *Ṛita*. 'Eternal Order'. The relation which the gods sustain to ṛita is variously stated. Heaven and Earth are called the ancient parents (*mātarā*) of *Ṛita* (VI. 17, 7), and in the same passage they bear the epithet devaputre 'whose sons are gods'. Heaven and Earth, then are parents of the gods and parents of ṛita. In other words, the devas, each in his own proper sphere, are *Ṛite*, express *Ṛita*, are guardians and cherishers of ṛita. For example, Uṣas is not independent of Eternal Order. She was born in *Ṛita* (ritejā I. 113, 12), and so her task is to cherish and protect it. She does not infringe the heavenly ordinances[87], the law of *ṛita*[88], but rather follows its rein (I. 123, 13), for day by day she returns to the place appointed. In the thought of *ṛita* being expressed by the daily recurrence of dawn we have the idea of the *uniformity* of *nature*. Of all the gods the two chief Ādityas, Varuṇa and Mitra, are most intimately connected with *ṛita*, so that what seems in some passages to be the work of *ṛita*, in others is referred to as the work of Varuṇa.

All the gods, then, are alike in either determining,[88] or expressing or guarding some aspects or other of *ṛita*, which may be translated as 'the course of things', 'nature', or 'cosmic order'. Through the great conception of *Ṛita* the multiplicity of nature is reduced to a unity and the multiplicity of the gods (corresponding to the multiplicity of nature) is seen to reflect a single will, because all are 'labourers together' in maintaining a single all-comprehensive cosmic order. Thus the tendency of Ṛigvedic religion was toward some form of unity, whether monotheistic or pantheistic.

**6. We may finally note the bearing of all this upon two recent theories of the Riveda:—**

(a) Max Müller's theory of '*Henotheism*'[89], namely 'the belief in individual gods alternately regarded as the highest'. We have seen that the gods from a heavenly 'caste'. All participate in deity. All possess in superabundant measure the qualities of power, sovereignty, wisdom, beneficence and beauty. Where there are so many gods, there must necessarily be considerable indefiniteness of outline; and, as we have seen, there is a tendency to the recognition of an underlying unity, and so the fusion. Hence the loftiest attributes might properly be ascribed to any and every deva, simply because he was a member of the 'clan of the devas', and because all alike participated in divinity. This did not simply in the least that a god thus addressed was regarded as the 'highest' in contradistinction all the rest, but simply that he had his full share of divinity. Of course, exaggerations, and inconsistencies are found in the Vedic hymns, but so are they in other religious literature[90]. Where there is more than one deity or divine perosn, it is difficult always to keep the right balance, especially when the one worshipped is an *ista devatā*.

Swāmi Dayānad Sarasvati's theory of '*Monotheism*' in the Ṛigveda. Taking his cue from the late passages Ṛv. I. 164. 46[91] and X. 114, 5[92] the founder of the Ārya Samāj held that all the gods mentioned in the Ṛv. are simply variant names for one god. This process of reduction from multiplicity of unity would have been easier, if there had been no dual gods or group gods mentioned in the Ṛv. It has apready been remarked that the tendency of Ṛigvedic polytheism was toward unity of some sort, either monotheistic or pantheistic. Swāmi Dayānand was not a pantheist. In reading into the Ṛigveda a monotheistic doctrine as opposed to pantheism, he virtually declares that instead of issuing in pantheism or at most in an unstable monotheism, Vedism ought to have issued in al clear-cut and definite monotheism. The monotheistic interpretation of the Ṛigveda involved on the part of Swāmi Dayānand much wild and unscientific exegesis. For this, however, we may be thankful that as between theism and pantheism Swāmi Dayānand took the side of theism.

**Foot Notes:**

1. Cf. James, *Psychology*. 1900, p. 358: "Reasoning is always for a subjective interest".
2. Macdonell, VM. 1.
3. Oldenberg, Ṛv. 39.
4. Usener, *Gotternamen*,.see above, p. 13.
5. Called by Usener 'Sondergott', op. cit. 75.
6. Schrader, Aryan Religion, ERE. II.
7. Cf. Hillebrandt, VII. III. p. Vii: Alles was die Einbildung erregt, Furcht, Frende crweckt, was den Geist im Traum oder Wachen bewegt, wird oder kann zum Ausgangspundte einer Gottheit oder "Damons werden", also Rhys Davids Buddhism (American Lectures), p. 12: "The gods were ideas, a rough kind of scientific hypothesis. The arrival of a new god meant the birth of a new ieda".
8. ERE. art. *Aryan Religion* 11.32.
9. VM. II. 12-13; III. p. XV.
10. *Gotternamen*, 75-122.
11. Baded largely on Roman *Indigatamenta*. See Art. by Wissowa in ERE. VII. 217-218.
12. Hillebrandt, VM. II. 14.
13. Macdonell, VM.; Keith. Indian Mythology.
14. Cf. Hillebradnt, VM. 11.19.
15. These names in *pati* might, so far as the form is concerned, belong to the Indo-European period. Compare the Greek 'lord of the house' and the Lithuanian *weisz-path* (= *Vispati*) 'lord of the clan'; also the Lithuanian divine names *Dimstipatis* 'lord of the house and home' (cf. Vedic *Dampati* 'house-lord' and *Stipa* 'household protector). *Raugupatis* 'lord of the leaven', Laukpatis 'lord of the field'. *Zemepatis* 'lord of the land' (Cf. Persian *zamin*), and the Litu-Prassian Wejo-patis 'lord of the wind'. Usener, *Gotternamen*, 89, 100, 105. There are many other names in *pati* in the Ṛv. such as *sadasaspati*, *gasapati*, *satpati*, *somapati*, *vanaspati*, *rathaspati*, *gathapati*, etc, but these are probably all used as epithets of the

great gods. It is conceivable, however, that prior to their use as epithets some of them may have been true 'Sondergotter'. Schrader (ERE. 11. 35 note) regards the Lithuanian divine names ending in *patis* as very old.

16. IV. 57, 4-5, 7-8.
17. One is impressed with the wealth of epithets which adorn such Vedic gods of the first magnitude as Indra, Varuṇa, Agni and Soma.
18. Macdonell, VM. 77.
19. *Taittiriya Samhita* IV. 5, 1-11. Translation, Keith (in HOS.), 11-353-362.
20. According to Oldenberg (ṚV. 216-224). Rudra is probably to be taken as a god who sends chills and fevers from his dwelling place in the forest and mountains of the North. Hillebrandt (VM. (II. 179-208) thinks that Rudra was a god of the terrors of the climate, connected very specially with the feverish time immediately following the monsoon. Such opinions doubtless hold good for the later Vedic period, but not so certainly for the Ṛigveda.
21. p. 21.
22. VM. III. p. XII.
23. X. 151.
24. This is regarded by Usener (Gotternamen 347-349) as the logical goal of all polytheisms, but he admits that in the case of Greece and Rome vested interests of the priesthood were too strong and that the monotheistic movement had to come from Palestine through the Christian Church.
25. Keith (*Indian Mythology*, 97), reffering to the new creations of the Brāhmaṇa period, remarks that "they serve to show full of semi-divine figures was the ordinary life of the people, who saw a deity in each possible form of action". This quite after the manner of the Roman *Indigatamenta* as interpreted by Varro.
26. Compare Rom. 1.20: "The invisible things of Him since the creation of the world are clearly seen, being through

the things that are made even His everlasting power and divinity".

27. *Buiti*, *yatu*, *druj* = Vedic, *bhūta*, *yata*, *druh*. See. p. 21.
28. Of whom *Vata* is mere doublet.
29. Also called *Kuyava* 'who causes bad harvests'. The Mussoorie hills at this time (May 1921) look as if they were under the power of Susna, the demon of drought. The spring crops have largely failed for lack of rain.
30. Indebtedness is also acknowledged to Hillebrandt's translation. LR. 112-114.
31. X. 87 and VII. 104 reappear in AV. VIII, 3, 4 with some changes in the order of stanzes and some textual variations. They are both distinctly Atharvanic in quality.
32. p. 82, n. 1.
33. VII. 104, 1, 4, 22, 23.
34. VII. 104, 21. Hindi derivative *jadu*, 'sorcery',
35. *Yatudhana*, *yātumant*, *yatumarant*, VII. 104, 15, 16, 20, 23.
36. Oldenberg ṚV. 263, n. 1 and 268. Compare the expressions *raksoyuj* 'yoker of the rakaus', *raksas*..... *Yatumavatam* 'ranksas of the sorcerers', etc. See Oldenberg ṚV. 272, as translated: "Every moment of life, every activity and every dwelling is threatened by troops of invisible fiends, the allies of human evil-doers'.
37. *Atrinah* VII. 104, 1, 5.
38. *Kracyad* VII. 104, 2; X. 87, 2, 19. Kravyād is applied to the corpse-devouing Agni in X. 16, 9-10. Agni is called in later Sanskrit the *all-eater* and at the same time the *all-purigier*.
39. X. 87, 16. This looks like a cannibal trait borrowed from the barbarous habits of the aborigines.
40. VII. 104, 18, 20, 21.
41. *Acitah*, v. 1.
42. Thus the Vedic like the Hebrew demon was conceived as a caluminator' (δικβολος) and an 'adversary' (* I. Sam. XXIX. 4.)

43. With ansita 'falsehood' the *Yatudhana* smites *ṛita* 'truth' (X. 87, 11). Compare: "He (the devil) is a liar and the father thereof" (John VIII. 44), and "without are the dogs and the *sorcerers*.... every one that loveth and maketh a *lie*" (Rev. XXII. 15). The worst charge the enemies of Christ could make against Him was to say He had a demon, that is, was in league with evil spirits (Matt. XII. 24, John VII. 48). Note that the same kind of accusation is mentioned in Ṛv. VII. 104, 15-16.
44. *Muradeva* 'whose god is a root', *mura* = *mula*, VII., 104, 24; X. 87, 2, 14. So Oldenberg, Ṛv. 266 n. 3, and Geldner *Glossar*. This epithet, like sisnadeva 'whole god is the phallus', doubtless reflects the religious beliefs and practices of the aborigines. We may compare *sahamula* III. 30, 17 and *Sahamara* X. 87. 19; also X. 87, 10 the Yatudhana's *root*' (*mula*).
45. Oldenberg, ṚV. 265.
46. Sapharuja either 'eleven-hoofed' (Hillebrandt, LR. 115), 'hoof-breaking' (Whitney-Lanman, AV. VIII, 3, 21), or 'hoof-armed' (Griffith). If 'eleven-hoofed' is correct, then there is a point of contact with the mediaeval representation of Satan.
47. VII. 104, 23; X. 87, 24.
48. VII. 104 and X. 87.
49. *Tamasi anarambhane* in the darkness which offers nothing to tame hold on', therefore bottomless (VII. 101. 3).
50. *Parsana*.
51. *Vavra* (*vri* 'to cover') 'hole', 'hell', with the *epithet ananta* 'endless' (VII. 104, 17, cf. v. 3).
52. VIII. 104, 4, 5.
53. *Sat and asat* VII. 104, 12.
54. The fixed religious formula tends to have a magical character. Not to mention the formula in the Roman Mass which causes 'transubstantition', reference may be made to the repeated use of the Lord's prayer in some forms of worship and to the closing formula of prayer 'for Jesus Christ's sake'. Whether a magical character

is attributed to these formulas depends upon the attitude of the worshipper.

55. Primitive IE. form postulated by scholars.
56. P. 14.
57. It was, of course, interrupted and modified during the Iranian period by the Zoroastrian reformation.
58. Or 'to King Sudas'.
59. VII. 53, 1; I. 185, 4; IV. 56.2.
60. Daivya jana VII. 53, 2.
61. Pitara, lit. 'two fathers' (VII. 53, 2; 1.160, 3) or matara 'two mothers' (1. 159, 3) explained in I. 160, 2 as 'father and mother.'
62. I. 160, 1, 3.
63. Tylor, *Primitive Culture*, London, 1871, 1.290 ff.
64. Ṛv. VI. 51, 5. Note that *Dyauspitar* is in the vocative, as are its equivalents in Greek and Latin.
65. P. 14.
66. Schrader (ERE. II. *Aryan Religion*) thinks that the IE. *Dyaus* had a position of honour as compared with the other heavenly ones. V. Bradke (*Dyaus Asura* 110) in like manner holds that IE. polytheims had a decidely monarchical character with Father Heaven as the patriarchal head. Oldenberg (ṚV. 34 n. 1), while admitting that presumably Father Heaven occupied a position of honour among the gods, hold that his fatherhood was not taken very seriously, and that the IE. gods were too fluid and shifting to permit us to think of them as an ordered pantheon (like the Greeks) ruled over by a supreme god. With this Macdonell (VM. 22) agress, criticing, V. Bradke's view that *Dyaus* was the supreme god of the Indo-European age, while at the same time admitting that he must have been 'the greatest among the deities of a chaotic polytheism. Meyer (GA. $I^2$, 755 ff.) refers tot the dominating position of the Heaven god in IE. religion, and holds that Dyāus in India was thrust into the background through the growth of a multiform naptheism, thereby losing much of his original greatness. The present

writer accepts Meyer's view as probable. Varuṇa in post-Vedic times was denuded and depersonalised. The pre-Vedic Dāyus may have been traced in the same way.

67. Macdonell, VM. 12.
68. Pp. 14-16.
69. Purvaje, VII. 53.2.
70. ṚV. 1. pp. VII-VIII.
71. *Daivya jaina, janus, janas, janiman, janta, janman and vis.*
72. *Manusa jana, janus, janas, juniman, jantic, jainman* and *vis.*
73. *e.g.* daivyani manusa janunsa 'heavenly and human tribes' VII. 4, 1., parthivani janma 'celestial and terrestial and terrestrial generation' V. 41, 44.
74. *dhisane, vodasi.*
75. Compare the tripartite Hebrew division into 'heaven above', 'earth beneath' and 'water under the earth' (Ex. XX. 4). The Vedic Indians had knowledge of rivers and of river-confluences (*Samudra*), but only slightly of the ocean. The Hebrew lived on the borders of the great sea (Mediterranean). Hence the difference.
76. *Cf. Yasna* I. 10 'thirty and three lords'.
77. Probably originally the voice of thunder. *Cf.* A.D. in PS. XXIX.
78. Reminds one of the Hindi *Bhumiya* 'land-lord'.
79. Macdonell, VM. 53.
80. 1.124, 3; 5, 10.
81. III. 3, 11; VI, 59, 2.
82. P. 82.
83. In the case of such terrestrial deities as Agni and Soma, their heavenly origin and subsequent 'descent' to earth is expressly stated. The deified 'Waters' and 'Rivers' manifestly descend from the sky in the form of rain. Deified terrestrial 'mountains' may be regarded as having their prototype in the cloud-mountains of the sky.
84. *Cf.* 'Who coverest thyself with light as with a garment', Ps. CIV. 2.

85. *Cf.* X. 33, 9, 'Beyond the will (*vrata*) of the gods lives not even the hundred-lived.
86. Like the multiplicity of Greek Roman and Lithuanian gods.
87. *Daivyani vratani*, I. 92, 12.
88. *Ṛitasya dhama* I. 123, 9.
89. Aś in the case of Varuṇa.
90. Oldenberg, Ṛv. 101, note; and Macdonell, VM. 16.
91. Farnell (*Greece* and *Babylon*, 1911, p. 84) refers to the "tendency very marked in the Babylonian liturgies, to exalt the particular divinity to whom worship is at that moments being paid above all other", with the result that "the ecstatic poet is always contradicting himself".
92. The one Being priests speak of in many ways: they call it Agni, Yama, Mātarisvan.'
93. 'priests and poets with words make into many the bird (= the Sun) that is but one.'

# twelve

## THE HYMNS OF THE VEDAS

I wish at the outset to make it clear that, although my object is to draw attention to the best, Indian writings, yet it by no means follows that every single extract from those writings will be put forth as an example of what is wise and just and true.

In point of fact, the following pages have a double object. They are designed as much to give a summary of the history of Sanskrit literature as to present the reader with examples of certain selected portions of that literature. In attempting this double task I am conscious of my inability to do justice in a single volume to the richness of the materials at command. An adequate idea of the luxuriance and varied character of Sanskrit literature can with difficulty be conveyed to Occidental scholars. Naturally, too, the severe European critic will be slow to acquiesce in any tribute of praise bestowed on composition too often marked by tedious repetitions, redundant epithets, and farfetched conceits; just as the genuine Oriental, nurtured under glowing tropical skies, cannot easily be brought to appreciate the coldness and severe simplicity of an educated Englishman's style of writing. We might almost say that with Indian authors merit is apt to be measured by magnitude, quality by quantity, were it not for striking thoughts and noble sentiments which often reward the student who will take the trouble to release them from the surplusage of matter under which they lie concealed; were it not, also, that[3] with all this tendency to diffuseness, it is certainly a fact that nowhere do we find the art of' condensation so successfully cultivated, as in some departments of Sanskrit literature.

Probably the very prolixity natural to Indian writers led to the opposite extreme of brevity, not merely by a law of reaction, but by the necessity for providing short summaries and epitomes as aids to the memory when oppressed by too great a burden.

However that may be, every student of Sanskrit will certainly note in its literary productions a singular inequality both as to quantity and quality; so that in studying Hindu literature continuously we are liable to be called upon to pass from the most exuberant verbosity to the most obscure brevity; from sound wisdom to little better than puerile unwisdom; from subtle reasoning to transparent sophistry; from high moral precepts to doctrines implying a social condition scarcely compatible with the lowest grades of culture and civilization.

In embarking, so to speak, on so vast an ocean of research, it will be necessary for me to start from that original source and fountain-head of all Indian religious thought, philosophy, and literature—the Veda.

Vedic literature, however, has been already so much written about, and so clearly and ably elucidated by other writers, that I shall be excused, if I pass very rapidly over this part of my subject.

In the first place, I think I may assume that most educated persons are aware that the Sanskrit word Veda means 'knowledge.' Some, however, may possibly need to be informed that the term Veda is properly only applied to divine *unwritten* knowledge, imagined to have issued like breath from the Self-existent (Brahman), and communicated to no single person, but to a whole class of men called Ṛishis or inspired sages. By them the divine knowledge thus apprehended was transmitted, not in writing, but through the ear, by constant oral repetition through a succession of teachers, who, as claiming to be its rightful recipients, were called Brāhmans. Manu (1.3) declares that the Veda is itself the Self-existent Brāhman. Sāyana, on the other hand, affirms that the Veda is his breath (*acchvasita*). There are, however, numerous inconsistencies in the accounts of the production of the Veda which seem not to have troubled the Brāhmans, or interfered with their faith in its divine origin. With reference to the statement that it issued from the Self-existent, like breath, one account makes it so issue by the power of A-drishta (see p.74), without any deliberation or thought'; on his part; another makes the four Vedas issue from Brāhman, like smoke from burning fuel; another educes them from the elements; another from the Gāyatri. A hymn in the Atharva-veda (XIX. 54) educes them from Kāla or 'Time.' The Satapatha-brāhmana asserts that the Creator brooded over the three worlds, and thence produced three lights, fire, the air, and the sun, from which respectively were extracted the Ṛig, Yajur, and Samaveda. Manu (1.23) affirms the same. In the Purusha-sūkta the three Vedas are derived from the mystical victim Purusha. Lastly, by the Mimānsakas the Veda is declared to be itself an eternal sound, and to have existed absolutely from all eternity, quite independently of any utterer or revealer of its texts. Hence it is often called *sruta*, 'what is heard.' In opposition to all this we have the Ṛishis themselves frequently intimating that the Mantras were composed by themselves.

Here, then, we have a theory of inspiration higher even than that advanced by Muhammad and his followers, or by the most enthusiastic adherents of any other religion in the world. It is very true that this inspired knowledge, though its very essence was held to be mystically bound up with Sabda or 'articulate sound' (thought to be eternal), was ultimately written down, but the writing and reading of it were not encouraged. It was even prohibited by the Brāhmans, to whom alone all property in it belonged. Moreover, when at last, by its continued growth, it became too complex for mere oral transmission, then this Veda resolved itself, not into one single volume, like the Kurān, but into a whole series of compositions, which had in reality been composed by a number of different poets and writers at different times during several centuries.

There is this great difference, therefore, between the Kurān and the Veda, that whereas the reading of the former is regarded as a sacred duty, and constantly practised by all good Muslims, the Veda, even after it had been committed to writing, became absolutely a sealed book to the masses of Hindūs, and with the exception of some of the later Vedic works, called Upanishads, is to this day almost entirely unread, however much it may be still repeated in religious services and its divine authority as an infallible guide nominally upheld.[1] In fact, the absolute and infallible authority of the Veda is held to be so manifest as to require no proof, and to be entirely beyond the province of reason or argument. Manu even extends this to Smriti (II. 10), where he says, By *sruti* is meant the Veda, and by *smṛiti* the books of tradition; the contents of both these must never be questioned by reason.

Of what, then, does this Veda consist? To conduce to clearness we may regard it as separating itself into three quite distinct divisions, viz.:—

1. *Mantra,* or prayer and praise embodied in metrical hymns and texts.
2. *Brāhmana,* or ritualistic precept and illustration written in prose.
3. *Upanishad,* mystical or esoteric doctrine appended to

the aforesaid Brāhmana, in prose and occasional verse.

To begin, then, with the Mantra portion. By this is meant those prayers, invocations, and hymns which have been collected and handed down to us from a period after the Indian branch of the great Indo-European race had finally settled down in Northern India, but which were doubtless composed by a succession of poets at different times (perhaps between 1500 and 1000 years B.C.). These compositions, very unequal in poetical merit, are highly interesting and important, as embodying some of the earliest religious conceptions, as well as some of the earliest known forms, of the primitive language of that Primeval Āryan race-stock from which Greeks, Romans, Kelts, Teutons, and the Slavonic races are all offshoots.

They are comprised in five principal collections of Mantras, called respectively Ṛik, Atharvan, Sāman, Taittirīya, and Vajasaneyin. Of these the Ṛig-veda-containing one thousand and seventeen hymns-is the oldest and most important, while the Atharva-veda is generally held to be the most recent, and is perhaps the most interesting. The Atharva-veda, in fact, seems in its present form to have been later than Manu. At least it does not appear to have been recognized as a fourth Veda in the time of Manu, though he mentions the revelation made to Atharvan and Angiras (XI. 33). In book XI., verse 264, he declares that the Veda is only threefold, thus: *Rico yajūnshi canyāmi sāmani vividhāni ca, esha jneyas trivrid vedo yo vedainam sa veda-vit.*. The Atharvans were a class of priests descended from a man named Atharvan. They appear to have been the first to institute the worship of fire before the separation of the Indians and Iranians, for there were priests called Atharvans in both India and Persia.

As to the Sāma-veda and the two collections of the Yajur-veda (Tāittirīya and Vajasaneyin, or Black and White), they all three borrow largely from the Ṛik, and are merely

Brahmanical manuals, the necessity for which grew out of the complicated ritual gradually elaborated by the Hiudū Āryans. A curious allusion to the Sāmaveda occurs in Manu IV. 123, &c., 'The Rig-veda has the gods for its deities, the Yajur-veda has men for its objects, the Sāma-veda has the Pitṛis, therefore its sound is impure. Kullūka, however, in his commentary is careful to state that the Sama-veda is not really impure, but only apparently so. This semblance of impurity may perhaps result from its association with deceased persons and its repetition at a time of A-sauca. The Sāma-veda is really a mere reproduction of parts of the Ṛik, transposed and scattered about piecemeal, only seventy-eight verses in the whole Sāma-veda being, it is said, untraceable to the present recension of the Ṛik. The greatest number of its verses are taken from the ninth Maṇḍala of the Ṛik, which is in praise of the Soma plant, the Sāma-veda being a collection of liturgical forms for the Soma ceremonies of the Udgātṛi priests, as the Yajus is for the sacrifices performed by the Adhvaryu priests. Hence we may affirm that the only two Vedic hymn-books worthy of being called separate original collections are the Ṛig-veda and Atharva-veda; and to these, therefore, we shall confine our examples.

To what deities, it will be asked, were the prayers and hymns of these collections addressed? This is an interesting inquiry, for these were probably the very deities worshiped under similar names by our Āryan progenitors in their primeval home somewhere on the table-land of Central Asia, or elsewhere, perhaps not far from the sources of the Oxus.[2] The answer is: They worshipped those physical forces before which all nations, if guided solely by the light of nature, have in the early period of their life instinctively bowed down and before which even the more civilized and enlightened have always been c6mpelled to bend in awe and reverence, if not in adoration.

To our Āryan forefathers in their primeval home God's

power was exhibited in the forces of nature even more evidently than to ourselves. Lands, houses, flocks, herds, men, and animals were more frequently than in Western climates at the mercy of winds, fire, and water, and the sun's rays appeared to be endowed with a potency quite beyond the experience of any European country. We cannot be surprised, then, that these forces were regarded by our Eastern progenitors as actual manifestations, either of one deity in different moods or of separate rival deities contending for supremacy. Nor is it wonderful that these mighty agencies should have been at first poetically personified, and afterwards, when invested with forms, attributes, and individuality, worshipped as distinct gods. It was only natural, too, that a varying supremacy and varying honours should have been accorded to each deified force—to the air, the rain, the storm, the sun, or fire-according to the special atmospheric influences to which particular localities were exposed, or according to the seasons of the year when the dominance of each was to be prayed for or deprecated.

This was the religion represented in the Vedas and the primitive creed of the Indo-Āryans about twelve or thirteen centuries before Christ. The first forces deified seem to have been those manifested in the sky and air. These were at first generalised under one rather vague personification, as was natural in the earliest attempts at giving shape to religious ideas. For it may be observed that all religious systems, even the most polytheistic, have generally grown out of some undefined original belief in a divine power or powers controlling and regulating the universe. And although innumerable gods and goddesses, gifted with a thousand shapes, now crowd the Hindū Pantheon, appealing to the instincts of the millions whose capacity for religious ideas is supposed to require the aid of external symbols, it is probable that there existed for the first Āryan worshippers a simpler theistic creed: even as the thoughtful Hindū of the present day looks through the maze of his mythology to the philosophical background of one eternal self-existent Being, one universal Spirit, into whose unity all visible symbols are gathered, and in whose essence all entities are comprehended.

In the Veda this unity soon diverged into various ramifications. Only a few of the hymns appear to contain the simple conception of one divine self-existent omnipresent Being, and even in these the idea of one God present in all nature is somewhat nebulous and undefined.

It is interesting to note how this idea, vaguely stated as it was in the Veda, gradually developed and became more clearly defined in the time of Manu. In the last verses of the twelfth book we have the following: 'Him some adore as transcendently present in fire; others in Manu, lord of creatures; some as more distinctly present in Indra, others in pure air, others as the most high eternal Spirit. Thus the man who perceives in his own soul, the supreme soul present in all creatures, acquires equanimity towards them all, and shall be absorbed at last in the highest essence.'

In the Purusha-sūkta of the Ṛig-veda (X. 90), which is one of the later hymns, probably not much earlier than the earliest Brāhmana, the one Spirit is called Purusha. The more common name is Ātman or Paramātman, and in the later system *Brahman,* neut. (nom. *Brāhma*), derived from root *biṛth,* 'to expand,' and denoting the universally expanding essence or universally diffused substance of the universe. It was thus that the later creed became not so much monotheistic (by which I mean the belief in one god regarded as a personal Being external to the universe, though creating and governing it) as pantheistic; Brahman in the neuter being 'simple infinite being'—the only real eternal essence-which, when it passes into universal *manifested* existence, is called Brahmā, when it manifests itself on the earth, is called Vishṇu, and when it again dissolves itself into simple being, is called S'iva; all the other innumerable gods and demigods being also mere manifestations of the neuter Brahman, who alone is eternal. This, at any rate, appears to be the genuine pantheistic creed of India at the present day.

To return to the Vedic hymns—perhaps the most ancient and beautiful Vedic deification was that of Dyauś,[3] the sky, as Dyaush-pitar, 'Heavenly Father' (the Zeus or Jupiter of the Greeks and Romans). Then, closely connected with Dyaus, was a goddess A-diti, 'the Infinite Expanse,' conceived of subsequently as the mother of all the gods. Next came a development of the same conception called Varuna, 'the Investing Sky,' said to answer to Ahura Mazda, the Ormazd of the ancient Persian (Zand) mythology, and to the Greek Ουπανος—but a more spiritual conception, leading to a worship which rose to the nature of a belief in the great. This Varuna, again, was soon thought of in connection with another vague personification called Mitra (= the Persian *Mithra*), 'god of day.' After a time these impersonations of the celestial sphere were felt to be too vague to suit the growth of religious ideas in ordinary minds. Soon, therefore, the great investing firmament resolved itself into separate cosmical entities with separate powers and attributes. First, the watery atmosphere—personified under the name of Indra, ever seeking to dispense his dewy treasures (*indu*), though ever restrained by an opposing force or spirit of evil called Vritra; and, secondly, the wind-thought of either as a single personality named Vayu, or as a whole assemblage of moving powers coming from every quarter of the compass, and impersonated as Maruts or 'Storm-gods.' At the same time in this process of decentralization if I may use the term-the once purely celestial Varuṇa became relegated to a position among seven secondary deities of the heavenly sphere called Ādityas (afterwards increased to twelve, and regarded as diversified forms of the sun in the several months of the year), and subsequently to a dominion over the waters when they had left the air and rested on the earth.

Of these separately deified physical forces by far the most favourite object of adoration was the deity supposed to yield the dew and rain, longed for by Eastern cultivators of the soil with even greater cravings than by Northern agriculturists. Indra, therefore-the Jupiter Pluvius of early Indian mythology—is undoubtedly the principal divinity of Vedic worshippers, in so far at least as the greater number of their prayers and hymns are addressed to him.

What, however, could rain effect without the aid of heat? A force the intensity of which must have impressed an Indian mind with awe, and led him to invest the possessor of it with divine attributes. Hence the other great god of Vedic worshippers, and in some respects the most important in his connection with sacrificial rites, is Agni (Latin *Ignis*), 'the god of fire. Even Sūrya, 'the sun who was probably at first adored as the original source of heat, came to be regarded as only another form of fire. He was merely a manifestation of the same divine energy removed to the heavens, and consequently less accessible. Another deity, Ushas, 'goddess of the down,'—was naturally connected with the sun, and regarded as daughter of the sky. Two other deities, the Asvins, were fabled as connected with Ushas, as ever young and handsome, travelling in a golden car and precursors of the dawn. They are sometimes called Dasras, as divine physicians, 'destroyers of diseases'; sometimes Nāsatyas, as never untrue. They appear to have been personifications of two luminous rays imagined to precede the break of day. These, with Yama, the god of departed spirits,' are the principal deities of the Mantra portion of the Veda.

We find, therefore, no trace in the Mantras of the Trimurti or Triad of deities (Brahmā, Vishṇu, and Siva) afterwards so popular. Nor does the doctrine of transmigration, afterwards an essential element of the Hindu religion, appear in the Mantra portion of the Veda; though there is a clear declaration of it in the Āraṇyaka of the Aitareya Brāhmṇa. Nor is caste clearly alluded to, except in the later Purusha-sukta.

But here it may be asked, if sky, air, water, fire, and the sun were thus worshipped as manifestations of the supreme universal God of the universe, was not the earth also an object of adoration with the early Hindus? And unquestionably in the earlier system the earth under the name of Pṛithivī; ' the broad one,' *does* receive divine honours, being thought of as the mother of all beings. Moreover, various deities were regarded as the progeny resulting from the fancied union of earth with Dyaus, 'heaven.' This imaginary marriage of heaven and earth was indeed a most natural idea, and much of the later mythology may be explained by it. But it is remarkable that as religious worship became of a more selfish character, the earth, being more evidently under man's control, and not seeming to need propitiation so urgently as the more uncertain air, fire, and water, lost importance among the gods, and was rarely addressed in prayer or hymn.

In all probability the deified forces addressed in the hymns were not represented by images or idols in the Vedic period, though, doubtless, the early worshippers clothed their gods with human form in their own imaginations.[4]

I now begin my examples with a nearly literal translation of the well-known sixteenth hymn of the fourth book of the Atharva-veda, in praise of Yaruna or 'the Investing Sky':[5]

> The mighty Varuṇa, who rules above, looks down
> Upon these worlds, his kingdom, as if close at hand.
> When men imagine they do ought by stealth, be knows it.
> No one can stand or walk or softly glide along

Or hide in dark recess, or lurk in secret cell,
But Varuṇa detects him and his movements spies.
Two persons may devise some plot, together sitting
In private and alone; but he, the king, is there—
A third—and sees it all. This boundless earth is his,
His the vast sky, whose depth no mortal e'er can fathom.
Both oceans[6] find a place within his body, yet
In that small pool he lies contained. Whoe'er should flee
Far, far beyond the sky, would not escape the grasp
Of Varuṇa, the king. His messengers descend
Countless from his abode—for ever traversing
This world and scanning with a thousand eyes its inmates.
Whate'er exists within this earth, and all within the sky,
Yea all that is beyond, king Varuṇa perceives.
The winkings[7] of men's eyes, are numbered all by him.
He wields the universe, as gamesters handle dice.
May thy destroying snares cast sevenfold round the wicked,
Entangle liars, but the truthful spare, O king[8]

I pass from the ancient Aryan deity Varuṇa to the more thoroughly Indian god Indra.

The following metrical lines bring together various scattered texts relating to this Hindū Jupiter Pluvius:[9]

Indra, twin brother of the god of fire,
When thou wast born, thy mother Aditi
Gave thee, her lusty child, the thrilling draught
Of mountain-growing Soma-source of life
And never-dying vigour to thy frame.
Then at the Thunderer's birth, appalled with fear,
Dreading the hundred,ointed thunderbolt-
Forged by the cunning Tvashṭri-mountains rocked,
Earth shook and heaven trembled. Thou wast born
Without a rival, king of gods and men—
The eye of living and terrestrial things.
Immortal Indra, unrelenting foe
Of drought and darkness, infinitely wise,
Terrific crusher of thy enemies,
Heroic, irresistible in might,

Wall of defence to us thy worshippers,
We sing thy praises, and our ardent hymns
Embrace thee, as a loving wife her lord.
Thou art our guardian, advocate, and friend,
A brother, father, mother, all combined.
Most fatherly of fathers, we are thine
And thou art ours; oh! let thy pitying soul
Turn to us in compassion, when we praise thee,
And slay us not for one sin or for many.
Deliver us to-day, to-morrow, every day.
Armed for the conflict, see! the demons come-
Ahi and Vṛitra, and a long array
Of darksome spirits. Quick, then, quaff the draught
That stimulates thy martial energy,
And dashing onward in thy golden car,
Drawn by thy ruddy, Ṛibhu-fashioned [10] steeds,
Speed to the charge, escorted by the Maruts.
Vainly the demons dare thy might; in vain
Strive to deprive us of thy watery treasures.
Earth quakes beneath the crashing of thy bolts.
Pierced, shattered, lies the foe-his cities crushed,
His armies overthrown, his fortresses
Shivered to fragments; then the pent-up waters,
Released from long imprisonment, descend
In torrents to the earth, and swollen rivers,
Foaming and rolling to their ocean home,
Proclaim the triumph of the Thunderer.

Let us proceed next to the all-important Vedic deity Agni, 'god of fire,' especially of sacrificial fire. I propose now to paraphrase a few of the texts which relate to him:—

Agni, thou art a sage, a priest, a king,
Protector, father of the sacrifice.
Commissioned by us men thou dost ascend
A messenger, conveying to the sky
Our hymns and offerings. Though thy origin
Be threefold, now from air and now from water,
Now from the mystic double Araṇi,[11]
Thou art thyself a mighty god, a lord,
Giver of life and immortality,

One in thy essence, but to mortals three;
Displaying thine eternal triple form,
As fire on earth, as lightning in the air,
As sun in heaven. Thou art a cherished guest
In every household—father, brother, son,
Friend, benefactor, guardian, all in one.
Bright, seven-rayed god ! how manifold thy shapes
Revealed to us thy votaries! now we see thee,
With body all of gold, and radiant hair
Flaming from three terrific heads, and mouths
Whose burning jaws and teeth devour all things.
Now with a thousand glowing horns, and now
Flashing thy lustre from a thousand eyes,
Thou'rt borne towards us in a golden chariot,
Impelled by winds, and drawn by ruddy steeds,
Marking thy car's destructive course, with blacknes&
Deliver, mighty lord, thy worshippers.
Purge us from taint of sin, and when we die,
Deal mercifully with us on the pyre,
Burning our bodies with their load of guilt.
But bearing our eternal part on high
To luminous abodes and realms of bliss,
For ever there to dwell with righteous men.

The next deity is Sūrya, 'the Sun,'[12] with reference to the variety of his functions, has various names—such as Savitri, Aryaman, Mitra, Varuṇa, Pushan, sometimes ranking as distinct deities of the celestial sphere. As already explained, he is associated in the minds of Vedic worshippers with Fire, and is frequently described as sitting in a chariot drawn by seven ruddy horses (representing the seven days of the week), preceded by the Dawn. Here is an example of a hymn (Ṛig-veda 1.50) addressed to this deity, translated almost literally:—

Behold the rays of Dawn, like heralds, lead on high
The Sun, that men may see the great all-knowing god.
The stars slink off like thieves, in company with Night,
Before the all-seeing eye, whose beams reveal his pres
ence,

Gleaming like brilliant flames, to nation after nation.
With speed, beyond the ken of mortals, thou, O Sun,
Dost ever travel on, conspicuous to all.
Thou dost create the light, and with it dost illume
The universe entire; thou risest in the sight
Of all the race of men, and all the host of heaven.
Light-giving Varuṇa ! thy piercing glance doth scan
In quick succession all this stirring, active world,
And penetrateth too the broad ethereal space,
Measuring our days and nights and spying out all crea tures.
Sūrya with flaming locks, clear-sighted god of day,
Thy seven ruddy mares bear on thy rushing car.
With these thy self-yoked steeds, seven daughters of thy chariot,
Onward thou dost advance. To thy refulgent orb
Beyond this lower gloom and upward to the light
Would we ascend, O Sun, thou god among the gods.

As an accompaniment to this hymn may here be mentioned the celebrated Gāyatri. It is a short prayer to the Sun in his character of Savitṛi or 'the Vivifier,' and is the most sacred of all Vedic texts. Though not always understood, it is to this very day used by every Brāhman throughout India in his daily devotions. It occurs in Ṛigveda III. 62 10,[13] and can be literally translated as follows:—

Let us meditate (or, we meditate) on that excellent glory of the divine Vivifier. May he enlighten (or stimulate) our understanding. [*Tat Savitur vareṇyam bhargo devasya dhimahi, Dhiyo yo nah praco-dayat*]

May we not conjecture, with Sir William Jones, that the great veneration in which this text has ever been held by the Hindus from time immemorial, indicates that the more enlightened worshippers adored, under the type of the visible sun, that divine light which alone could milhmine their intellects?

I may here also fitly offer a short paraphrase descriptive of the Vedic Ushas, the Greek 'Ηως, or Dawn:—

Hail, ruddy Ushas, golden goddess, borne
Upon thy shining car, thou comest like
A lovely maiden by her mother decked,
Disclosing coyly all thy hidden graces
To our admiring eyes; or like a wife
Unveiling to her lord, with conscious pride,
Beauties which, as he gazes lovingly,
Seem fresher, fairer each succeeding morn.
Through years on years thou hast lived on, and yet
Thou'rt ever young. Thou art the breath and life
Of all that breathes and lives, awaking day by day
Myriads of prostrate sleepers, as from death,
Causing the birds to flutter from their nests,
And rousing men to ply with busy feet
Their daily duties and appointed tasks,
Toiling for wealth or pleasure or renown.

Before leaving the subject of the Vedic deities I add a few words about Yama, 'the god of departed spirits.' It appears tolerably certain that the doctrine of metempsychosis has no place in the Mantra portion of the Veda,[14] nor do the authors of the hymns evince any sympathy with the desire to get rid of all action and personal existence, which became so remarkable a feature of the theology and philosophy of the Brāhmans in later times. But there are many indirect references to the immortality of man's spirit and a future life, and these become more marked and decided towards the end of the Ṛig-veda. One of the hymns in the last Maṇḍala is addressed to the Pitṛis or fathers, that is to say, the spirits of departed ancestors who have attained to a state of heavenly bliss, and arc supposed to occupy three different stages of blessedness, the highest inhabiting the upper sky, the middle the intermediate air, and the lowest the regions of the atmosphere near the earth. Reverence and adoration are always to be offered them, and they are presided over by the god Yama, the ruler of all the spirits of the dead, whether good or bad. The earlier legends represent this god as a kind of first man (his twin sister being Yamī), and also as the first of men that died. Hence he is described as guiding the spirits of other men who die to the same world. In some passages, however, Death is said as he his messenger he himself dwelling in essential light to which the departed ore brought, and where they enjoy his society and that of the fathers. In the Veda he has nothing to do with judging or punishing the departed (as in the later mythology), but he has two terrific dogs, with four eyes, which guard the way to his abode. Here are a few thoughts about him from various hymns in the tenth Maṇḍala of the Ṛig-veda:—

To Yama, mighty king, be gifts and homage paid.
He was the first of men that died, the first to brave
Death's rapid rushing stream, the first to point the road
To heaven, and welcome others to that bright abode.
No power can rob us of the home thus won by thee.
O king, we come; the born must die, must tread the path
That thou hast trod—the path by which each race of men,
In long succession, and our fathers, too, have passed.
Soul of the dead! depart; fear not to take the road-
The ancient road—by which thy ancestors have gone;
Ascend to meet the god—to meet thy happy fathers,
Who dwell in bliss with him. Fear not to pass the guards-
The four-eyed brindled dogs—that watch for the de parted.
Return unto thy home, O soul! Thy sin and shame
Leave thou behind on earth; assume a shining form-
Thy ancient shape-refined and from all taint set free.

Let me now endeavour, by slightly amplified translations, to convey some idea of two of the most remarkable hymns in the Ṛig-veda. The first (Maṇḍala X. 129), which may be compared with some parts of the 38th chap. of Job, attempts to describe the mystery of creation thus:—

In the beginning there was neither nought nor aught,
Then there was neither sky nor atmosphere above.
What then enshrouded all this teeming Universe?
In the receptacle of what was it contained ?
Was it enveloped in the gulf profound of water?
Then was there neither death nor immortality.
Then was there neither day, nor night, nor light, nor darknes,
Only the Existent One breathed calmly, self contained.
Nought else than him there was—noght else above, beyond.
Then first came darkness hid in darkness, gloom in gloom.
Next all was water, all a chaos indiscreet,
In which the One lay void, shrouded in nothingness.
Then turning inwards he by self-developed force
Of inner fervour and intense abstraction, grew.
And now in him Desire, the primal germ of mind,
Arose, which learned men, profoundly searching, say
Is the first subtle bond, connecting Entity
With Nullity. This ray that kindled dormant life,
Where was it then? before? or was it found above?
Were there parturient powers and latent qualities,
And fecund principles beneath, and active forces
That energized aloft? Who knows? Who can declare?
How and from what has sprung this Universe? the gods
Themselves are subsequent to its development.
Who, then, can penetrate the secret of its rise?
Whether, twas framed or not, made or not made; he only
Who in the highest heaven sits, the omniscient lord,
Assuredly knows all, or haply knows he not.

The next example is from the first Maṇḍala of the Ṛigveda (121). Like, the preceding, it furnishes a good argument for those who maintain that the purer faith of the Hindūs is properly monotheistic:—

What god shall we adore with sacrifice?[15]
Him let us praise, the golden child that rose
In the beginning, who was born the lord—
The one sole lord of all that is-who made
The earth, and formed the sky, who giveth life,

Who giveth strength, whose bidding gods revere,
Whose hiding-place is immortality,
Whose shadow, death; who by his might is king
Of all the breathing, sleeping, waking world-
Who governs men and beasts, whose majesty
These snowy hills, this ocean with its rivers
Declare; of whom these spreading regions form
The arms; by whom the firmament is strong,
Earth firmly planted, and the highest heavens
Supported, and the clouds that fill the air
Distributed and measured out; to whom
Both earth and heaven, established by his will,
Look up with trembling mind; in whom revealed
The rising sun shines forth above the world.
Where'er let loose in space, the mighty waters
Have gone, depositing a fruitful seed
And generating fire, there *he* arose,
Who is the breath and life of all the gods,
Whose mighty glance looks round the vast expanse
Of watery vapour-source of energy,
Cause of the sacrifice—the only God
Above the gods. May he not injure us!
He the Creator of the earth—the righteous
Creator of the sky, Creator too
Of oceans bright, and far-extending waters.

Let me now give a few verses (not in regular order and not quite literally translated) from the celebrated Purushasukta, one of the most recent of the hymns of the Ṛig-veda (Maṇḍala X. 90). It will serve to illustrate the gradual sliding of Hindū monotheism into pantheism, and the first foreshadowing of the institution of caste, which for so many centuries has held India in bondage:—

The embodied spirit [16] has a thousand heads,
A thousand eyes, a thousand feet, around
On every side enveloping the earth,
Yet filling space no larger than a span.[17]
He is himself this very universe,
He is whatever is, has been, and shall be.
He is the lord of immortality.

All creatures are one-fourth of him, three-fourths
Are that which is immortal in the sky.
From him, called Purusha, was born Virāj,
And from Virāj was Purusha' produoed[18]
Whom gods and holy men made their oblation.
With Purusha as victim they performed
A sacrifice. When they divided him,
How did they cut him up ? what was his mouth!
What were his arms! and what his thighs and feet ?

The Brāhman was his mouth, the kingly soldier[2]
Was made his arms, the husbandman his thighs,
The servile Sūdra issued from his feet.

I close my examples of the Mantras with slightly amplified versions of two hymns one in praise of Time, personified as the source of all things, taken from the Atharva-veda; the other addressed to Night, from the Rig-veda.[20]

The following is the hymn to Time (Atharva-veda XIX. 53. A few verses at the end are omitted, one or two lines transposed, and a few inserted from the next hymn on the same subject:—

Time, like a brilliant steed with seven rays,
And with a thousand eyes, imperishable,
Full of fecundity, bears all things onward.
On him ascend the learned and the wise.
Time, like a seven-wheeled, seven-naved car, moves on.
His rolling wheels are all the worlds, his axle
Is immortality. He is the first of gods.
We see him like an overflowing jar;
We see him multiplied in various forms.
He draws forth and encompasses the worlds;
He is all future worlds; he is their father;
He is their son; there is no power like him,
The past and future issue out of Time,
All sacred knowledge and austerity.
From Time the earth and waters were produced;
From Time, the rising, setting, burning sun;
From Time, the wind; through Time the earth is vast;

Through Time the eye perceives; mind, breath, and name
In him are comprehended. All rejoice
When Time arrives-the monarch who has conquered
This world, the highest world, the holy worlds,
Yea, all the worlds—and ever marches on.

The hymn to Night is my last example. It is taken from the tenth Maṇḍala of the Ṛig-veda (127):-The goddess Night arrives in all her glory,

Looking about her with her countless eyes.
She, the immortal goddess, throws her veil
Over low valley, rising ground, and hill,
But soon with bright effulgence dissipates
The darkness she produces; soon advancing
She calls her sister Morning to return,
And then each darksome shadow melts away.
Kind goddess, be propitious to thy servants
Who at thy coming straightway seek repose,
Like birds who nightly nestle in the trees.
Lo! men and cattle, flocks and winged creatures,
And e'en the ravenous hawks, have gone to rest
Drive thou away from us, O Night, the wolf;
Drive thou away the thief, and bear us safely
Across thy borders. Then do thou, O Dawn,
Like one who clears away a debt, chase off
This black, yet palpable obscurity,
Which came to fold us in its close embrace.
Receive, O Night, dark daughter of the Day,
My hymn of praise, which I present to thee,
Like some rich offering to a conqueror.

**Foot Notes:**

1. The want of accuracy in repeating the Mantras of the Ṛig-Veda is illustrated by the native editions of Manu. An edition (with the Commentary of Kullūka) in my possession is a scholar—like production, but almost in every place where the Mantras of the Ṛig-Veda are alluded to by manu (as in VIII. 91, XI. 250, 252, 253, 254) errors disfigure the test and commentrary.
2. Professor Whitney and other doubt this usual assumption. Some even lean to the theory that somewhere in the North of Europe is the primeval home of the Aryans.
3. From *dyu or dyo*, the same as the Old German Tiu or Ziu, who, according to Professor Max Müller, afterwards became a kind of Mars (whence Tuesday). For Dyaush—pitar see Ṛigveda VI. 51.5.
4. See Dr Muir's Sanskrit Texts, vol. v. p.453.
5. Ably translated by Dr. Muir (Sanskrit Texts, vol.v. p.63) and by Professor max Müller. It may be thought that in giving additional translations of this and other hymns I man going over ground already well trodden; but it should be borne in mind, that, as the design of the work is to illustrate *continously* the development of Hindū Knowledge and literature by a selection of good examples rendered into idiomatic English, I could not, in common jústice to each a subject, exclude the best massages in each department of the literature merely because they have been translated by otehrs. I here, however, once for all acknowledge with gratitude that, while making versions of my own, I have derived the greatest assistance from the translations of other scholars. It must be understand, too that my examples are not put forth in offering rival translations. They are generally intended to be as literal as possible consistently with the observance of English idiom, and on that account I have preferred blank verse; but occasionally they are paraphrases rather than translations, sentences and words being here and there omitted or transposed, or fragments joined together, so as to read like one continuous passage. In fact, it will be seen that my main design has been to offer English versions of the text for general readers, and for those

students and educated men who, not being necessarily Sanskṛitists, are desirous of some insight into Hindū literature.

6.That is, air and sea.

7.The winking of the eye is an especial characteristic of humanity, distinguishing men from gods; cf. Nala V. 25, Māgha III. 42.

8.Compare Manu VIII. 82: 'A witness who speaks falsely is fạt bound by the snares of Varuṇa.' These snares are explained by Kullūka to be 'cords consisting of serpents' (*Pāsaiḥ sarpa-rajjubhih*).

9.The texts which furnish the basis of these and the succeeding verses will be found in the 5th volume of Dr. Muir's work, and there will also be found a complete poetical sketch of Indra (pp.125-139).

10.The Ṛibhus (Grek 'see language ) were the celestial artisits of the Veda.

11.Two pieces of the wood of the *Ficus religiosa* used for kindling fire.

12.Yāska makes Indra, Agni, and Sūrya the Vedic Triad of gods.

13.Note that the Rishi or author was Viśvamitra, a *Kshatriya*.

14.In Mandala I. 164, 32, *bahu-prajah* is explained by *bahu-janmabhak*, 'subject to many births,' but it may mean 'having abundant offspring.'

15.In the text this question is repeated at the end of every verse. A literal translation will be found in Muir's Sanskrit Texts, vol. iv. p.16.

16.According to the Upanishads and the Tattva-samasa the all-pervading self –existent spirit is called Purusha, *puri* sāyanāt, from dwelling in the body.

17.Dr. Muir translates (literally), 'He overpassed the earth by a space of ten fingers.' The Katha Upanishad (II. 4.120 says that Purusha, 'the soul', is of the measure of a thumb (*angushṭha-mātraḥ*).

18.This is tantamount to saying that Purusha and Virāj are in substance the same. Virāj, as a kind of secondary creator, is sometimes regarded as male, sometimes as female. Manu (I.11) says that Purusha, ' the first male', was called Brahmā, and was produced from the supreme self-existnt Spirit. In I.32 he says that Brahmā (see Kullūka's commentary), having divided his own substance, became half male, half female, and that from the female was produced Virāj, and that from Virāj was born manu – the secondary prognitor and producer of all beings.

19.The second caste or Kshatriya is here called Rajanya. By 'husbandman' in the next line is of course meant the third or Vaiśya caste.

20.Both literally translated into prose by Dr. Muir, Texts, vol.v. p.408, vol.iv. p.498.